Reprint Publishing

For People Who Go For Originals.

www.reprintpublishing.com

A QUAKER SINGER'S
RECOLLECTIONS

THE MACMILLAN COMPANY
NEW YORK · BOSTON · CHICAGO · DALLAS
ATLANTA · SAN FRANCISCO

MACMILLAN & CO., LIMITED
LONDON · BOMBAY · CALCUTTA
MELBOURNE

THE MACMILLAN CO. OF CANADA, LTD.
TORONTO

DAVID BISPHAM
From a Photograph by Hartsook, Los Angeles

A
QUAKER SINGER'S
RECOLLECTIONS

BY

DAVID BISPHAM

David Bispham Memorial Edition

Issued Through the Courtesy of

THE MACMILLAN COMPANY

PREFACE TO SECOND EDITION

A Heart to Heart Talk with Students of Singing—and their Teachers

The possession of a real singing voice coupled with real musical ability is a very rare and, seemingly, a chance gift granted to but one in ten thousand. The voice may exist without the requisite intelligence, or the musicianship minus the necessary vocal equipment. The possessor of both voice and brains is a most fortunate mortal and should be afforded every opportunity to make a career; the partially endowed, however, while entirely at liberty to cultivate their talents for personal and amateur use, should be carefully steered away from all thought of a public career and not lured toward it.

Children should hear and be taught to sing good music in all schools as a delightful natural pastime, not as a matter of dull routine, until Nature determines whether, in special instances, further musical study is advisable. Though more women than men turn to music for their livelihood, marriage and family cares divert many from further thought of it as a profession. Boys' voices, touchingly pellucid as they often are, seldom retain their former charm after the time of change; with manhood and its cares come thoughts, desires and urges in other directions, until most youths consider singing, after all, not to be a man's work. So we see that the number of contestants in the field is rapidly being reduced by the operations of that same Power that gave the gift and still offers the prize to all such as are strong enough to persevere in the contest. Yet there are multitudes of all sorts and conditions of men and women pressing in, lured by the prospect of what they consider to be easy gain, but these require further weeding out if even a tolerably good standard is to be maintained in the profession.

I once was, for a short time, President of an Association of Singing Teachers, and, during my speech at the annual banquet, my views upon two subjects caused such a storm of protest that I was good-naturedly hissed, and another reigned in my stead thereafter. The points to which exception was taken were, first, that no one should teach singing who could not sing, or who had not been a singer; and, second, that no one should teach people who had not enough voice to become, at least, fairly good amateurs. The outcry took the concrete form of—"How are we, then, to earn a living?" To this my reply was—"Do something else; that is what most pupils have to do after wasting time and money on an Art in which they never had even a remote chance of success."—Then came the hissing. I am uncompromising in my opinion upon these matters and try to make them plain early in my association with vocalists who seek my advice.

Civilization of the present is built up on models of the past. In every field of endeavor, we use the experiences and accomplishments of those before us in point of time as stepping-stones to still further accomplishment. Just so it is essential to add to the precept of the teacher the example of the performer, and we may paraphrase the old proverb by saying,—an ounce of example is worth a pound of precept. The student may learn more from the model held before him by a competent artist than by the unproved ideas of a teacher personally inexperienced in singing.

Nothing is truer when applied to singing than that "Many are called, but few are chosen." But now let me take counsel with those who have demonstrated the possibility of ultimate success—given Luck and Health, Opportunity, Natural Refinement and Level-headedness. At all costs singers must henceforth strive to avoid the general reproach of "Vox, et præterea nihil"—Voice, and nothing much besides. What must they do in the struggle to attain a high place in so exalted a calling as that of a singer? What must they know? What must they undergo?

Would-be-vocalists must continue carefully and rigorously to train their voices in strength and agility so that the very delicate mechanism of the larynx may endure the strain of the long hours of practice in the studio and of rehearsal, before a public performance of any dignified character is to be thought of. Vocalists must know

how to read music well and should be as thoroughly
trained for the requirements of vocal art as instrumentalists have to be for the reading and rendering of violin,
piano and organ music. Orchestral players working for
Union wages usually despise high-priced songbirds whose
technical shortcomings are so obvious.

Singers must acquire a full repertoire of classic songs,
oratorios and operas. These things should be learned
first, learned rapidly and learned well; they are the stock
in trade of the singer, but it is scarcely realized owing to
the regrettable but quite frequent debasement of taste
of the present time. Singers should learn Italian, French
and German for the great music of those schools, and
they *must* learn English for the magnificent music of our
own tongue—and for very shame's sake,—for not one
singer out of ten today can be understood when singing
English, except in musical comedy where, unfortunately,
good singing is not a requisite, but where, owing to the
lack of other operatic opportunities, the very best available talent could be chosen, and should be heard.

The artist should realize that he may have to undergo,
beside what has been said about training for his work,
a very hard life of early hours and late hours, with all-
day work between; of unavoidable travel in cold, heat
and discomfort; and of performance under stress of ill
health. But, worst of all, the artist must endure the
very general and equally undeserved reproach of lax
morals, because Music and the Stage in Puritan times

acquired a bad name from which, in the esteem of many otherwise sensible people, they have by no means recovered.

All these things, however, are set forth in the following narrative by one who has had long and close personal experience with every phase of his profession, and who therefore knows of what he speaks. To have acted in twenty-five plays and to have given as many recitations to music, to have performed fifty-eight operatic rôles, to have rendered over two hundred oratorios, cantatas, and kindred works, and to have sung to date some fifteen hundred songs, making a grand total of over eighteen hundred titles is no mean achievement for an American Quaker Singer, but it is not a circumstance to what has been done by many of my colleagues in the cities of Europe where artistic work is so highly systematized. Such an advance is, I hope, possible in the United States where all musical art would be vastly improved by the initial careful selection of talented executants and by more intelligent study of a wisely chosen curriculum and preparation in all branches of vocal art before any aspirants would be permitted to inflict themselves upon the public.

September, 1921.

PREFACE

IN overlooking a lifetime one may overlook many things in it; I have forgotten some, I suppose; it is often convenient to have a memory that forgets, but how inconvenient not to have one that remembers!

Memoirs — they are what may come when we have shuffled off this mortal coil; Reminiscences — the word is too high-sounding, unless one sings it; but Recollections may be spoken; they belong more to the present.

Recollections, then, let these be. Some of mine are subconscious, as of times far and far away, when my ancestors were, as Professor Huxley said, " sitting in trees and painting themselves blue "; or of a later time when Christianity brought Rome, her art and her language, again to Britain; or of a nearer day, when Freedom was demanded for the folk; or of that time still more near, when for Freedom's sake my own kindred sought a freer life in a newer world.

These things are ever present in my thought, and of my life it should be an easy thing to tell; yet it is not, for am I not the concentrated essence of the experiences of my ancestors, as well as of myself? And so of my own self to tell the plain, unvarnished tale, I find it hard.

Friends are a necessity for an artist: without them, be he never so good, he fails; with them, he stands at least a chance of success. It has been my good fortune to be blessed with many friends in private, and I owe nothing but thanks to the encouragement of the critical

PREFACE

fraternity; but to the public after all I owe everything, for to it, in the last analysis, is an artist beholden most. At present, however, I wish to express my gratitude to those who have so kindly helped me with this little volume, not the least among these being my good friend Wallace Rice, to whom I owe my delivery from the toils and fascinations of the dictaphone.

In this book I have refrained from going into many particulars of my artistic career, preferring to give a general survey of its principal points, for my object is not only to interest music lovers by giving them a glimpse into an artist's life, but to provide a stimulus for amateurs who contemplate entering the professional arena, and to show them how necessary it is to have, in the first place, the natural ability, then the inner urge to prosecute their studies intelligently, the impulse to continue against opposition, and the determination to endure to the end.

To the profession of music, many are called but few are chosen. Of those who do achieve success, some are born to the purple, and so have the avenues of approach thrown open to them. But most of us are obliged to struggle in the press of those who throng the Muse even to touch the hem of her garment, and we may be thankful if she stretches forth her hand to help us on our way.

DAVID BISPHAM.

New York,
November 15, 1919.

CONTENTS

CHAPTER I

PAGE

INFANCY AND ORIGINS I

CHAPTER II

THE YOUNG IDEA 15

CHAPTER III

MUSIC'S GOLDEN TONGUE 28

CHAPTER IV

THE WORLD'S A STAGE 38

CHAPTER V

STEPPING-STONES 47

CHAPTER VI

DECISION 55

CHAPTER VII

SERIOUS STUDY BEGINS 62

CHAPTER VIII

OPERA FROM AFAR 72

CHAPTER IX

SPIRITS AND SOOTHSAYING 76

CHAPTER X

CONCERTS IN LONDON 82

CONTENTS

CHAPTER XI

PAGE

OPERA FROM WITHIN 92

CHAPTER XII

THE THRESHOLD CROSSED 102

CHAPTER XIII

PLANCHETTE AND PROPHECY 110

CHAPTER XIV

CLIMBING THE STEEPS 117

CHAPTER XV

WITH MANY TONGUES 123

CHAPTER XVI

FESTIVAL AND UNIVERSITY 131

CHAPTER XVII

THE FAT KNIGHT 139

CHAPTER XVIII

ARTS AND LETTERS 146

CHAPTER XIX

PHANTOMS OF HARMONY 157

CHAPTER XX

FROM GRAVE TO GAY 168

CHAPTER XXI

SWIMMING WITH THE TIDE 177

CHAPTER XXII

MY AIN COUNTRIE 185

CONTENTS

CHAPTER XXIII

PAGE

FORTUNE GOOD AND ILL 196

CHAPTER XXIV

CYCLES OF SONG 204

CHAPTER XXV

BEETHOVEN IN DRAMA 215

CHAPTER XXVI

MY NATIVE TONGUE 224

CHAPTER XXVII

ENTER DANNY DEEVER 230

CHAPTER XXVIII

WHERE ANGELS FEAR 238

CHAPTER XXIX

HAPS AND MISHAPS 247

CHAPTER XXX

THE UNFLYING DUTCHMAN 259

CHAPTER XXXI

A BAFFLED IDEAL 269

CHAPTER XXXII

ACROSS SEAS AND CONTINENTS 280

CHAPTER XXXIII

GOING TO AND FRO 290

CHAPTER XXXIV

COMPOSER AND CRITIC 301

CONTENTS

CHAPTER XXXV

PAGE

WOMAN AND SONG 309

CHAPTER XXXVI

THREE PRESIDENTS 317

CHAPTER XXXVII

SCULPTOR AND STAGE 326

CHAPTER XXXVIII

SPEAKING WITH TONGUES 336

CHAPTER XXXIX

PROGRAM MAKING 347

CHAPTER XL

IN REDWOOD FORESTS 353

CHAPTER XLI

DIVERSE INTERESTS 364

ILLUSTRATIONS

David Bispham . . . . *Frontispiece*

PAGE

William D. Bispham, Jane S. Bispham, David S. Bispham,
aged three . . . . *Facing page* 2

Myself when Young 5

Bispham Coat of Arms 9

Scull Coat of Arms 13

David Bispham, as the Duc de Longueville, in Messager's
Opera, "The Basoche" . . . . . *Facing page* 80

David Bispham, as Kurwenal, in Wagner's "Tristan and
Isolde" . . . . *Facing page* 114

David Bispham, as Alberich, in Wagner's "Niebelungen
Ring" . . . . *Facing page* 114

David Bispham, as Beckmesser in Wagner's "Meistersingers"
. . . . *Facing page* 124

David Bispham, as Schickaneder in Mozart's "Impresario"
. . . . *Facing page* 124

David Bispham, as The Vicar, in Lehmann's "Vicar of
Wakefield" . . . . *Facing page* 142

David Bispham, as Falstaff, in Verdi's "Falstaff"
. . . . *Facing page* 142

David Bispham, as Wotan, in Wagner's "Valkyrie"
. . . . *Facing page* 208

David Bispham, as Gomarez, in Floridia's "Paoletta" . .
. . . . *Facing page* 342

Gomarez rejuvenated in Floridia's "Paoletta" *Facing page* 342

David Bispham — The Death of Gomarez — in Floridia's
"Paoletta" . . . . *Facing page* 343

David Bispham, from a sketch by J. A. Cahill 344

A QUAKER SINGER'S RECOLLECTIONS

CHAPTER I

INFANCY AND ORIGINS

My heart leaps up when I behold
A rainbow in the sky;
So was it when my life began;
So is it now I am a man;
So be it when I shall grow old.
— *William Wordsworth.*

My earliest recollection — and what could be a more beautiful one? — is of seeing a perfect rainbow after heavy storm. I was a child of two and a half years, spending part of a summer with my parents at Atlantic City, so convenient to us of Philadelphia. At the close of a rainy afternoon, when most of the guests were indoors and we small fry unwillingly cabined in the parlors of the old Clarendon House, a friend of my father's came in and, picking me from the floor, said, " Come, my little man, I'll show thee a rainbow."

Carrying me on his shoulder, he bore me outside and stood me on the railing of the porch overlooking the sea. There, both its legs in the water, glowed a perfect rainbow against the black cloud that had been pelting us with its floods shortly before. My father's friend, and mine, explained to me about the shower, about the sun's shining out through the rain after the passing of the cloud, and how " that makes the rainbow." Many a time since

I

have I found — as who has not? — that there is beauty awaiting us after duress and storm, and a lesson withal!

As I look back, Arch Street in Philadelphia seems very important to me. A dignified street it was; one of private houses with an occasional necessary " store " on a corner; but now, alas, how changed! I was born near it, at No. 30, North Seventh Street, on January 5, 1857, though my birth seems to be recorded nowhere, except possibly in a family Bible which long search has not revealed.

The reason for this lack of record is simple. My mother was Miss Jane Lippincott Scull before her marriage to my father, William Danforth Bispham, and both were of old Quaker families; but as my father had left the Quaker body, my mother was in consequence " disowned for marrying out of meeting," and I was born before she was received back into the fold. Hence there is no record of my birth in the archives of the Society of Friends, and all effort has been unavailing to discover where my father, though a most particular and methodical lawyer, set down the fact of the arrival of his son and heir.

Another early memory and my first recollection of the " Sabbath " is of bowed window shutters on a summer day and of going forth with my parents, led by my mother's hand, to Arch Street half a " square " distant, and so to Meeting. As we went, we three together, on many a happy " First Day," we stopped to look at the grave of Benjamin Franklin in the corner of the cemetery at Fifth and Arch. Below Third Street, across the way from the Meeting House, was the old shop of Betsy Ross, where the first Stars and Stripes is said to have been made. At Seventh and Market was the house where Thomas Jeffer-

WILLIAM D. BISPHAM   DAVID S. BISPHAM   JANE S. BISPHAM
                              AGED THREE

From Photographs by Gutekunst, Philadelphia

son wrote the Declaration of Independence. At Sixth
and Chestnut stood the State House with the Liberty Bell.
How often have I climbed the belfry tower! And how
well I recall the coming of the boys from the Civil War,
cheering their lungs out as they swung past the sacred
place of the nation's birth!

The quietude of my earliest years was too soon broken
in upon by wars and the rumors of wars. Fort Sumter
and Bull Run were in every one's mouths, to be followed
by the names of McClellan, Sherman, Sheridan, and
Grant. Men were drilling everywhere with canes and
broomsticks. I even remember seeing men armed with
shot-guns jumping on the Market Street horse-cars, to
take the first train for Gettysburg during Lee's invasion
of Pennsylvania. My father had already volunteered
for the Blue Reserves, so called, and had two months of
soldiering before the crisis was over.

When he returned, to our surprise he preferred sleeping on the little grass plot in our yard to repose in his
bed. But he was a rather original man — he played
the flute, for instance, ran to fires with the Diligent Engine company, read Darwin and Huxley, and was called
a freethinker. He had been educated at the Lawrenceville School and at Princeton University, studying law at
the latter. He freed himself so completely from Quakerism that he would not be married in the Friends' Meeting. My mother must have been, as indeed she was,
deeply attached to one whom she followed to the disapproval of her parents and of the Meeting, but time
heals all things and she returned to the fold after my
birth.

The little Seventh Street house fell from its estate and
is no more. I often visited it in its decline, calling back

visions of my father as a volunteer fireman hurrying out in helmet, cape, and boots. I can still hear the soft notes of his flute. I remember the room where I was born, the red-headed sulphur matches I ate and the convulsion that followed, the torture of learning to read at my mother's knee, and the nightmare I used so often to have which was an unholy combination of the Fourth of July and the Book of Revelation — pin-wheels and rockets and the end of the world consumed in fervent heat!

My father and I got on well — very well as I grew older and music began to grow within me; but, what a fright he gave me once! Unknown to me he put on a wig while having his head shaved to stop the falling of his hair. He was in his easy chair when I came in to climb into his lap. As I thrust my fingers into his curly brown hair he suddenly bowed his head and left the wig in my hand. Poor child, I nearly died of fright, thinking I had pulled my father's head off! It was my first venture with wigs, and little did my parents think when soothing me that I should wear so many of them in after life. My first sight of a boy in a false face was little better. I was quieted only when I put it on myself — the first of how many disguises!

I saw Abraham Lincoln as he passed in the procession on the occasion of an official visit to Philadelphia and, though but a child of five or six, my mental picture of the tall man seated in his open carriage as he raised his hat and bowed to the shouting throngs about him is as clear as if it happened yesterday. Several years before there was any question of the accuracy of George Gray Barnard's conception of Lincoln I was able to enter my personal protest to the sculptor himself while visiting his studio and seeing the sketch of the statue that has

Myself When Young

since made such a stir. The head was a fine study, but in my opinion he entirely misunderstood the body of Lincoln and wrought out his conception in evident and utter disregard of what he actually looked like.

I vividly recall the time of President Lincoln's assassination, for I, a lad of eight, came home from school to find my mother upon her bed in a paroxysm of grief, sobbing out, " Our savior has been killed! "

Soon after this we moved from Philadelphia to Moorestown, New Jersey, to live until after my graduation from college in 1876. I had often been there before on the old stage-coach, and used to be shown the place under the bank of Pennshawken Creek where the first members of my family to pass that way had slept in a cave. William Penn had granted lands to my people, and they were going to them through the forests that then covered the country to take up their land and settle down among the Indians. But the aborigines were never hostile to Friends and were well treated by them, to the mutual advantage of both.

We lived not far from the two Bispham farm houses that my forebears had built long before, one of which still stands. My two grandsires, born in 1795 and 1798 respectively, lived, one to be eighty-five and the other to be eighty-nine. Both were large men, six feet tall, with the simple education of their ancestors. They had been New Jersey lads, the Bispham family belonging to Burlington, and the Sculls to Salem County. By honest work and business integrity they made themselves well off, both accumulating fortunes considerable for those days. These properties were divided equally among their rather numerous children, so that no large portion of either remains in any single pair of hands.

Grandfather Scull had for many years a house at Germantown as well as one in Philadelphia, and there he used to spend the summers, six miles from the city and, as I used to think, at the end of a long journey. The old dwelling still stands on the site of the Battle of Germantown in Main Street, nearly opposite the Chew mansion and a few hundred yards above the Johnson house. Many a happy time have I had there as a boy, wondering over the scars of war still visible then: the cannon-ball break in the stone at the corner of the house, the marks of musketry upon the heavy doors, and the famous " bullet-hole fence " in the garden.

Once in London at the height of my operatic life, sitting by an open window on a warm summer day, an old four-wheeler crawled by and the odor of the horse drifted to my nostrils. On the instant I saw again and vividly, as if before my eyes, the old Germantown place where I had been so often in early boyhood: the stable, brown painted, the big bay horses in their stalls, the harness in its appointed place, the oval duck-pond in the stable-yard, the currant-bordered garden-walk, the grape-vined arbor, even the comet of the early Civil War time, and finally myself, full of watermelon, before my amused grandfather, waddling — a bit of an actor even at that early age — to make him laugh the louder.

The smell from that antiquated London " growler " even brought back to me the memory of the brogue of the Irish serving-maids in the family, who lived out their lives in my grandfather's service, and of the rich Lancashire burr of the English coachman, and of the broken English of a German nurse. My knack of picking up and imitating foreign accents and modulations of speech, so useful upon many later occasions, was doubtless acquired at this time. One of the few actors whom I have found it difficult to imitate successfully, was my friend the late Beerbohm Tree, whose peculiar blend of German officer, Jewish actor, and Anglo-French society dude I never could accomplish.

Tastes and predilections, quite as much as physical characteristics, have ancestral origins, and it is no small part of my good fortune that in inheriting a sound constitution and rugged health from these grandparents of mine, I came also into possession of certain literary and artistic leanings, from which my love for music and the stage may well be derived, through the evident gifts in such fields which were apparent in my mother's family. Manuscript poems by my grandfather and by his eldest son, my uncle Gideon Scull, are still in my possession, and this uncle of mine wrote a number of books of a biographical character, and in addition showed considerable cleverness by his drawings in pen-and-ink. There is a family legend that as a youth at table, Gideon would fashion from bread little animals, beasts of the field and denizens of the farmyard, for the amusement of his younger brothers and sisters. My uncle David, too, wrote books, choosing religious subjects which had puzzled him and every one before him, and which seem as far from solution as ever; while Edward, the youngest brother, exhibited in early manhood so considerable a talent for drawing and painting that he entered the classes of a celebrated Parisian artist. He found the life distasteful, however, and later painted only for his own and his family's enjoyment, devoting his years to good works. David Scull, the second brother and my mother's favorite, was the handsomest man I have ever known, and I loved him deeply. All these uncles were great

Bispham.

Coat of Arms of the Bispham Family

travelers, though my father's family were by preference stay-at-homes.

The name of Bispham is one of great antiquity in the north of England and exists to this day in Lancashire and in the Lake District, where it was known long before the time of William the Conqueror. It is to be found in the Domesday Book, in 1086, written as Biscopham, since contracted into its present form, derived from the far more ancient name of the noble Saxon family of Biscop with the addition of the old word *ham,* meaning *home,* the combination signifying "The home of the Biscops."

The earliest extended mention of an individual bearing the name is to be found in the Chronicle of the monk Florence of Worcester, who gives a long account of Benedict Biscop as living between the years A. D. 628 and 689. He became a monk and founded the famous monastery of Jarrow at Wearmouth. There he educated to become his successor, the cleric known as the Venerable Bede, who also tells of his friend the Abbot as having made many journeys to Rome and as bringing back with him not only artificers in glass from Venice, but also "John, precentor of the church of St. Peter the Apostle, to Britain to teach his monks the course of chanting throughout the year."

I like to think that I bear the name of a family to which is thus directly due the introduction into England of the earliest examples of its superb cathedral glass, and the introduction, too, of the noble Gregorian strains which afford so precious a basis for its ecclesiastical music.

Thirty miles north of Liverpool and a few miles west of the smoky town of Wigan stands ancient Bispham Hall, from whose precincts, it is traditional in the American branch of the family, the Bispham men shook

the dust of their feet after having turned Quaker, in order
to cast in their lot with William Penn and their fellow
colonists of like belief and aid him in the foundation of
the new Commonwealth of Pennsylvania near the end
of the seventeenth century, a thousand years after the
days of Biscop and Bede.   The family name has, from
the time of its earliest recordings in church registers and
upon legal documents, been subject to a variety of spell-
ings, natural enough when phonetics were the rule, and
from the Biscopham of the Domesday Book came
Biscopem and *Biscopeym,* finally settling into *Bispham,*
pronounced *Bispam,* as indeed it was often to be found
written in England.   From this came *Bispame, Bispen,*
and *Bispin.*

With the departure of the original Quakers from their
mother country to Philadelphia came a further gradual
exodus of the clan to Boston, Virginia, and the West
Indies.   Indeed I have found representatives of the
ancient name all over the United States and in Australia.   But few remain in England, and those are in
Lancashire about the villages and ancient Hall of the
name, or in the Lake District to the north.   Besides my
own but one other Bispham was for many years to be
found in the London Directory, and I have never seen it
among the lists of any choral body with which I sung
during the whole of the time I assisted at festivals in
England.

In America my patronymic began to be spelled *Bisphame, Bisphan, Bisphen, Bisphain,* and *Bisfan,* and was
often not only written but spoken as *Bisfam,* the letters *p* and *h* being mistaken as intending the sound of *f.*
The correct pronunciation is Bis-pam, the *h* being silent.
Although I have been addressed as Mr. *Bispum,* which is

not so far away in sound, I am more often called *Bisham,*
which is not at all correct.   There is an old house on the
Thames known as Bisham Abbey, but no one in the
mother country confuses the two names, or mispro-
nounces my patronymic.   Sometimes it is written in the
United States as *Bicham, Bishham, Bishamp, Bishpban,*
and *Bishpham,* the last being rather an ordinary mis-
conception of the name.

I have kept many letters, telegrams, and the like, from
which the following examples will show that the elder
Mr. Weller's advice has been adopted and my surname
set down "according to the taste and fancy of the
speller."   What an iniquity to manufacture out of seven
simple letters such contortions as these!— *Beechman,
Bisparn, Besphain, Besphourm, Besthon, Biftham,
Bipham, Biskham,* and *Biscamb.*   Others have contributed *Bistam, Bisthiam, Bixham;* with *Bisthan,
Bispthan, Bispthane, Bisplain,* and *Bisplian.*   One of my
friends, who should have known better, could never get
her tongue untwisted from *Bipsham.*   I have been described on my own program as Mr. *Dispham,* and
from being called "a household word" my poor cog-
nomen has degenerated at times to a state perilously
near that of a household utensil, as in *Dispam* and
Dishchan!

The name of my mother's family, Scull, or Skull, possibly derived from the Norse *skald,* a herald or crier, is
also of great antiquity, and belongs to the west of England, near the Welsh border.   The first of the name to
come to America was the Quaker, Nicholas Skull, who became William Penn's surveyor and made the first map of
Philadelphia.   On the maternal side I am proud of being descended from a long line of Norman ancestors, as

VITAM IMPENDERE VERO

Scull

Coat of Arms of the Scull Family

set forth in the annals of the Order of Runnymede, comprising nine of the signers of Magna Charta, viz:— Roger and Hugh Bigod, Henry de Bohun, Richard and Gilbert de Clare, John de Lacie, William de Mowbray, Saher de Quincey, and Robert de Vere.   Good American as I am, I see nothing to be ashamed of in such researches or in their results, agreeing with the old writer who said: " No man despiseth family save him who hath it not, or is unduly proud thereof who hath aught else to be proud of."

My mother never permitted ·a piano in her house, though she was not unmoved by the " concord of sweet sounds," and eventually accepted a cabinet organ as a gift from my father.   I fancy he felt in me the beginnings of something like an accompanist for the strains of his flute, and so it turned out, for I soon began to pick out the harmonies with which my soul was filled, but of whose devious ways along the keys my fingers were ignorant.

Though my own home was so largely unblest by the music which my mother's faith forbade her to enjoy, I found what I craved as I grew older in the house of my grandfather, Samuel Bispham, at No. 263, North Sixth Street, opposite Franklin Square.   The good Samuel and his wife Maria, who was one of the Stokes clan, came of less strait-laced stock than the Sculls and Lippincotts, and a piano with music was to be found there, not of a high order, to be sure, but of a healthy sort.   The numerous grandchildren were welcome in the house, which was a second home to us.   Grandfather himself used to troll many a lusty English ditty, and sang to us every Christmas Day until he had passed eighty, and I in the home circle there first lifted up my voice in song.

CHAPTER II

THE YOUNG IDEA

What will a child learn sooner than a song? — Pope.

THE little red-headed fellow of eight went from the big city and the quiet Friends' School at Twelfth and Chestnut streets, from the constant and almost sole companionship of his dear mother, to live in the country at Moorestown, and meet a larger circle of acquaintances.

An English journalist, writing a few years ago for a London paper upon American cities, described Philadelphia as a city on the banks of the Delaware River "opposite Camden." Yet, as an American writer said of Edmund Gosse's visit to the United States, he, the fastidious critic and friend of the living world's great litterati, upon being summoned by a penciled post card to call upon Walt Whitman, proceeded to Camden, the last town in the world, made his way to the last street in the town, and to the last house in the street and there found in the American Sage one whom he was fain to call the greatest man he had ever met!

As Mark Twain called a girl's red hair "Skaneateles color, because it was ten miles from Auburn," so Moorestown was ten miles from Camden. All around that countryside were fine sturdy descendants of British yeomen. They did not mingle with the world, these Quaker folk, for they seldom married out of Meeting, and many of them had never been to Philadelphia at all until the railroad was put through; then the old village with its Main Street lined with noble trees began rapidly to change.

At first we lived at Mrs. Higbee's house at the far end of the long street, and there began to come to me one by one the experiences of life. At Mrs. Higbee's there was an antique piano that stood harp-like against the wall; sitting by Miss Beulah's side at it, "turning over" for her as she played, I gained my first idea of musical notation.

But "Miss Lill" was my favorite among the girls. She was the widow of a gallant officer in the Civil War, Major Morris, who had escaped all harm during many campaigns, only to die of heart disease as he stood leaning against the fence at home after the war was over. I was much impressed by this and never have ceased to feel keen sorrow for that pretty young widow who was my teacher at her mother's house while we lived there.

Nor shall I forget the readings, "Woodman, spare that tree," "Excelsior," and the like, with which she led my young mind to a knowledge of polite literature and *belles lettres*. Though I could not remember the rules of grammar she sought to instill into me, I possess to this day the very "Student's Companion" she gave me, and often think of the numerous English words of Latin derivation with which I became acquainted in that truly admirable compendium of useful knowledge.

Then came a home of our own and a real school for me. I was a willful lad, and after a while was placed with Bartram Kaighn, an aged man who had been my father's teacher when he was a boy in Philadelphia, and had prepared him for Princeton. As fate would have it this worthy Friend moved to Moorestown, and I was sent to my father's preceptor, who struggled manfully to instill into me a few of the many things he knew. Though fond of me, he often punished me, and I have always marveled at his patience, rattle-brained as I was. He prepared me for Haverford College, of which institution my grandfather Scull had been one of the founders, and there my mother's brothers had all been educated. I have many things to thank Bartram Kaighn for and nothing to regret in my association with him, except circumstances for which I alone was to blame.

As a boy I was, in many respects, a shy youngster; indeed, appearances to the contrary notwithstanding, I am shy still. Circumstances alone have forced me to appear to have a virtue which I do not possess, the assumption of which has caused many to think me a calm man in the presence of the public or elsewhere.

My first lessons in French were with Bartram Kaighn. I had heard other boys speaking their lessons before I began to study the language, and with my quick ear I caught the correct pronunciation at once. But when first called upon by Mr. Kaighn to read a paragraph from " Télémaque," my diffidence so overcame me that instead of pronouncing as I knew I should, I read the passages as if they were so many English words, realizing full well that I was condemning myself in the eyes of my master. Upon the conclusion of my efforts, he wearily said, " That will do, David; it is as well as I could have expected of thee."

At that moment my British blood had spoken and whatever kinship I may have with the French was in abeyance, hiding its diminished head in the corner to which I expected Bartram to remand me as a punishment; for in his school the stool, the corner, and the fool's cap were still institutions, dating back to the time of the whipping post and stocks which my father remembered well as existent at Moorestown in his boyhood.

I have always been ashamed of this first attempt at pronouncing French. My ability to pronounce the foreign tongues in which I have been compelled to sing has been of the greatest service to me. It goes without saying that I have a full knowledge of the meaning of all that I sing in other languages, but I cannot sail far upon the sea of philology without fear of foundering, my vocabulary being limited to the words which will supply me with the necessaries of life, the conventions of conversation, or the language of song.

All the book learning I knew good Bartram Kaighn made sufficiently available to enable me to pass the preliminary college examinations, and I went from Moorestown gayly enough. I remember, however, being homesick and longing for the companionship of that dear mother whose only child I was. For a day, or maybe two days, I thought I should not be able to endure the anguish of separation. With all my high spirits, I was at first as lonely as a cat in a strange garret. All the boys seemed to walk about on their toes and look at me as dogs do when they are getting acquainted.

Fortunately for me, however, I found at Haverford some of my old schoolmates and some of my cousins besides, so I was not altogether alone. By these I was soon introduced to others with whom I formed life-long friendships, though none of a musical nature.

Scholastic work was immediately entered upon and was composed of a curriculum dignified in its simplicity, but noted then, as ever since, for its thoroughness and high objective.

During my time at Haverford my deficiency in mathematics was noticeable, though for a period I had a good enough will and memory to advance even as far as the study of trigonometry, conic sections, astronomy, and dear knows what!— all things that I dislike to remember. Finally I was given my choice between mathematics and the study of German, and I am glad that I was wise enough to take up the latter. It subsequently proved to be of the greatest use in my operatic career.

At college our principal game was cricket, and Haverford had the finest team among American colleges, its reputation being kept up to the present day through the efforts of my kinsman, Henry Cope, who for years took an eleven to England to play with the schools and colleges there. Though I constantly played cricket I was not a good player. I could bowl fairly well, but somehow or other my opponent always bowled better than I and, as the ball had a way of getting under my bat and knocking down my wicket, despite my best efforts to prevent it from doing so, I was not given a place upon the first eleven and I fear but feebly adorned the ranks of the second.

I suppose the ways of boys at Haverford were just the same as boys of any other school and I do not remember that any one indulged particularly in things that he should not have done, though perhaps owing to the strict rule of the Quakers we were not permitted to do many things which we might otherwise have done with perfect propriety. We all had to go to meeting on Sunday, " First Day," as they call it, and to the midweek meeting on " Fourth Day." We assembled outside the college on these occasions and marched, the Seniors first, the Juniors second, and the Sophomores and Freshmen bringing up the rear, solemnly along the little boardwalk across the bridge which spans the cut through which used to run the old Pennsylvania Railway trains.

Into the little Friends' meeting we filed, all sitting in silence the greater part of the time, though among the professors there were several admirable occasional speakers.

At Haverford there were sometimes mock trials and the like, taking the place of stage plays. In these I participated with the rest, and look back upon the evenings thus spent with a great deal of pleasure; but the meetings of the quasi-secret society I joined I recollect with greater interest, for at some of these I made my first efforts at declaiming from Shakespeare such selections as Hamlet's Soliloquy, the speeches of Brutus and of Mark Antony or the quarrel scene from " Julius Cæsar " and The Seven Ages of Man.

I remember vividly my first hurt from criticism, for one of my friends took me off admirably, both in manner of delivery and in style of gesture. I have thought of this travesty upon myself hundreds of times since and have felt grateful to have been so early shown how I sounded and appeared to others.

I left Haverford College at last after much anguish in cramming for my final examinations, for I was ever something of a dullard at study, and I thanked my lucky stars that I should never again have any examinations to pass, little dreaming that before long I would find myself on the way leading to constant examinations before the greatest tribunal imaginable, namely, the great public.

That summer of 1876, when I went back to Moorestown after a little travel with young companions, seeing such native beauty as the Hudson and Niagara, I had to face the question of what to do with myself. My parents being of moderate means it was, of course, necessary that I should work for my living. As I had friends who were physicians, I thought I should like to become a doctor, and therefore visited hospitals with my acquaintances, went through dissecting rooms, and was present at clinics and operations performed upon those suffering from accidents. The experience of the hospitals was not easy, and that of the dissecting room certainly gruesome; yet before long my nostrils became accustomed to the peculiar odor of the dissecting room; but I could not stand seeing operations performed upon mangled humanity, brought into the theatre of the hospital for treatment before the students. I was carried fainting from the place on more than one occasion, to the amusement of those who had already become hardened to the work of mercy. It was therefore presently decided that I had better go into the wool business of my uncle David Scull, founded by his father many years before.

And so, at $4 a week, I was put to learning the wool trade, and spent seven years in that establishment at No. 125, Market Street, occupied with the intricacies of my business, both in the office and in the warehouse among the workmen and the bales and fleeces of wool.

One morning my uncle David called me into the office and said that he was considering going abroad and wanted my mother and me to go with him; and so early in 1878 I had the good fortune to take this trip.

Eight months in Europe to a youth of twenty-one is no light matter, and I look back upon it as being in reality the beginning of my education, for then only was I able to comprehend the value of what I had learned at school and college and be thankful that it was an education classical in character. Few young men had then been given the opportunity to leave Quaker Philadelphia and see Europe under conditions as favorable as those I enjoyed.

We landed in Liverpool and I well remember seeing in the Mersey River that gigantic steamship, the *Great Eastern,* which had long been used in laying ocean cables. Indeed I had the opportunity of going aboard of her before she was broken up and of seeing the tanks in which the cable had been coiled, but which were then devoted to the base uses of circus rings and of what is nowadays called Vaudeville.

Great was my delight to discover in the cloister of Chester Cathedral the gravestones of monks bearing the name of Bispham. Upon climbing into the belfry tower I found that the oldest and largest bell in the chime had been given it by one William Bispham centuries before, as evidenced by the Latin inscription running around the lip of the bell. Near the Lady Chapel of the Cathedral is also a memorial tablet set into the wall bearing the name of William Bispham, another member of the family, who was born in 1597. This was restored in 1888 by my kinsman, William Bispham of New York.

Fascinating it was to me to visit Bispham Hall, that ancient home of my people in Lancashire, a land that had been the cradle of my race. Nowhere in the world could a youth have more thrust upon his receptive mind than during an intelligent visit to England, where we saw most of the celebrated abbeys, castles, and ancient cities, many of which I was afterward to know so well through journeys taken as a professional singer during my several years' residence in England.

On our way from London and Paris to Italy, we visited Switzerland, where occurred an incident I shall never forget, which was vividly recalled to my mind by events in the late war, when our party, having arrived in the little railway station on the way to Zermatt, left the train in order to take horses which had been ordered for us and which we found waiting.

Having arranged my mother's traveling pack upon the saddle of her horse behind the station, and all being ready for our party to go up the valley, I left the animal and went into the station for my mother; but what was my surprise on returning to find a large military German calmly mounting my mother's horse — furnished with a sidesaddle, by the way — and riding off upon the animal, from whose back he had taken my mother's traveling pack and thrown it upon the ground. Of course, all my protests were unavailing. The horseman paid not the slightest heed to me or to the objections of our party; but went on his way with such rejoicing as he may have had in his inward heart, followed as he was by some good Anglo-Saxon talk, which I have no doubt he understood perfectly well. The rigidity of his back as he rode off forced me to think that he was bracing himself against something which was hitting him hard.

I was afterward to come into contact with a good many such persons in the course of my professional career, and I have always found it interesting to speculate upon the reasons that cause clever men who ought to know better to do so many obviously disagreeable things. However, that is the way of some people, I suppose. Breeds of men have their manners and customs, just as breeds of dogs have theirs.

From Switzerland our little party went down among the Italian lakes, and thence through Verona to Venice and on through other ancient Italian cities to Florence,

where I was afterward to live for some time, and so to
Rome.

Beyond the singing of popular songs by street musicians
and by gondoliers on the canals of Venice, I heard little
music during my early visits to the Land of Song.   I
did go once to the Costanzi Theatre in Rome to hear
Verdi's opera " Don Carlos," too seldom given nowadays,
and for reasons I cannot make out.   Verdi was identified in his younger days with the cause of Italian unity,
and his very name was used as a rallying cry, its letters
standing for the patriotic toast, " Vittorio Emanuele Re
D'Italia," V-E-R-D-I!   But this, and the political opinions expressed in " Don Carlos," should have no influence
on the public to-day.   The eminent composer was fond
of this opera, issuing a second and even a third edition
of it, each time with considerable changes which make
it all the better as a work of art.

In Roman churches I also heard on festivals the voices
of male singers who had been in the Pope's choir at St.
Peter's, which had been dispersed among the other
churches some time before, where they were to be heard
by an admiring public, that would actually applaud well-
rendered selections in the masses as if they had been given
in the concert room.   This seems strange to us of to-
day, but the period of which I speak is now recognized
as having been one in which the music of the Roman
Church reached almost its deepest debasement.   It was
the time when the organist would play such pieces as the
" Brindisi " from " Lucrezia Borgia " or " La donna é
mobile " from " Rigoletto " at the elevation of the Host.

When in Rome, my uncle made up his mind to go to
Athens, where I was greatly impressed by the Greek theatres, cut into the slopes of the Acropolis.   Fortunately

I had read Greek tragedies in college, and so vividly did their stories return to me when treading the stone platforms from which they were originally delivered, that my natural love for the stage was greatly enhanced. Perhaps without knowing it I inwardly resolved to become an actor, or a singer; perhaps both. At any rate I felt called to express myself before the public in the high-sounding vocal phrases that I loved so well. Strange to say, the experiences of those days in Athens so powerfully affected my mind that my endeavors toward the foundation and maintenance of a Classic Theatre resulted after many years in the building of what is known as the Greek Theatre at the University of California in Berkeley.

I had abundant opportunity when in Constantinople of hearing the Turkish music which so unpleasantly assails the ear in the bazaars, clanging instruments and high-pitched voices uttering tuneless phrases. It was indeed strange enough, but it gave me no pleasure whatever, and I was glad to leave early such entertainment as I had attended.

Of what Europe calls music there is next to nothing in the Mohammedan religion, and I found none when I attended the service of the Dancing Dervishes. Yet their worship is intended to be a praise of God, by means of such long-continued gyrations as would put almost any athlete to shame.

Great was my surprise when those simple, almost Quakerish-looking, men arose from " facing the meeting," exactly as at home in Philadelphia, and started slowly to twirl on their toes about the previously empty floor space between them and the congregation. Fast and faster they turned until their gray and Friendly coat-tails stood out from their bodies at right angles, for all the world like ballet dancers' skirts; and, as their motion gradually subsided, the coat-tails assumed a more seemly angle and finally hung down as circumspectly as any well-behaved coat-tails should do. No expression whatever appeared upon the stolid countenances of the worshipers, who seemed to vie with each other in the length of their choregraphic exertions.

If the service of the Dancing Dervishes is as barren of music and as silent as a Quaker Meeting, the experience that I had of the Howling Dervishes was quite the reverse. It was indeed more than barbaric; it was savage in its intensity. From a latticed balcony we looked down upon a rather large room, the floor of which was bare; in the corner was a raised throne upon which sat one who was evidently a dignitary of the sect. Around the room ran low divans upon which were seated the worshipers, young, old, and middle-aged, white, black, and tawny. These, excited by the beating of drums and the sounds of a strange chant, and urged on by a leader who arose and went to the middle of the room, finally stood in line with him and went through extreme physical contortions, loudly chanting the while. One great black eunuch in particular I shall never forget, a giant in physique, who outdid all competitors; yet ultimately puffing and sweating, he was himself led from the room rejoicing in the strength that enabled him so to assail Heaven with his cries, and to dance before the Lord in pious orgies.

I looked forward to the autumn of that year with anything but pleasure, for I knew that it would take me back again to the warehouse and office of my good uncle; but I shook from my mind all such unpleasant thoughts as wool fleeces and wool bales, and buying and selling that oily but necessary commodity, and gave myself up to the enjoyment of the hour. It is better for us all not to cross bridges until we come to them, but at last I found my way back by way of Marseilles and gay Paris to smoky London, and thus home to what Benjamin Franklin called " my dear Philadelphia."

CHAPTER III

There is no truer truth obtainable
By man, than comes of music.
— *Robert Browning.*

DESIRE to enter upon a musical career came to me, I am sure, through the influence of the music I heard in the Episcopal Church at Moorestown, where now and then I went with my father, who sang occasionally in the little choir. The majesty of the pealing organ, played by my grand-aunt Emma Stokes, the choir behind the green baize curtains of the organ loft, the dignity of Doctor Weld with his black gown and snowy sleeves, all so far removed from the simplicity of Friends' Meeting, wrought mightily upon my mind. Yet High Church practices were little known about Philadelphia, and I did not then dream of St. Mark's and my future participation in services which might have been Roman Catholic, for all the difference apparent to a casual observer.

My uncle John Bispham had given me a zither, on which I had lessons from a German " professor," by occupation a saloon-keeper. I had also a few lessons on the guitar from a woman, and I learned to strum on the banjo from my pal Will Chamberlain, who had given me some notion of chords on the piano. His parents were not Quakers; not they! — and under their hospitable roof my youthful eyes and ears were opened to many things which the larger world smiles upon. My mother,

I am sure, thought all music a wile of the Evil One, the
stage a snare for every foot, old or young, and the combination, as in opera, something too appalling to contemplate. She had once been to an opera, and the ballet shocked her beyond expression!

Yet even as a boy I could not believe there was essential wrong in either music or the drama; the only wrong
lay in their debasement, their unworthy presentation or
immoderate and inconsiderate use. In this last respect
I am in entire agreement with Fox and the early Quakers,
who formed their estimates on the excesses of the Restoration Period.

I often journeyed from Moorestown to Philadelphia
on Saturday, to hear an occasional concert, or perhaps to
go to a matinée to see some celebrated actor in a good
play; poor music, poor plays, and poor acting I held in as
little favor then as I do now. It was at the Academy that
my delighted ear first heard " Pat " Gilmore and his band
play the " William Tell " overture and similar popular music. Theodore Thomas, whom I was afterward
to know so well and with whom I was to sing so frequently, gave me my first acquaintance with the symphonies of Beethoven, Schubert, and many others. I shall
never forget the rhythm in the beat of his right arm or
the dignity and grace of the movements of his left hand
as he modulated the strains of his orchestra.

On summer evenings in Philadelphia I used to listen
to such open-air concerts and music as could be found in
those days, chiefly in the German districts of the city,
where small orchestras were to be heard in the beer gardens. It was in one of these that I first heard the Hungarian violinist, Remenyi, whose acquaintance I sought.
The principal piece that I recall he played was a Hun-

garian gypsy selection, for the adaptation of which he
assumed the credit, though he told me with evident vexa-
tion that a man named Joachim had also made an arrangement of the same airs, which he was proclaiming
all over Europe as the only genuine one.

At another concert during this period I heard the famous Ole Bull, the diamond in the end of whose violin
bow still flashes in my mind's eye. I recall the wizard's
slender figure and long white hair and his somewhat antiquated style of dress coat and neckcloth. Ever since, I
have rather curiously connected this vision with Paganini,
his world-renowned predecessor.

My uncle John also took me to my first opera. How
I loved him for it! We heard Clara Louise Kellogg,
that charming lady who was to be one of my artistic
friends many years later, sing in " Martha " and subsequently in other parts. I shall always remember the exquisite silvery tones of Joseph Maas, the English tenor
whose career was cut short all too soon by death. The
operas sung by Miss Kellogg's company, " Mignon,"
" The Bohemian Girl," " Faust," and kindred works,
were done in our good English language, and brought
fame to all concerned.

I also became well acquainted — from the distance of
the " peanut " gallery — with members of the Richings-
Bernard opera company, and I heard the fascinating
Zelda Seguin as Carmen, one of the best it has ever been
my pleasure to hear, and Charles Santley, the celebrated
English barytone, in " Zampa." Who would have
thought that I was to have Zelda Seguin acting with me,
and be privileged to sing on many a program with
Charles Santley?

During my years in college, my opportunities for education through music and the drama were largely to remain outside the prescribed curriculum. Among the impedimenta which I took from Moorestown to Haverford was my beloved zither, which I played upon when occasion offered in spare moments. I had not counted upon the strict authorities at Haverford forbidding such harmless music as was made upon this rather primitive instrument; but to my great chagrin I was soon informed that music was against the rules, and that if I must needs play at all, I would have to do so off the college grounds. I therefore packed my zither in its little case and took it over to the Haverford station on the Pennsylvania Railway where, through the kindness of the ticket seller, I was enabled to keep it, and where I went daily to practice. I never took it back to the college. Indeed when I began to hear something of other music I deemed practice upon it almost a waste of time, it was so limited in its scope; though for social occasions I was not unwilling to show my skill and perform such selections as I knew at sociables, Sunday-school concerts, and the like, during the holidays when I was entertaining and being entertained among my young friends.

The scarcity of musical opportunities naturally tended to cause me to seek elsewhere that diversion which my nature so craved. As naturally as a duck goes to the water, I endeavored to make the acquaintance of people who were musical. I was advised to go to a large hall in Vine Street where there was a stage upon which a variety performance was carried on during the evening, when Teutonic families gathered for their supper and beer, and where a young German barytone could be heard singing to his own accompaniment at the piano.

I often went to hear this singer, Max Heinrich by

name, and from that remarkable artist obtained my first
introduction to the greatest song writers of the world:
Schubert, Schumann, Mendelssohn, Brahms, while pieces
rendered in the English language flashed upon my ear,
and all this brought a message new and strange to me.   I
recognized in it what I needed, and straightway determined to make the acquaintance of this Heinrich and to
learn from him, if possible, some of the songs which I
had heard him sing.   This led me into contact with a
great artist, from whom I afterward gleaned a knowledge of many things of value to me in my profession,
and I am glad to say that Max Heinrich remained my
friend until the day of his death.

He told me about his early career — he was only a
young man himself at the time, and I was but eighteen.
He said he had had an opportunity to sing in the Royal
Opera at Berlin, that his voice had been brought to the
attention of the old Emperor William, and that he had
received a command to go and sing in private for his
Majesty.   He confessed to me, however, that when the
evening arrived, he, having pawned his dress coat and being unable to find the wherewithal to release it, was
playing billiards with some companions when an emis-
sary came from the Palace looking for Heinrich, and ex-
citingly demanding his attendance, saying that the Emperor and members of his party were waiting to hear
him.   Heinrich, however, declined to go, as he was not
able to dress for the occasion — indeed, he could not
be admitted in his ordinary clothes to the presence of
royalty in the drawing-room of the Palace.   And so, regretfully and with a shrug of his shoulders, he dismissed
the court messenger.   But he said to me, " I vas a
damned fool, as usual."

After that, Heinrich told me, he went concertizing through Germany; made a little money, kept some of it and, after wandering with Hungarian gypsies, he, himself, the most delightfully wandering of all the wanderers, found his way to America about 1873 and deposited what savings he had in the bank of Jay Cooke, which failed soon after, and Heinrich found himself stranded. To keep body and soul together, he sang in the beer hall of which I have spoken.

Not long after, Heinrich became the bass soloist in the choir of the Roman Catholic Cathedral on Logan Square, where the organist was Michael H. Cross, whom I afterward knew intimately for many years, and who told me that one day after service a young German came up into the organ loft, asking " Do you vant a singer? " Mr. Cross said, " What can you sing? " He replied, " I vill sing at sight anything you gif me." Cross handed him a difficult barytone solo from a mass, playing the accompaniment, while Heinrich rendered the number to his entire satisfaction, obtaining the position and remaining at the cathedral for several years.

Fortunately for me, there came to live at Haverford one Ellis Yarnall and his English wife, a rare couple indeed, whose house was filled with books and pictures, and whose eldest daughter was a good pianist and sang nicely herself. She and her mother introduced me to old English songs, in which I at once began to revel. I have used them ever since, deeming them to be of the highest quality in their class and in no wise inferior to music of other nations merely because they happen to be in the English language and by English composers, who, strangely enough, were not by many persons considered the equals of those born on the other side of the English Channel.

It turned out that I, who could not be kept away from music, and vocal music in particular, influenced the young men about me who, notwithstanding the fact that they were of Quaker blood, were just as apt to enjoy music and to sing as those who belonged to other religious denominations. A little glee club was formed before I left Haverford and it was but a short time after my graduation that the authorities, some of the elder of whom had passed away, came to the conclusion that musical instruments might be permitted to the students, who at once began to bring guitars, banjos, and mandolins to the college, to the good, I doubt not, of every one of the student body; though music was not taught then at Haverford, nor has it ever become part of the curriculum.

Years later I was privileged to give at my Alma Mater several concerts, which were partly made up of the songs I had learned from Max Heinrich and the Yarnalls. These concerts were largely attended and were the first that had ever been heard at Haverford.

In that early part of my experience I remember well hearing the celebrated Emma Abbot in " Paul and Virginia " and one or two other things. The fact that she introduced " Home, Sweet Home " into any opera at her own sweet will did not interfere with the enjoyment of her performances by the audiences of that time; indeed they rather looked for the familiar strains, expecting them before they wended their way to their own sweet homes.

For all my enjoyment of the people that I heard in my youth, nothing could compare with the real thrill that I received one afternoon when, going to one of these very performances, I heard a girl singing up an alley. This unseen, unknown woman had indeed a God-given voice.

I was not too young to have heard Brignoli, but somehow I never did hear him, though my father often spoke
of his silvery tones and of his clumsiness upon the stage,
where his gait was said to be so awkward that he once
tripped over his own feet and fell down.

Backed up against the Twelfth Street Meeting House
where I went to school as a child, stands the Roman Catholic Church of St. John in Thirteenth Street, the organist of which was a friend of Brignoli's, who used to go and
sing the Offertorium there now and then.   It is told that
once, the sermon being long and Brignoli perturbed lest
he should be late at a luncheon party, the celebrated tenor,
after nervously walking up and down the choir loft for
some time, suddenly tore aside the curtain and called
down to the priest, who had not yet finished his discourse,
" Stop-a de preach!   Stop-a de preach!   I sing-a now! "
And the mandate of the eccentric singer was duly obeyed
and the song sung.

There are so many instances of eccentricity among artists that the world at large is not far wrong in considering that some of them may be not quite *compos mentis,*
as the Latins would say.   Indeed the fine old basso, Castelmary, said to me one day toward the close of his
career at Covent Garden, where I was just beginning
my own, " How are you to-day, my dear? " and tapping
my head with his forefinger he questioned, " Just a leetle
mad, eh?   Just a leetle mad? "   I suppose he wanted
to know where he stood with me, as he was the *régisseur*
of the company and I was plunging in " where angels
feared to tread "; such an act could but be, to him, that
of a madman.

Madame Titjens I heard but once, and nothing remains in my memory of the sound of her voice; I can

only recall her enormous figure. My sense of hearing
seemed to have been blotted out by that of sight.

Long after Christine Nilsson had left the operatic
stage I used to meet her socially in London. She had
become too portly to adore, though her voice was said to
have retained all its power and beauty. During my early
manhood I had heard her in " Faust " and I was once
taken behind the scenes to the greenroom at the Academy of Music in Philadelphia by a friend of the great
prima donna, to whom I was introduced. She was no
longer appearing in opera and was singing in what was
one of her last concerts in America.

Nilsson was still superb of figure and looked most
regal in a purple velvet gown with a long train. I believe she was of peasant origin, though she was said to
be patrician, but I had never seen such extremes of
behavior as in that few minutes before she was called
on the stage about the middle of the program. During
the intermission she had been conversing in a dignified
manner with a group of friends. When she was told
that the time had come for her to sing, she suddenly
turned upon her accompanist and gave him such a blow
upon his back with her hand that it nearly prostrated the
little man, saying with a loud laugh, " Come along, what
are you standing there for? "

She proceeded from the greenroom to the stage, I
walking close behind her. Just as she stepped into view
of the audience her train caught upon a nail in the floor
and in one instant she had turned and was tearing at
it with the ferocity of a tigress. Seeing the trouble, I
was fortunately able to disengage her dress from the
obstacle, when she, with instantaneous composure, walked
upon the stage like a queen.

That same greenroom is still adorned with litho-
graphed portraits and photographs of all of the artists
whom I saw and heard in my youth, but I have never entered this room nor gone upon that stage without thinking
of that afternoon, to me so memorable, when I first came
into anything like personal contact with a great representative of the lyric profession.

CHAPTER IV

THE WORLD'S A STAGE

That noise or sound which musicians make while they are in tuning their instruments . . . is nothing pleasant to hear, but yet is a cause why the music is sweeter afterwards.— Bacon.

My father had decided that I ought to see Edwin Booth in " Hamlet," somewhat against the wishes of my mother, on condition that I should read the play. This I made haste to do, needless to say. My imagination had already been stirred by the visit of a traveling troupe to Moorestown and I remember to this day the villain, the lover, and the bee-yoo-ty-ful lady of the piece. I had also been taken surreptitiously to enjoy the gorgeousness of a Christmas pantomime, but I think my mother never found this out.

It was at the Walnut Street Theatre that I had the never-to-be-forgotten experience of hearing and seeing Edwin Booth. I say " hearing " advisedly, for I as distinctly recall the melody of his voice and his perfect diction as I do the beauty of his figure and face. On that stage I afterward saw Mr. Booth in several parts, when I grew older and my mother ceased objecting to what she could not very well control. It was there, too, that I saw Charlotte Cushman, Ristori, Lawrence Barrett, John McCullough, a Philadelphian, and the lovely Adelaide Neilson, whose methods more nearly matched those of Booth than those of any one else I have ever seen or known of.

The Philadelphia public never needed to be treated with such consideration as that of Boston. There fashionable folk would attend nothing that called itself a theatre, but came later to patronize the company of eminent actors that flourished for so many years at the Boston Museum. And it not only had to call itself a " museum " to secure the attendance of respectable people, but it had to have enough museum curiosities, however incongruous, to justify the name.

I had cousins and friends in my native city who did not approve of the theatre, and yet would induce me to go with them to the negro minstrels. I laughed heartily then, as I have done since, at the stories told by the black-faced comedians; but what I truly enjoyed was the harmonious chorus-singing of those men. Such antics upon the stage as by many are considered nothing worse than innocent merriment, I am still Quaker enough to think a serious waste of time and money, and I marveled in my boyhood, as I do now, at the state of mind which approves of negro minstrels and variety shows and disapproves of some fine legitimate drama well played by an accredited company of actors.

Philadelphia, notwithstanding the number of Quaker families, gave good support to such play-houses as the Walnut Street and Arch Street Theatres, at the latter of which Mrs. John Drew and her husband, surrounded by a distinguished company, played for many years.

It is not strange, considering my upbringing, that, as a boy, I never met John Drew the younger, or any of his family. One of my uncles lived near them; but they were classed among " people of the world," and, being " actor-folks " besides, did not come within the social scope of my strict-principled relations. John Drew went to school at the Episcopal Academy in Locust Street, we grew up and were educated only a stone's throw apart, and yet, though in after years we learned that we had many friends in common, in our boyhood we never met. My father knew the Drews and, as he used to tell me, had the entrée of their theatre, though he never made use of it.

In my father's library were many volumes of English plays which I read with avidity, and in Tenth Street near Chestnut stood the Mercantile Library. Upon the ground floor of this building there was about midway along the reading room on the north wall a section devoted to dramatic literature. After hearing Edwin Booth, Madame Ristori, and the few other great players whom I remember as a boy, I often went there to spend hours, standing before these shelves with the biographies of David Garrick, Edmund Kean, Macready, or the Kembles in my hands, reveling in the plays of the theatre and the romances of real life that clustered about the romances of fancy.

This was to me a magic country indeed, and from it came a clear call in a voice akin to that of music. These two voices joining in a fascinating duo, as it were, summoned me to join the circle haunted by the shades of those long gone, though as yet nothing was further from my mind than an actual association with those whose acquaintances I was then making, in an artistic way, across the footlights.

During these times I saw the visiting actors, Barry Sullivan and Charles Fechter. Years later Fechter toured America, when I heard him read the play of "Hamlet." He had a slight German accent that was soon forgotten and I have always remembered with great interest not only his rendering of the title rôle, but of the minor characters of the play which so frequently are obliged to suffer at the hands of artists of quality inferior to that of the star. But Fechter rendered all the parts superbly, especially that of the King, whose soliloquies he gave with great effect and whose mental anguish he depicted in a manner that I have never seen equaled. About this time, too, Edwin Booth and Lawrence Barrett, as Brutus and Cassius respectively, toured the country and performed " Julius Cæsar," with a cast and in a manner always to be remembered by any one who had the fortune to see the tragedy with so many well-chosen men in the principal parts.

E. L. Davenport afterward assumed the part of Brutus, and it is no treason to say that I preferred him in that character to Booth who, to my mind, lacked the physical and vocal power at that stage of his life to give the noble lines their requisite weight.

Another heroic figure upon the stage of my early manhood was F. C. Bangs, whom I vividly remember as Mark Antony with Booth, and in the sumptuous revival of Byron's " Sardanapalus," in which he was magnificent.

From hearing such plays as these I was beginning to appreciate the value of our admirable language, when so ably rendered as it was by these distinguished men.

The first time that I was ever in love with an actress was when I saw the wonderful Adelaide Neilson in some of her Shakesperian characters, notably as Viola and as Juliet. But my interest in this woman was really more intellectual than physical. Lovely as she undoubtedly was in face and figure, her voice was more entrancing than that of any actress I remember, while her diction was absolutely perfect. Had the phonograph been invented in her day the subsequent generations would indeed have had an object lesson in the correct use of the English language. With her played the beautiful Jack Barnes, as manly a figure in Romeo and other parts as one could wish to see, and a perfectly fitting companion upon the stage to even so great a woman as Miss Neilson.

While I still lived in Moorestown and before I graduated from college I met at an evening party two talented young men, Robert and William Neilson; both were lawyers and graduates of the University of Pennsylvania; and both were excellent musicians, playing the piano and singing on the evening in question with light tenor voices, in a beautiful manner, selections from the earlier operas of Gilbert and Sullivan and of Offenbach. When I came to live in Philadelphia and mingle in the musical and dramatic circles I naturally sought, I fell in again immediately with " Billy " Neilson, whose remarkable ability as a comedian caused him to be in demand in all amateur theatricals that went on in our city, and it was not long before he enlisted my services also, in plays and operettas given at the Amateur's Drawing-Room in Seventeenth Street above Chestnut, now occupied by a branch Post-Office.

One summer during my holiday in New York, I remember visiting the delightful little Madison Square Theatre in Twenty-fourth Street, west of Broadway, where upon its elevator stage I saw a charming performance of Frances Hodgson Burnett's play " Esmeralda," which I had already read in the magazine where it first was published, and in which I longed to play the part of the old man. Indeed, from that time I realized that I was fitted for character parts, and when soon after I saw Charles Wolcot as the French professor in " To Parents and Guardians," more than ever was I determined to emulate the example of this admirable artist, and, if I ever did go on the stage, to play such parts as he performed so truthfully. Wolcot could do anything from farce to tragedy and was one of the most accomplished actors I ever saw.

It was not long before I found myself performing with my friend Billy Neilson in a variety of pieces at the Amateur's Drawing-Room, and as a member of the Pilgrims Dramatic Society at the Working Men's Club in Germantown, which had an excellent auditorium and stage.

After assisting in various minor affairs I had the opportunity of singing in " Golden-haired Gertrude," an operetta by Miss Elinor Parrish, in the author's private house, a performance so successful that it was repeated at the Amateur's Drawing-Room on the evening of Monday, December 27, 1880, really my first appearance before the public in a work of this nature. This was soon followed by Arthur Sullivan's musical adaptation of Burnand's old play called " Cox and Box," with Billy and Robert Neilson in the cast with me, and this I repeated the next summer at the opening of the ballroom at Rodick's Hotel in Bar Harbor. Neilson was the printer; I was Cox the hatter, and Bouncer was admirably performed by Elliott Pendleton of Cincinnati. We finished the evening with W. S. Gilbert's delightful comedy " Sweethearts," in which I was the gardener, while the young lover, who is many years older in the second act, was well done by Reginald de Koven, already known as the composer of excellent songs. It is pleasant to remember him in those days as being so much in demand in social and musical circles, not only because he played his own compositions so well on the piano but because he was even then recognized, by those who knew, as having a fresh touch which was soon to leave its mark upon the music of the day.

I was fast making up my mind at that time that business, other than theatrical or musical, was not for me; but I did not yet see my way toward the leaving of it. My uncle was doing his best to interest me, though I fear he must have been sadly disappointed when he found my real thought wandering so far from the occupation he had planned, for like the stenographer of a friend of mine, I did not let my work interfere with what I was thinking about.

During this time I was, indeed, too busy with the musical and dramatic activities of the various clubs to which I belonged to do much more than learn my numerous parts.   My own share of them possesses a certain interest in showing how much stage experience I was gaining.

I played in " Nan, the Good-for-Nothing "; as the husband in " A Husband in Clover "; as Sir Bloomfield Brambleton in " Who's Who "; as Sir Charles Seymour in " A Cup of Tea "; as Colonel Berners in " Cut Off With a Shilling "; as General von Rosenberg in " Her Bitterest Foe "; as Jeremy Crow in " Meg's Diversion "; as Mr. Babblebrook in " A Lesson in Love "; as Doctor Fleming in " Weak Woman "; as Lord Touchstone Pepper in " A Reformer in Ruffles "; as Hawkesley in " Still Waters Run Deep "; appearing also in William Dean Howells's " The Parlor Car " and " The Postal Card," and taking the part of Sir Peter Teazle in a scene from " The School for Scandal."

After singing as Pigeon in " Golden-haired Gertrude," already mentioned, I sang also the Foreman of the Jury in Gilbert and Sullivan's " Trial by Jury "; in " The Sorcerer," by the same brilliant collaborators; as Griddly

in Offenbach's " Sixty-Six," and in " Choufleuri," by the
same composer. Most memorable to me of all these
varied activities upon which my youthful energy was ex-
pended was my taking the part of the Apothecary in the
remarkable travesty of " Romeo and Juliet " given at the
Germantown Opera House on Friday evening, April 4,
1882, for the benefit of the Young America Cricket Club,
and on other occasions also. Written by Charles C.
Soule of St. Louis and first presented before the University Club of that city five years previously, its undergrad-
uate buoyancy and witty rhymed dialogue secured from
Horàce Howard Furness, the distinguished editor of the
Variorum Shakespeare, the high praise of being the best
travesty of Shakespeare within his wide and profound
knowledge.

During one of the performances I distinctly remember
seeing my good friend, Mrs. Caspar Wister, the novelist,
in the front row in company with her brother Doctor
Furness, who was evidently amused by the performance,
to which he listened with the aid of his ear trumpet, for
he was, even at that time, growing very deaf.

The morning after, I received a letter from him asking
me, if possible, to procure for him a copy of the libretto
of our play in order that he might keep it in his famous
collection of Shakespeareana. In his library at his house
in Wallingford, Pennsylvania, he showed it to me years
afterward, and I have seen the same book more than once
in the same collection, now in Philadelphia, which was inherited by his son.

My own collection of memorabilia numbers by this
time many volumes, and in looking these over I find that
during the course of those years of unconscious preparation, I had arrived by way of sociables, reading circles,

music with my father, and through affairs at college, to the little plays and operettas that I have mentioned; and through these, by degrees, to more important plays and more important music.

As I look at it now from a distance, such means of acquiring a knowledge of the stage and music as a profession is not by any means one to be followed by every other person; but it happens to have been what I did, and it led me to a professional life.

CHAPTER V

STEPPING-STONES

Music strikes in me a deep fit of devotion, and a profound contemplation of the First Composer. There is something in it of Divinity more than the ear discovers.— Sir Thomas Browne.

DURING all this time of activities upon the amateur stage, though most of my parts were spoken, it must not be supposed that my prime devotion to music fell into abeyance. On the contrary, as it was amateur singing that led to acting, so in the years soon to come it was my preparation for singing in oratorio that led me to the final combination of singing and acting on the operatic stage.

While I was in my uncle's wool house, I sought and found a vocal teacher, Edward Giles, an admirable basso, holding a position as organist in one of the city church choirs. To him I went frequently, using either my lunch hour or skipping off a little earlier in the afternoon and having a lesson with him before going home to supper. The drudgery of the wool business, which caused me to be at the store by eight o'clock, was wonderfully mitigated by the thought of the joy that would presently be mine, when I should be able to quit for the day and learn the great parts written by Handel, Haydn, and others of the master musicians.

Through Mr. Giles I was introduced to Michael Cross, the organist of the cathedral where Max Heinrich sang, and I soon became a member of the Orpheus Club, an ag-

47

gregation of men with good voices who were glad to
come together on Monday evenings to practice glees and
part songs under the leadership of Cross, an enthusiast
about such music.   I lived through the week in anticipation of the rehearsals for these concerts, three of which
were given at Musical Fund Hall each season.

This was the room in which Jenny Lind had sung when
visiting Philadelphia, and she had then declared it one
of the most perfect auditoriums in which she had ever
lifted up her exquisite voice.   My father and his sister
had heard her and were never tired of speaking of the
beauty of her singing.   It appears that the crowds that
assembled to hear her were so great that request was
made in the newspapers that ladies should come without their crinolines in order that more persons might be
seated in the hall.

Not until long after my younger days did people tire
of speaking of Jenny Lind and the beauty of her art,
only eclipsed by the later appearance of Adelina Patti.
When a girl Patti had been a good deal in Philadelphia,
where her kinsman Ettore Barili had been her master
and was still teaching the art of singing.   I was afterward
to meet Madame Patti, and also Jenny Lind, when the
latter was an old woman, a few years before her death.

Michael Cross became my musical guide, philosopher
and friend, and as I was so keen about the rehearsals of
the Orpheus Club he suggested that I should join the
Arion, a similar club, holding its rehearsals and concerts in Germantown.   I also belonged to a Madrigal
Society and an Oratorio Society, the Cecilian, all under
the direction of Cross, and about a year after I returned
from Europe I found myself in the midst of musical affairs in Philadelphia, rehearsing under Cross's baton

several times each week, and at the concerts of his clubs at least fifteen times a year. The more I sang the better I liked it and the less interest I had in business, which notwithstanding I stuck to for seven years.

It was because of my evidently serious interest in the art that Cross invited me to become a volunteer member of his new choir at Holy Trinity Church, Rittenhouse Square, where I sang from 1879 to 1882; and I am sorry that no particulars of the work done there have been kept. Suffice it to say that while Cross did not indulge in the more classical music of the Roman Catholic Church, yet in the quite " low " service of Holy Trinity he was able to use much of that of the Church of England, with which I became acquainted for the first time.

I soon became a proficient reader of vocal music, and was learning to play well upon the instrument called the human voice; though my unwieldy fingers would accommodate themselves to the keys of the piano as little as ever. Nearly every Saturday for several years I spent the evening at Cross's listening to him and his associates playing string quartettes, and though I could do nothing but admire their performances, I devoted myself with the greater assiduity to the cultivation of the gift which Heaven had been pleased to bestow upon me, studying enthusiastically with Cross the bass and barytone rôles in the best oratorios.

Frequently in those days I met Max Heinrich who heard me sing such songs as " The Erl King " and " The Two Grenadiers "; but, as he afterward confessed, he did not think I could ever make anything of myself as a singer.

On one occasion I had the opportunity of meeting Ulysses S. Grant. The Orpheus Club sang at a reception

given him in the galleries of the Academy of Fine Arts,
and I was presented to the distinguished soldier-citizen.
The chief hostess of the occasion, turning to the President and indicating with a wave of her hand the assembled
men of the Orpheus Club, said, "And now, Mr. President, what would you like these gentlemen to sing for
you?" Grant, in his blunt and rather callous way, replied, "Anything you please, madame; I don't know one
note from another." We sang none the better, I suppose, for knowing that the guest of the occasion had no
enjoyment in our performance; however, we sang for the
President of the United States, and that was something.

The whole neighborhood of the city where I daily
worked was full of historic memories. Old Christ
Church, which Washington used to attend when he lived
in Philadelphia, was just around the corner in Second
Street, and though many memories of the past smiled
upon me as I went to and fro in the Philadelphia streets,
yet I did not consider in my youth the possibility of meeting face to face persons of prominence in my later life.

To my delight I frequently had the pleasure of seeing
the aged poet Walt Whitman as he walked past our place
of business in his shapeless shoes and light tweed suit of
no cut at all, several buttons of his waistcoat open, and
what was apparently his nightshirt, with its collar lying
loose over that of his coat, likewise open at the neck
and showing his gray and hairy breast. Crowning a
superb and rather massive Homeric-looking head was a
broad, light felt slouch hat. Thus Whitman proceeded
in serene indifference to the attention of passers-by, who
would almost have stared him out of countenance had
he deigned to notice them.

My native city had in those times two Episcopal

churches where the services were very " high ": St. Clement's, which, but for the English language used, might as well have been a Roman church for all I could see, and St. Mark's, where the English organist, Minton Pyne, invited me to become a member of his choir, offering me at the same time a moderate salary to insure my attendance. I accepted with pleasure, feeling that it might be the stepping-stone to something more than the $6 a week I was now getting in my uncle's office. I, therefore, donned the cassock and cotta and for about four years participated in most of the music rendered by that vested choir. Several of its members were English singers who had been brought up in cathedrals in their mother country and knew well the kind of music performed at St. Mark's Church. The weekly rehearsals were long and arduous, but none the less interesting, as they introduced me to a phase of the art which so far I had not known.

The first program I have of services in St. Mark's Church is that of Easter Day, 1882. After a year or more, upon the departure of our English precentor, his mantle fell upon me, and I rejoiced in lifting up my voice in this kind of praise to the Power who had bestowed upon me the gift for which I was becoming increasingly thankful. Minton Pyne had been a pupil of the great organist S. S. Wesley of Gloucester Cathedral, and had brought with him to America the very best churchly traditions. To him I owe a debt of gratitude for the great assistance he was to me in my musical life in introducing me to so many of the finest sacred works, such as the Masses of Mozart, Beethoven, and Schubert, which were constantly rendered by us, in addition to the noblest of English music.

Simultaneously I belonged for about four years to the

Cecilian Oratorio Society, and assisted as one of the
basses of the chorus in the productions of "The Messiah,"
"Israel in Egypt," "Judas Maccabæus," and "Samson"
by Handel; in "The Creation" and "The Seasons" by
Haydn; in "Elijah," "St. Paul," and "The Hymn of
Praise" by Mendelssohn; the "Passion Music" by Bach;
the "Odysseus" and "Frithjof" by Bruch; the "Stabat
Mater" by Rossini; "The Redemption," "Mors et
Vita," and "Gallia" by Gounod, and the oratorio
"Moses in Egypt" by Rossini.

At last I became proficient enough and well enough
known as an amateur soloist to be asked by the committee to sing some of the smaller bass solo parts, which,
of course, I was only too proud to be able to assume.
I find, for instance, from the programs before me, that at
the Academy of Music in March, 1883, I sang the part of
the Steersman in Max Bruch's "Odysseus" to the Ulysses
of Heinrich; and on March 12, 1885, I took the part of
Judas, Peter, and the High Priest in Bach's St. Matthew
"Passion Music," while Max Heinrich sang the part of
Christ.   This was my first appearance as a soloist in any
large public way in oratorio; and on April 9, 1886, I sang
the part of the bass Narrator in Gounod's "Redemption,"
again with Heinrich as Christ.   I was beginning gradually to get my musical feet under me.

Somewhere along in these years Theodore Thomas
issued a call to members of all oratorio societies to come
to New York to assist there in a Festival, to take place
at the Seventh Regiment Armory.   I went from Philadelphia with most of the members of the Cecilian and
sang in Handel's "Israel in Egypt," thus performing for
the first time under the baton of one whom I so revered
and whom I was to know so well in later life.

On this occasion that noble singer, Myron Whitney, of Boston was one of the basses, and I shall never forget the singing of his part in " The Lord is a Man of War." I had admired Whitney from the first time I ever heard him, at the opening of the Centennial Exposition in Philadelphia on May 10, 1876, when in the open air before a vast concourse of people, he held his own superbly in the bass part in " The Centennial Cantata," by Dudley Buck. Whitney was an ideal oratorio singer and, better than any one I ever heard, except Santley, could negotiate the runs required of the Handelian singer, as well as the dramatic rendering of its recitative, in which so few are acceptable.

Some years ago the late Gustave Kobbé, he, perhaps somewhat my senior, in speaking of those times of our youth, said, " I have a story of you which I doubt if you have ever heard "; and proceeded to tell me that he, too, was in business in Philadelphia when young, and that one morning while he was talking to an elderly Friend, I went by, humming what seemed to be a vocal exercise. The elderly Friend stopped in his conversation and pointed to me as I passed, saying: " Does thee see that young man going along there singing? Well, he is the grandson of an old friend of mine, but I tell thee he isn't going to come to any good, for he is always fooling around after music."

I have thought often since of Kobbé's story and how essential it is for a person in order to make a success in anything to be always thinking of it and doing it, as far as lies in his power, and not to fool around after it.

Music is not only a fine art but a science, and should be learned scientifically and accurately. Otherwise it amounts to next to nothing and is likely to lead to the

stupid waste of time against which my Quaker ancestors
so feelingly inveighed.   As a matter of fact I was trying
to master one of those Handelian passages I had just
heard Whitney sing.   I thought more of that than of my
raise to an $8 weekly wage.

CHAPTER VI

The soul of music slumbers in the shell,
Till waked and kindled by the master's spell;
And feeling hearts — touch them but rightly — pour
A thousand melodies unfelt before.— Rogers.

HIGH aspiration and some little accomplishment in music; lack of ambition and no accomplishment in commerce; these two phrases well express my groping toward the pathway of a career in those days. The work of Sir George Grove, editor of the *Dictionary of Music and Musicians* and director of the Royal College of Music in London, had long attracted me. I wrote him for a prospectus of his institution, fondly hoping to prepare myself there for a professional career. To my chagrin the prospectus informed me that I was already too old to enter its classes. As there was no source of information nearer than London, I wrote Sir George again, stating my case. A prompt answer contained an introduction to his friend Georg Henschel, conductor of the newly founded Boston Symphony Orchestra.

By appointment I went to Boston, soon to find myself standing before the famous singer, whom I had so often admired in my native city. No one could have been kinder than Henschel, but I found myself afflicted with a bad case of stage fright and he, realizing how little justice I was doing myself, asked me to return the next day when, after another hour of song and conversation with him, I felt much more at my ease.

After full inquiry into my experience and capabilities he told me, to my keen disappointment, that he thought them quite inadequate as a basis for professional work, for what I had done had been done entirely as an amateur and without serious study. I was listening to an accomplished pianist, conductor, composer, and singer. I could not play the piano. I had never conducted. I could not compose, but I thought I could sing. Henschel, however, told me that though I had a good natural voice, my inability to play the piano left it fairly impossible for me to learn even a little of the music I must know if I wished to take up a singer's career with any reasonable hope of success. Disappointed as I was, I nevertheless determined from that night to be a singer. So far as my inability to play the piano was concerned, most of the singers I had heard could not play and had been accompanied by some one else. What audience ever knew what a singer's pianistic talents might be? Its judgment is based on the beauty of his voice and the interest he arouses by his songs and his singing.

I decided never again to waste time by touching a piano, but to devote myself all the more to the cultivation of my voice, and thereafter sought the assistance of those who played the piano well, and with their aid I worked up a repertory of classical songs such as I had often heard Henschel, Heinrich and others perform and which I knew I, too, could sing.

Among operatic artists I took as models the barytones Galassi and Del Puente; the former possessing, in a somewhat lighter voice, the grand manner which I so admired in the oratorio singing of Myron Whitney; the latter, the same delightful verve and animation I so enjoyed in the work of Max Heinrich.

There were a number of musicians in the social circles of Philadelphia who had a marked influence upon my career; through them I joined a coterie of amateurs which led to my acquaintance with many persons whom I might not otherwise have known, and certainly gave me an opportunity to sing as often as I cared to. I may say frankly that I was in demand for my vocal solos; my enthusiasm being such as to win the confidence of my associates. I was fast becoming enamored of music, not only as a pleasurable thing, but as a means of making a livelihood not afforded by the wool business, where by this time I was getting as much as $10 a week, which I frankly confess I did not deserve, and where as time went on I was rapidly demonstrating my unfitness for such work as I had to do. My thoughts were never upon it for one moment; I was always living in the past and hoping for the future. Each musical evening was a fresh inspiration for me; each concert in which I took part I looked upon as a higher rung on the ladder.

Temporarily abandoning business in 1885, I revisited Europe, steeping my heart as well as my head in the beauty and mystery of art, my whole nature yearning toward a public career. What was almost a loathing filled me at the thought of the fleecy treasure at home which so wholly failed to capture my imagination. I was longing for the time to come when, if I returned to America, it would be not for business, but to mingle once more with my companions of the musical circles which I had enjoyed so greatly, the professionals, amateurs and dilettanti, association with whom, indeed, made up my real life.

While abroad I had heard opera in London, attended concerts, and on one occasion became a volunteer member of the giant chorus at the Handel Festival at the Crystal Palace under the conductorship of August Manns. This participation in "The Messiah" was effected by means of the not unknown course called bribery; an attendant yielding to the lure of half a sovereign to let me in among the basses.

I heard opera in Paris, in Milan, and in Rome. Naturally enough I was impressed more by the performances I heard at Bayreuth than by any other operatic function which I had ever attended. The singing of Rosa Sucher, then in her prime, stands out in my memory beyond anything else. Isolde in her hands became the acme of operatic grace and intensity; she seemed to me even to surpass Lilli Lehmann in that particular character. Gura was, to my mind, the finest Hans Sachs I had ever heard, while Friedrichs as Beckmesser was unapproachable. Though I laughed at Beckmesser I longed to sing the melodious and gracious vocal passages allotted to Sachs, and heard " Die Meistersinger " often.

On returning to Philadelphia in the autumn of 1885 I again attempted to take up a business career, not this time in my uncle's establishment, though offered an advance of $2 a week, but as a clerk in the Lehigh Valley Railway office, the examination for which I was barely able to pass. I received there something like $12 a week, I think, for doing nothing that I liked, and doing that badly, with the prospect of $14 five years afterward, if I could pass the further examinations required.

The thought of this was enough, and I immediately determined to get away as soon as I could, making plans to return to Europe and study there with the distinct intention of becoming a singer in oratorio and concert. I had not yet learned a single operatic rôle for professional use, aware as I was of my mother's aversion to such a career. I thought she was wrong, yet respected her wishes. Beyond a few operatic arias which I used occasionally in concert, I had no acquaintance whatever with operatic literature, except as I had heard it from the seats of an opera house. If I had been preparing for anything, it was for concert and oratorio.

During the winter I resumed my attendance upon the rehearsals of my musical clubs and went on as before as precentor of St. Mark's Choir. These for a time sufficed to give me all the vocal exercise I could spare from my business and social life.

I returned to Europe in the spring of 1886, severing at that time all immediate connections with Philadelphia for many years. Indeed, it was a full decade before I appeared again in my native city.

Crossing to Europe for the third time I met on board the steamer the well-known Chicago singing teacher, Frank Baird, a pupil of William Shakespeare of London; meeting this great master soon after my arrival I felt that I could do no better than entrust my musical and vocal education to so eminent an authority. I cannot be sufficiently thankful for the good fortune which thus brought me into contact with so fine a man, so admirable a musician, and a teacher who was also a singer.

During his time at the Royal Academy of Music in London he had won the Mendelssohn scholarship, and at first intended to make a career as a concert pianist, but finding that his own beautiful tenor voice was developing, he began to study with the elder Lamperti in Milan, and upon returning to London one Sunday, as he told me, he found a letter addressed to him in an emergency and almost at the last moment from the committee of one of the festivals, requesting him to assume an important part in a work with which he was entirely unfamiliar. Being an excellent reader he was able to go immediately to the dress rehearsal, where he carried through his part without a mistake, a feat the accomplishment of which would have been almost impossible to any one else in England.

This led to Mr. Shakespeare's frequent engagement as tenor at the principal English musical festivals. His taste did not, however, lead him to enjoy public singing; and, as his voice was very light in quality, it was not long before he gave up all participation in concerts and devoted his entire time to teaching.

It was at this period that I fell in with the master whose name, of course, had attracted me. As I learned from himself he came from the Warwickshire family from which the dramatist had sprung; indeed " Shakey," as we called him, bore a marked resemblance to the bust of Shakespeare in the church at Stratford-on-Avon; yet he laid no claim to direct descent from the poet, and was quick to laugh out of court the Teutonic contention that he was of German origin.

Shakespeare's name as a teacher is quite as highly thought of and as widely known in the United States as it is in England, where he had many competitors, and where his musicianly and extremely careful method of teaching was less the vogue than that preferred by many artists who sought the advice of masters who were not themselves vocalists, who did not know the classics well, whose stock in trade was the popular ballads of the day. Shakespeare, on the contrary, inculcated a love for the classics, and nothing else found acceptance in his studio. Having taught his pupils how to sing, he educated them in the literature of song, and in the manner of rendering such selections as fitted their individual voices. In fact he taught us the three essentials: *how* to sing, *what* to sing, and how to *sing* it!

Informing Shakespeare of my intention to study in Italy for the concert stage in England, he urged me to study there with him at once. I preferred, however, to do as I had planned, and I am glad that I did so, desirous as I was to obtain more knowledge of French, German, and Italian.

At the Birmingham Festival, before leaving England, I met B. J. Lang, the celebrated conductor of Boston. I had known him in America and he had heard that I intended to make a career of music. At that time grand opera was looming large in New York, and he greeted me with the question, "Why have you chosen oratorio?" I explained to him that I knew no opera, owing to my mother's dislike of that phase of music. But he still persisted, assuring me that opera was the thing. "Oratorio," said he, "is only opera spoiled." Amusing and possibly true; but according to my wont, after satisfying myself as to the right course to pursue, despite Mr. Lang's and Shakespeare's advice, I went my way to Florence, where I put myself under Maestro Vannuccini.

CHAPTER VII

SERIOUS STUDY BEGINS

For sure no minutes bring us more content
Than those in pleasing, useful studies spent.
— *John Pomfret.*

WHEN the celebrated actor Sir Johnston Forbes-Robertson was last in America, he reminded me of my visit to him in England in 1886. After forwarding a letter of introduction, I had called at his studio — he is a painter as well as an actor — telling him during our conversation that I was about to go to Italy, but would before long appear upon the boards in London. He listened attentively and assured me that I should not find it an easy thing to do. He had been upon the stage since his youth, had mingled with artists and with the most distinguished actors and musicians of his day; he had lately been taken into Henry Irving's company, where he was highly esteemed; and yet he was far from standing where he wished to be.

Referring to that time he said: " I thought when you had gone: ' Poor fool! he little knows what there is in store for him, brought up in Philadelphia with no musical or artistic antecedents, not being able to play the piano, knowing no one and having no pull in London; yet he is going to try it. Poor fool!'" Turning to some one who sat with us, he suddenly said, "Yet, by gad, he came back and did it!" As a matter of fact, that is what happened.

Five years from that time I was back in London and on the stage under the best of auspices; and that is why this book is being written, for I want those who follow me to know just how it came about that I have accomplished whatever I have done, and to realize that nothing can be done at all unless one sets out to do it oneself, relying upon nobody at all, yet scorning no assistance. Every aid for advancement must, of course, be seized, but for all the aid that may be extended, no one can accomplish anything if he himself lacks the inner urge that animates all who do things in the world, even to the salmon that rush against the current up the most torrential streams, struggling through rapids, leaping waterfalls. Though thousands die in the attempt, yet some succeed and get to the wished-for haven and spawning ground, where they are at peace. Thus they accomplish what the inner impulse of their nature prompts them to do, and by paths they know not, through ways never traversed before, they reach their goal through the guidance of that Providence to whom the rise of the artist and the fall of the sparrow are one.

Upon leaving London I went to Florence by way of San Remo on the Italian Riviera, and there, on Ash Wednesday in the spring of 1887, occurred one of those dreadful convulsions of nature that leave puny man weak, trembling, and helpless before the majesty of Nature and the power of Nature's God. Never shall I forget the horror of being aroused in the early morning by the whole earth quaking in a manner that reminded me of nothing so much as a dog shaking a rat to death. Imagine the Hound of Heaven with the earth in His teeth!

Thousands of persons were killed or maimed for life

in those two shocks, which took place about five minutes apart and reduced to ruin scores of villages which had for centuries withstood the ravages of time. Fortunately, my hotel was strongly built and suffered no material damage. But how heart-rending it was to see, as I did upon the relief expeditions in which I took part, the ruined towns surrounded by mediæval walls, still standing to be sure, but concealing behind their ramparts and ancient defenses the havoc wrought among the defenseless! In most of these places the devout had been at early mass, during which the earthquake shook the churches so dreadfully that the heavy masonry of the roofs fell in, burying the congregations, though leaving the priest unhurt beneath the half dome over the chancel.

In one place I remember the story of an aged cleric, who stood serene, and lifted up his voice among the shrieks of the dying and injured, saying, " My children, I baptized you when you entered this sinful world, I now absolve you as you leave it for Paradise."

I have loved Italy from the time I first visited it and am particularly fond of the Italian Lakes; indeed who is not? The Plains of Lombardy had a fascination for me so great that it seemed as if I had frequented that part of the world in some former state of existence. I fancy that every one feels that he should like to be in that locality for ever, and therefore has a sort of reflex mental action; for many consider they have been there before.

On the day of my arrival in Florence I noticed a tall old man, bare-headed and with flowing hair and beard, carrying a beautiful little girl upon his shoulder as he went about the streets. Every one turned to look at the quaint but charming sight of the happy child and the equally happy grandfather, who turned out to be the well-known American song writer, George F. Root, author of " The Battle Cry of Freedom " and other Civil War songs.

Into the American Colony at Florence I was soon introduced, to meet among others the novelist Constance Fenimore Woolson, a niece of Fenimore Cooper; F. Marion Crawford, the writer of romance; William Cooper, the sculptor, whose wife was a brilliant musician; and her father, Thomas Ball, also a distinguished sculptor. These friends lived on the hill a little back of Michael Angelo's statue of " David," and it was at their house that I renewed the acquaintance of Salvini, that mighty actor, whom I had met in Philadelphia a few years before at the Penn Club, an organization which exists in part in order to do honor to the distinguished men who visit the Quaker City.

I had been thrilled as never before by Salvini's impersonation of Othello, which was the greatest piece of tragic acting that ever I have seen. Salvini never fell from his high estate, remaining to his end noble and impressive in every ·movement and in the majesty of his voice, superb beyond the power of words to tell.

I had met Henry Irving also at the Penn Club, and recall a story of him, told me by the man to whom it happened. He was deep in conversation with Sir Henry when some one was brought up and introduced and the conversation was not resumed. A year later, when Irving, again at the Penn Club, met my friend he stretched out his hand, called him by name, saying, " As I was about to say last year when we were interrupted," and went straight on with the conversation from the point at which it was broken off the year before. Despite such extraordinary powers Irving was still human and therefore liable to err. After playing Mathias in "The Bells" hundreds of times during his career, one night when alone upon the stage in the midst of a soliloquy, he suddenly stopped, unable to recall what followed. Not in the least disconcerted, he looked toward the prompter and was heard by the audience to say, "Line, please." The prompter, never thinking that Irving could be in need of him, was not attending to his business but was talking to some one behind the scenes, when the actor taking a step toward him said in a louder tone of voice, "Line, please!" The audience, observing that their favorite was in difficulties, was tense with excitement. The prompter, at last realizing Irving's plight, hurriedly consulted his book; and when Irving for the third time requested "Line, please!" the sound of the hastily turned pages was clearly distinguishable, with the frightened voice following, "Which line, Sir Henry?" The house gave a shout of laughter and the tragedian, recovering himself immediately, went on with his part.

I found in Italy, as elsewhere, that possession of a voice proved to be an open sesame to every circle, and during a visit to Venice, at the hospitable house of Mrs. Bronson, I met Robert Browning and had the interesting experience of singing one of his wife's sonnets to him. I have often wondered why great people cannot, in their appearance, live up to their reputations. This very usual-looking gentleman gave no hint of the genius within him. In Florence I met the great American painter, John Sargent, who was visiting his sisters at the house that had once been occupied by Elizabeth Barrett Browning. Not the least interesting of my acquaintances in the lovely Italian city was a neighbor, the novelist Madame Ouida, whom I came to know quite well. She lived in a palace said to be haunted by the victim of an ancient murder, whose ghost went shrieking through the court-yard and rooms which Ouida chose for a dwelling, in spite of her distaste for this gibbering relict of an older day.

When I went to call upon her in the great drawing-room on the second story of her habitation, filled as it was with a multitude of chairs and stools, screens and cabinets, stands and little tables, the sudden passage from the radiance of an Italian day to the dim rays of light which filtered through the closed Venetian blinds left me feeling like a Columbus setting forth upon uncharted seas.

Ouida's old-fashioned style of dress and slippers, of the sort my mother used for my occasional chastisement, square-toed with ribbons tied over the instep, are still a picture in my memory. She had never been beautiful, but was always fascinating. Her feet and hands, all that remained small about her, were always in evidence: her dainty toes rested upon a small stool before her, her hands in becoming gestures accompanying her speech; yet I judged from her girth and much augmented complexion that the dim light was a concession to the ravages made upon her by advancing years. She was a strange creature to me, with curious ideas about paying bills and about getting married, escaping both with unvarying consistency. Her creditors began suing her, one by one; and, acting on this hint, she began suing her former suitors, whose tender promises had been unable to survive the strain of her idiosyncrasies. She seemed to be as erratic as she was erotic, and shocked my Quakerly belief in the sanctity of the matrimonial bond by assuring me that the only certainty of married happiness lay in treating one's wife as if she were one's mistress.

During the years I was in Florence much music was to be heard both in public and in private, and I often sang for my friends.

Enormously pleased was I one day when my master, Vannuccini, asked me if I cared to sing the Offertorium the following Sunday at the famous church of the Santissima Annunziata. It appears that some one connected with the church had heard me and had asked Vannuccini that I, his young American pupil, be allowed to sing in the church. Vannuccini was willing and, much elated, I held forth on the Sunday from the interior of that high marble-walled choir beneath the dome of the church, surrounded by monks in their sandaled shoon and shaven heads, who sang the rest of the service from an enormous illuminated parchment volume of Gregorian chants, which stood upon a high lectern where all could see it. This led presently to a request from the clergy of the Santo Spirito to render them a similar service, which of course I was proud to do.

I also took part in several concerts at the Sala Filarmonica, a delightful little concert room, and at the request of the distinguished pianist Buonamici, I became the soloist at one of his orchestral concerts at the Pagliano Theatre.

Matters so progressed with me indeed that I was invited to Bologna and took part with the noted pianist Barbirolli in one of his concerts there, in the long narrow hall of the Liceo Musicale, which centuries before had been the refectory of a monastery. At these concerts I naturally sang the songs I was learning in preparation for my intended career as an oratorio singer; namely, the music of the older Italian School. In securing Vannuccini as a master, and in studying later with the elder Lamperti, and also with Shakespeare, his pupil, I was highly fortunate in having such eminent teachers, related in the line of direct succession to the masters of a century or more before them, who in their time were deemed the best of the day in which the art of song was at its highest point.

While the Italians are proverbially critical, yet sometimes vocal sinners, such as Vannuccini deemed his pupil Tamagno to be, were accepted by the public and indeed idolized by it for mere strength of voice, which in his case seemed to be enduring as brass. I remember hearing him render the tenor part in Rossini's " Stabat Mater " at a Sunday evening concert in the Pergola Theatre. The audience rose at him, for no one was ever known to sing the " Cujus Animam " with such a volume of tone as his; but at my lesson next day, Vannuccini was highly displeased with what Tamagno had done. He said he did not think it singing at all. He called it " bleating like a goat," and asked what could be done with a singer who knew nothing but operas. To my amazement he told me that Tamagno had not only never sung the " Stabat Mater," but until a fortnight before had never so much as heard of the work, which he had first studied with Vannuccini for this occasion.

That night I had a great lesson in deportment from the quartette who participated in the concert. The dignity with which they walked upon the stage from the wings, bowed first to the occupants of the royal box, then to that on the other side occupied by the Sindaco or mayor of the city, and last to the audience as a whole; the grace of their demeanor, as they sat in their chairs beside the conductor, rose to sing, resumed their places without fidgeting, or acknowledged in a restrained manner the applause of the audience, were indeed worthy of praise. Singers in costume on the operatic stage behave operatically, but in this instance no operatic airs were either sung or assumed, and the native simplicity of a wonderful people seemed to shine through every movement of the artists of that extraordinary quartette.

While in Florence I saw the funeral procession of an old woman locally celebrated, though she never sang outside of Italy, who was said to have had one of the most extraordinary voices of her day. For her several of the Italian composers had written operas and though she became an idol of the public, which she served faithfully for many years, the story was that she was nearly hissed off the stage upon the occasion of her first appearance.

Italians are particular, not only about voices but about the personal appearance of their singers. However fine her voice may be, if a woman has not fairly good looks she stands a poor chance of success. The artist to whom I refer was so plain that she was notorious throughout her quarter of the city for her " homeliness," as we say in America. They considered her *bruta,* ugly, and frankly said so, though every one along her little street knew and loved the splendid tones which they could hear rolling from the open windows of her apartment.

When it became known that she was going to make her début, all laughed and shook their heads, declaring her too plain for the stage, however beautiful her voice might be. She persisted, for she had found a manager who was willing to take the risk. The great night came, the whole town was present, the tradespeople among her friends and all in her quarter of the city thronged the gallery and the pit, the *bourgeoisie* sat in the better places, and fashion was well represented in the boxes. The house was indifferent to the other artists on the play bill, but became tense with excitement as the moment approached for the appearance of their much heralded Florentine woman, for Florence does not differ from other cities in its refusal to honor its own artists before they have made a reputation.

When this singer appeared at last the whole audience burst out in jeering laughter, crying *" Bruta! Bruta! "* booing, and whistling through their fingers, but not in the least disturbing the singer's poise. After trying in vain to make herself heard, she walked to the footlights, motioned to the orchestra to cease playing, shook her fist at the audience, and in good round *lingua Toscana* informed her townsfolk that she had not come there to be looked at but to be listened to, and that, by all the gods, she was going to be heard! At this the audience burst out into good-natured laughter and, delighted with her frankness, shouted back *" Brava! Brava!* Go ahead and let's hear you! " Settling down to the enjoyment of a voice which immediately captivated them, they forgave her every feature of her bad looks and for the remainder of her long life she was the idol of the Florentine populace.

CHAPTER VIII

OPERA FROM AFAR

For know my heart stands arméd in mine ear,
And will not let a false sound enter there.
— *Shakespeare.*

I WAS making up my mind to cease studying in Florence and go to London to put into practice what I had learned — for if I was to begin at all it was high time to set about it, as I was now thirty-two years of age — when I met with a curious accident. I was walking on the Lung' Arno and carelessly running my walking stick along the top of the stone wall bordering the river, when the cane struck an obstacle, went through my hand, and the head of it came violently against my Adam's apple, the bruise rendering me practically voiceless for some time.

I went to England by way of Switzerland, and while staying in the Engadine, was given the rare opportunity of becoming well acquainted with Professor Thomas Huxley, the great English scientist, with whom I had many walks and long conversations, not about music, but about what interested him. He talked exactly as he wrote, as I discovered when I read his books, with which I had not been well acquainted, and was being widely maligned because of his refusal to concede that the Bible as it stands is, as a whole, inspired by God. Upon this subject he spoke to me with great frankness, defending, at the same time, his distinguished brother scientist Darwin in most of his deductions as to the origin of species and the ascent of man through infinite ages from lower forms of life to what he is at present. He declared himself frankly and frequently to be what the world called him, an Agnostic, one who does not know; he had plenty of opinions, but he never made pronouncement as to their infallibility.

A little way along the lake where I was staying, I learned that the English actor, Squire Bancroft, was spending the summer. Recalling my visit to Forbes-Robertson, I determined to make the acquaintance of Bancroft and to obtain his opinion as to the likelihood of my success upon the metropolitan stage. Accordingly I made a little pilgrimage to Bancroft, who received me courteously, but with more insistence than Forbes-Robertson gave me to understand that London was full of singers and actors, and that if I were not already preparing for Italian opera, at that time the only opera performed at Covent Garden, I had in his opinion but a poor chance of success. When I told him I had not thought of going into opera, he naturally enough expressed great surprise, saying, " If you are studying at all why don't you study the whole thing? Why limit yourself to oratorio?"

I came away from him a more thoughtful if not exactly a sadder man, realizing how foolish I had been in allowing myself to be influenced, as I now knew I had been, by my Quakerly bringing up and my good mother's unreasoning dread of the stage as a stepping-stone to hell. But as the deed as done was only half done, I went back and told my predicament to Huxley, who gave me sound fatherly advice, counseling me to make the most of whatever opportunities came my way, to let the past bury its dead, and to apply myself in the future all the more assiduously to whatever my hand might find to do that would lead me to the attainment of my desire.

By way of Bayreuth, where I met some of the best German singers and where I reveled once more in Wagnerian performances and rejoiced in the part of Hans Sachs, I again found my way to London in 1889. Once there, I set about making all the musical acquaintances possible by means of letters of introduction. My accident had left me unable to sing well enough to make any attempt to do so before the public. Even Shakespeare, whom I sought at once, gave me little encouragement and told me that the blow on my voice box might have sufficed to deprive me of voice altogether.

Nothing is more wearing upon the voice than worry and apprehension, and realizing this, I did my best to counteract the mental depression which I was feeling. I stated my case to the eclectic, Doctor Tuckey, whom I had met in Florence, and unreservedly put myself into his care for hypnotic treatment, which he advised as useful in ridding my mind of the fear that I had lost my voice. I was asked to recline comfortably upon a couch where I lay looking upward and squinting at the spot of light upon the shining object before me. At such times Tuckey would quietly reassure me by saying: "As a medical man I know there is nothing seriously wrong with your voice. My one object is to relieve your mind. Rest quietly, go to sleep if you wish; but when you wake do not worry about the condition in which you have been. Think cheerfully of the future and of the success you will undoubtedly make when you regain your vocal power. I know you can sing; I heard you in Florence before your injury, and I am sure you will soon have the success that is your due."

As a matter of fact I never slept at all; such talk kept me wide awake. One day, however, when called from the room he gave into my hand the glass ball which he had been holding and said, " Hold this over your eyes yourself." I did so when left alone and my eyes soon closed. I dropped the ball, and when the good doctor returned he found me in a deep slumber. I began to get well soon after and I sought my friend the distinguished English composer, Sir Alexander Mackenzie, principal of the Royal Academy of Music, whom I had met on several occasions in Florence, and told him of my disappointment in not being able to sing. He said, " Let me hear you. You used to sing all right; I remember you in Italy." After I had done my best for him, he said in his kindly Scotch manner: " There is nothing the matter with you. Go ahead and try it. There is nothing worse for a singer than not to sing."

CHAPTER IX

SPIRITS AND SOOTHSAYING

There needs no ghost, my lord, come from the grave
To tell us this.— *Shakespeare.*

THROUGH Doctor Tuckey and his friends I had invitations to attend the meetings of the Society for Psychical Research, held in Westminster Town Hall, and there I heard a number of the papers which had been carefully prepared by Professors F. W. Myers, Sidgwick, Crookes, Mr. Gurney, Sir Oliver Lodge, and their associates. While not going into these matters to any extent myself, I look back with interest upon having heard the first public reading of papers which have since become so famous. In the good faith and earnestness of these distinguished men of science I have the utmost confidence, though with Madame Blavatsky, whom I also met at this time, I had no patience; but the cleverness of the beautiful Mrs. Anne Besant almost persuaded me to become whatever she was. Fortunately, my head had been screwed on pretty tightly by my Quaker ancestors, and I was not to be easily blown by every wind of doctrine; I must confess however that though I once went to an exponent of the New Thought for the toothache, it was not long before I sought the aid of an accredited American dentist, realizing the truth of the conundrum then current in London, " What is matter? " to which the answer was " Never mind," and " What is mind? " the reply being " No matter."

I went to two spiritualistic séances eager to test for

myself what Hamilton Aïdé had both told me of and
written about shortly before in a magazine article called,
" Were We Hypnotized? "   The query was intended to
solve the problem whether or not a select company of
clever men could have been deceived by the medium
Hume through hypnotism, or by some other means, into
believing that what they saw, in full light and with every
opportunity to investigate, had actually taken place.
If these things happened it must have been by the opera-
tion of a law so far unknown.   If they did not happen —
though the company took oath that they did happen,—
then they must have been subtly deceived into believing
to the end that they saw what could not have taken place
at all, for it was contrary to all human experience.

I went with my friend Francis James, the artist, who
had known Hume, to my first séance.   On the way there
James told me that he did not believe in Hume, and yet
that in broad daylight he, and the others assembled in a
London drawing-room, saw performed the act of levitation.   Hume by some agency was lifted six or eight
inches from the floor, carried through a long, open window out to the balcony, along the whole length of the
balcony, and in at the open window at the other end,
where he was deposited again upon the drawing-room
floor.

When we arrived at the house of the professional
medium and the gas was turned out strange noises began; the rattling of pictures and maps hanging on the
wall, knockings upon the table and the doors leading
into the passage and into the front drawing-room.   I felt
hands touching me; heard a voice speaking to me through
a cardboard tube such as is used to carry music through
the mails.   Before the lights were extinguished I had

noticed my old friend the zither, which presently arose, as of its own accord, and could be seen to move about the room over our heads as we sat, its position clearly indicated by a large spot of luminous paint on its under side, playing as it went a jingling tune. As the eye followed it down the room it reached the door and disappeared with a thud, and through the folded doors could be heard playing, seemingly in the front room. The sound began getting louder as it again approached the dividing doors; another thud and suddenly the bright spot reappeared in the back room. I uttered an exclamation of astonishment and incredulity, when to my amazement the instrument settled down on top of my head and played " Yankee Doodle "!

I came away mystified but not in the least converted, and to me the whole thing was hocus-pocus.

One of my companions, however, more impressed than I, declared to me subsequently: " Of course it's all nonsense; but there's a lot in it! " My judgment is, that whatever there is " in it " goes to the alleged spiritists. Nevertheless, sometimes the spirits, or whatever they are, manage to hit off something so startlingly true as to make one thoughtful.

I used to visit a country house near London, where the daughter of the hostess, a woman socially distinguished, was one of the most remarkable psychic subjects ever known. The brothers of the young lady were officers in the Life Guards, and every one in that household of the greatest refinement would have frowned upon anything bordering upon chicanery; yet no one could explain, and all stood in awe of the manifestations which quite unexpectedly might happen through the hand of their sister. Though not normally an artist, she would on a sudden paint pictures indistinguishable from those of Blake, write in foreign languages with which she was unacquainted, or extemporaneously compose poetry of great grandeur. In one instance, the poem thus produced afterward proved to be the translation of a papyrus found upon the body of an Egyptian mummy in the British Museum.

This lady, who knew nothing of my private affairs, once seated herself in the large hall of their house with a crystal ball in her hand. As she looked into it she soon began to say the names of a number of the letters of the alphabet, in no apparent order or with any connection with each other. Her mother, herself writing down what was said, called hastily to another member of the family and to one of the brothers, " Note carefully what she says." For years the family had recorded everything coming from her in this way. Presently the sensitive ceased speaking, and the three after comparing notes and deciphering the message, every word of which was spelled backward, presented a paper to me which I read with amazement. Let me say that I had been puzzled by the non-arrival of a sum of money due to me through the hands of an American agent, whose honesty had been questioned by an acquaintance. The message received from the crystal-gazer read as follows:

You must not be concerned that you have not heard from your agent. He has been ill and unable to attend to your business, about which you need have no fear whatever.

This was on a Sunday afternoon. Upon returning to my home in London, the first letter I opened in the mail Monday morning was from this man, enclosing the expected draft and apologizing for the delay, which was due to his ill health.

Another and even stranger thing took place for which I always have been at a loss to account. I had been in London but a few months, was quite unknown to the public, and it is altogether unlikely that I should have been heard of by the old phrenologist to whose quaint little book shop I was taken one evening somewhat against my will, but I am glad to have had an experience which has always remained a mystery to me.

We dived into a narrow street off Oxford Street, near the British Museum in Dickens land, and climbed a stairway littered with books, as was the passage from the front door. The old man, for all the world like the figure standing upon the top of the library ladder in the well-known picture called " The Book Worm," led us upstairs. His bald pate was covered with a black skullcap; his long broadcloth frock coat was so shiny that he could have seen himself in it, if he could have looked into his own back as well as he did into other people's brains. He was a gentle old soul, spoke quietly, confidentially, and almost affectionately to each of those who had sought him out, as they sat about the center table under the gaslight in his little parlor over the shop.

He walked about among us, quietly placing his hands upon the heads of each as he passed. When he had given each person a somewhat intimate review of his nature, he said that we were all surrounded by the spirits of those whom he called our guardians. Every other person in the room accepted his descriptions of relations or friends who had passed on, except myself, for I was unable to recognize the presence he minutely described as being my guide at the time. He said he saw an elderly, clean-shaven man with gray hair, dressed in a beautiful garment of red brocade with large puffed sleeves over a

DAVID BISPHAM
as The Duc de Longueville in Messager's opera "The Basoche."
From the portrait in oils by Herman G. Herkomer

lighter colored vest of satin, with a sword by his side and around his neck a heavy gold chain from which depended a great jeweled locket. I assured the old phrenologist there was no such person among my ancestors. My forefathers were, as I well knew, such as Michael Angelo declared his to be, "Simple persons who wore no gold on their garments." Standing with his eyes lifted ceilingward and gazing into vacancy, the old man persisted that he knew nothing about that and could only tell me what he saw.

I thought no more of the matter for a year and a half. Then, upon the occasion of my first professional appearance at the Royal English Opera in Shaftesbury Avenue in the *opéra comique* by Messager entitled, "The Basoche," I, as the Duc de Longueville, found myself, though I had for years worn a beard from which I tried hard not to part, clean-shaven at last, and bewigged and costumed with sword and chain and locket — every detail of the dress that the old phrenologist had described. Let who will explain this; I cannot.

CHAPTER X

CONCERTS IN LONDON

I do but sing because I must.
— Tennyson.

MY first actual appearance in London as a singer was upon February 23, 1890, at a concert in the rooms of the Grosvenor Gallery. That spring I sang there upon several occasions in association with well-known artists, among whom were Johannes Wolf, the violinist, and Joseph Holman, the 'cellist. It was there, too, that on April 15, I had the honor of bringing out at their first performance Stanford's magnificent "Cavalier Tunes," set to Browning's words for barytone solo and male chorus. I cannot too heartily recommend them to my barytone confrères.

I appeared on April 30, for the first time at the Orchestral Concerts at Crystal Palace under August Manns, and a fortnight later I was performing upon the stage of the Savoy Theatre in an operetta by Lady Arthur Hill called "The Ferry Girl," a charming little Irish story in which a number of well-known amateurs and ex-professionals took part for a charity in which the best of London society was interested. My work in this as Count Montebello attracted the attention of Ernest Ford, who was then composing a light opera called "Joan; or, The Brigands of Bluegoria," in which he asked me to perform, the book written by the brilliant Irish wit and parliamentarian, Robert Martin. It was given from

82

July 19th to 24th, inclusive, at the Opéra Comique in the Strand with my name at the head of the cast. Had it been performed by a regular company of professionals I believe it would have had a long run; as it was it was played for six performances to crowded houses. In it I enacted the part of Bilboss, " a bass brigand," supported by George Power, afterward Sir George, who had been for some time upon the stage in the early days of the Gilbert and Sullivan performances, by Cosmo Gordon Lennox, a collateral descendant of Lord Byron, Kinsey Peile and Paul Monckton, the playwrights, and the author, who was an admirable comedian. The leading lady was Mrs. Godfrey Pearse, a musical hostess with an exquisite though small voice, whose parents were none other than the famous tenor Mario and his equally celebrated wife Madame Grisi.

I sang in several other concerts in London, Liverpool, and elsewhere, before appearing for the first time at Covent Garden Theatre in the autumn series of promenade concerts being given in the historic auditorium that year. It was at one of these that I first sang with Sims Reeves, then approaching his sixty-eighth birthday. He had been upon the stage since his seventeenth year, when he made his first appearance as Count Rudolfo in " La Sonnambula." Reeves had expressed his intention of retiring from the stage in 1882; but 1890 found him still singing, as he continued to do so for several years longer. It is interesting to note, in view of the fact that Reeves so often disappointed his admirers, that upon the occasion to which I refer, an ample array of artists had been engaged in order to satisfy the most fastidious among the audience which was expected and which duly gathered. Against the chance of Mr. Reeves's treating the

management to one of his frequent " indispositions " fourteen soloists had been engaged, besides the military band
of the Scots Guards and an orchestra of a hundred and
fifty pieces. But Reeves appeared and sang, as only
Reeves could sing, " When Other Hearts and Other
Lips " from " The Bohemian Girl " and, by special request, Charles Dibdin's fine old ballad, " The Bay of Biscay." Being unusually good-natured, he added as encores " Sally in Our Alley," sung with exquisite grace,
and his favorite " Tom Bowling."

I had first endeavored to hear Reeves in 1878, at St.
James's Hall where he was announced to sing surrounded
by a galaxy of other great artists. When the time came
for his appearance, some one read a telegram from him
announcing, with much regret, that he had caught a severe cold and would not be able to fulfill his engagement.
There was breathless silence until the end of the message,
when loud comments and laughter, almost jeering laughter, arose from all parts of the concert room. Inquiry
proved that it was Reeves's custom thus to treat his audiences, though they invariably crowded to hear him.
Though disappointed three times out of four, their devotion was such that they returned upon the next an-
nouncement of his singing in the hope that at last they
might be lucky enough to listen to the celebrated man.
I was amazed to learn that Reeves was paid the sum
of sixty guineas (about $300) for singing and that it
was also stipulated that in the event of his not singing
he was still to have forty guineas. The management
could rely with such confidence upon the drawing power
of this remarkable gentleman that they had only to
guard against any great number of persons leaving the
hall and demanding their money back by the excellence

of the rest of the concert, for which several popular favorites were always engaged.

The reason for his frequent disappointments of the public was said to be his good wife's solicitude for his health. He would get up in the morning and sing a little while dressing. Naturally his voice was not in prime condition then, but Mrs. Reeves would say: "Oh, Gardy dear" (she never forgot that he had been Edgardo in "Lucia"), "I am sure you have a dreadful cold to-day. I will send a telegram saying it is impossible for you to appear this evening." Indeed it is said she almost wrought his ruin by the undue care she took of him.

It has been my luck to miss very few engagements, but once I missed my train to Ipswich through Queen Victoria's return to London, which halted traffic in the street I had to take to the station. Greatly concerned, I sent a telegram of abject apology, only to receive the cutting reply: "A Reeves can scarcely afford to disappoint an audience; certainly not a Bispham." I was crushed!

Less than three weeks after the Covent Garden promenade concert at which Reeves appeared, I was called upon suddenly to join his concert company on tour, replacing a singer who had been taken ill. This so-called "farewell tour" was arranged by an astute manager who in his contract expressly stipulated that Mrs. Reeves should not travel with him, knowing full well that the aged lady would exercise her old-time wiles and, if she could do so, would prevent him from singing.

As it was, we younger people of the company were charged with the duty of keeping our chief amused and pleased, never crossing him in any way, taking walks or drives with him, playing billiards and otherwise causing him to forget that he was a tenor. The results were eminently satisfactory to every one concerned, for during my connection with his company he never disappointed an audience, though we sang every night and traveled to some other city the next day. So much for the sensible management of a singer.

While with Reeves, I found myself associated with Miss Amy Sherwin, soprano, Percy Sharman, violinist, and an excellent one he was, and the erratic pianist, Mlle. Janotha, who was always designated on the bill as "Solo Pianist to H. I. M. the Emperor of Germany." This was probably the reason why she rarely if ever spoke to any of us except at the concert, and then as little as possible, devoting her time to a magnificent cat which she took everywhere with her, spending the intervals at concerts in conversation with this animal, or in telling her beads, for she was a devout Catholic.

Many public performers have fads or mannerisms which are their specialties, their trade-marks, as it were. One of Reeves's was his persistent determination to give no encore in response to the applause after his first appearance upon the program. If down for two selections, one in each part of the concert, he asserted that the audience had no right to demand more of him than these two pieces; but, if he chose to give an encore, as of course he did after the second selection, that was his gracious donation, and no concession to any demand the audience might make. The fact is, "Needs must when the devil drives," as the old proverb has it, and Reeves did not want to sing any more than he actually had to. But if he felt well and was sufficiently flattered he would often respond to two, sometimes three encores, as he had frequently done on our concert tour.

Reeves used to recount to us many tales of his days upon the operatic stage, when he was without a peer among tenors and was also in the heyday of his glory as an oratorio singer. Among his experiences in the concert field, he told with great glee of an occasion in Scotland when he was the soloist for a choral society which assisted him in one or two numbers as he sang the solo parts. One of the selections was Spofforth's charming madrigal, " Hail, Smiling Morn," at one part of which the tenor sings " At whose bright presence darkness flies away " and the chorus should reply " flies away." What was the tenor's amusement to find the echo repeated by the accompanying choristers in a broad Scotch burr. " At whose bright presence darkness flies away " sang Reeves; but the chorus replied " flees awa'! " and broke up the sobriety of even a Scottish audience.

Upon this tour I had an opportunity of seeing for the first time Burns's country and of making acquaintance with the bagpipes upon their native heath; and Reeves told me the story of the Scot who meets in the street a friend broadly smiling. " Eh, Sandy, what it is makes ye look sae happy the day? " says he, and Sandy answers, " Eh, mon, I dreamit that I was in Heeven. I dreamit there was seeven-an'-thirrty pipers a' playin' deeferent tunes at the same time in a sma' room. Eh, it was just Heeven! "

The statement I once heard that the Scotch are very earnest but hardly serious enough is contradicted by the tale of the man who came down an Edinburgh street on a Sunday morning with a lilt in his walk and a tune on his lips. A friend stopped with " Eh, mon, have a care, have a care. You'd better mind what you're aboot! "

" What is the matter? " asked the smiling man.   " Have a care, mon," warned the other.   " You look a'most as happy as if it were Monday."

Although Reeves's repertory was becoming limited, it sufficed him to the end.   Besides the pieces mentioned it comprised " The Death of Nelson " by Braham, " Come into the Garden, Maud " by Balfe, " The Message " by Blumenthal, and " My Pretty Jane " by Bishop.   Yet when his wife died two years later Reeves was not only still singing, but he soon married quite a young woman by whom he had a bouncing baby, after which he went on a vaudeville tour through the British Isles.   The last time I heard him was at a Sunday concert in Queen's Hall, London, October 6, 1895, in which I assisted. Though the power of his voice was sadly diminished, he gave a most touching rendering of the Passion music from " The Messiah."   A grand old boy he was!

There being no engagements in prospect after the Reeves tour, I went again to my beloved Italy to study with Lamperti at San Remo, where he spent the winters, and profited greatly by association with the master, whose rooms were crowded every morning with pupils, who sang and were listened to by their fellows.   I ever since have believed that method to be effective in any studio.   He sat there in his easy chair, in slippered feet with a rug across his knees, mitts on his hands, a shawl about his shoulders resembling in his drooping, rough-clad form, some lean and slippered pantaloon sitting in sackcloth and ashes.

He invariably held a conductor's baton in his hand, and with it would alternately drub the arms or shoulders of some careless girl, or point to the portrait of Marcella Sembrich, whom he considered the greatest of his pupils and one of the greatest singers before the public of the day — as, indeed, she was. He had no patience with incompetency. Turning to his wife as she played for him, he would complain of the stupid possessors of beautiful voices, " What can you do with these people when they have no brains? "

It was on this visit that I met the novelist Mrs. Frances Hodgson Burnett, who had already attained fame with " That Lass o' Lowrie's " and " Little Lord Fauntleroy." By her I was taken to Bordighera, a few miles along the coast, to meet at the home which had been built for him by his admirers, the Scotch poet George Macdonald, who lived there with his family, friends and servants, in a manner fairly patriarchal. He had a great deep room across the whole front of the house; and opposite the door as one entered stood a massive stone fireplace beside which was placed his huge high-backed armchair. The floor at the end of the room at the right was raised and there stood the dining table at which family, guests, and servants all sat together at every meal. Toward one end of the table was a large saltcellar from which every one helped himself by dipping his fingers in at will, and " below the salt," in the old fashion, sat the servants, one of whom arose as need required to attend to the wants of others.

During the afternoon our host read to us, as was his custom, from Milton, Shakespeare, the Bible, or selections from Greek tragedy, in a superbly simple and yet grandly massive voice. The whole effect of the old man in his great chair impressed indelibly any one fortunate enough to hear such a reading. On the broad mantelpiece above the poet's head stood a wooden bowl into which I saw one of his servants reach and draw forth money; it seems

that our host would never permit any bills to be contracted in his house, and insisted upon immediate payment being made for every purchase sent from the shops,
out of the bowl, which he kept supplied with small coins.

My stay in Italy was interrupted by a summons to
London from Mlle. Janotha, whom I had promised, when
on tour with Reeves, to assist at her concert in St. James's
Hall whenever it might take place.   As the occasion was
to be a more than ordinary one, I was only too glad to
make the journey.

The concert was given under the auspices of Queen
Victoria and almost all of her daughters, including the
Queen-to-be Alexandra, and I was proud, indeed, to find
myself again with Sims Reeves and the veteran Italian
violoncellist Signor Piatti, one of Joachim's quartette.
The reason for my appearance at this affair was in reality that I might sing certain songs written by Lady Tennyson, the wife of the Poet Laureate, to words by her
husband.   Mlle. Janotha had edited these songs, and
I had the honor of giving them not only their first — and
probably their last — hearing upon any stage, but of
doing so before one of the most distinguished audiences
that it was possible to gather in all London, Janotha having made as much as possible of her connection with royalty and the friends of the friends of royalty.   Though
Tennyson himself was not present, he was represented
by his wife and son Hallam, and many distinguished personages announced as patrons of the concert were in
actual attendance.   To me it was an auspicious occasion
and the first of many appearances on that platform.

Who, having been in St. James's Hall, will ever forget that wonderful room consecrated by the greatest artists of the world?   Yet the auditorium on the ground

floor of the same building was occupied every afternoon and evening by Christie's negro minstrels. One of Leach's most amusing drawings in *Punch* was that of the musical amateur who had issued from one of the classical Monday " Pops " at the same time that the crowd was pouring out from the minstrels. Climbing upon an omnibus beside a man whom he had shouldered in the crowd, he asked the stranger if he had enjoyed the concert, and received the rejoinder, " Concert be blowed! Christie's for me."

CHAPTER XI

OPERA FROM WITHIN

Music bright as the soul of light, for wings an eagle, for notes a dove.
— Swinburne.

THE night after Mlle. Janotha's concert, I attended a performance of Sullivan's " Ivanhoe " at the Royal English Opera House, Shaftesbury Avenue. Before the evening was over I was bidden to the office of the manager, D'Oyley Carte, where I was offered the part of Cedric the Saxon, in place of one of the members of the cast who was unreliable because of his erratic disposition and intemperate habits.

Consulting my master Shakespeare the following morning, I was besought by him and his good wife not to " ruin " this artist's career. I replied that I was not to be accused of ruining the career of a man who could not hold his position, but I promised that I would not give an affirmative answer until they had tried to bring him around and reëstablish him in his part at the opera. In this they were successful. The management gave me a copy of the work, however, with instructions to learn the part, and to be ready to return at a moment's notice to fill the vacancy if the artist should yield to his besetting sin. Though nothing more came of it, I had many hours of serious thought and regret for my lack of foresight in having left opera out of my calculations.

In London I found myself associated with many artists, among them the pianist Leopold Godowsky, then coming into prominence, and met the American contralto, Antoinette Sterling, whose majestic appearance was, if I am not mistaken, derived from American Indian ancestors. She was a serious woman and highly religious, considered opera wrong, for herself at least, and had devoted her talents to oratorio and later to the sort of ballad that points a moral and adorns a tale if it does not adorn the artistic side of the concert platform. If half a hymn the better a song pleased her.

Madame Sterling had been under the influence of Quakers in America, and I believe had joined that body, but she deemed that Friends were doing wrong by not having music in their places of worship, and at the time of which I speak had suddenly made her appearance at the Friends' Meeting in St. Martin's Lane in London, where, moved by the spirit as she declared, she arose and sang, without accompaniment, Mendelssohn's " Oh, Rest in the Lord," to the dismay of the worshipers. Some of them tried to silence her, and others supported her, deeming it better to hear the song through than to have an unseemly disturbance in the quiet precincts of the Meeting House. She ended and sat down, assuring me that after the meeting she was surrounded by many persons, who, with tears in their eyes, thanked her for what she had done, devoutly wishing that such singing might be heard regularly among them.

In the summer of 1891 my mother again crossed the ocean to visit me, interested as she was in my study and career, but filled with apprehension, dear soul, lest I should be enticed upon the stage. She knew that I had been successful in the two amateur operas of which I have spoken; and, having heard of the offer made me by Sullivan, looked forward with dread to a time when I might be tempted and fall into the wiles of the Evil One, as he lay concealed behind the scenery or beneath the boards of the iniquitous theatre.

Reassuring her, I made her realize that I had at her particular desire not studied any operas at all for professional purposes, and that were I offered an engagement I should have great difficulty in accepting it; yet, at the same time, if such an engagement should come, I should be the most foolish young man in the world not to accept it. It would be unlike the spirit of an American to hold back from anything honorably ambitious, and unwise from the point of view of business, for as a family our means were rather small, and though I lived quietly my early earnings were scarcely adequate to my needs.

My mother left England saying that she fully realized my position, and while she wished me well in my chosen career, she earnestly hoped that it might continue in the way of concert and sacred music such as oratorio, and prayed that the temptation of opera might never be offered me. As I bade her farewell, I said, " Mother, what would happen if opera should be offered me?" "Oh! my dear son," she said in alarm, " let us not think of that, I almost hope it may never come; but if it does, please write me at once and I will take the matter in prayer to a Higher Source and let thee know my decision." It was not long before I had the offer.

Through my friend the composer, Ernest Ford, my name was urged upon Arthur Sullivan's consideration and I was requested to come to the Savoy Theatre and have my voice tried. The outcome might possibly be my engagement as the Duke in Messager's opera "The Basoche," which had already been translated.

On arriving at the theatre I found about fifty aspirants

for operatic honors sitting about the stage or in the body of the house. These were called one by one, young men and young women, who proceeded to sing the songs they had brought with them, everybody being nervous. Particularly good voices were made note of, the names and addresses of their owners set down in a book, to be called upon if parts were vacant in any of the companies on the road. The Savoy Theatre had been an institution for years, companies from it went not only over Great Britain but over the whole English-speaking world. Everything was done in a businesslike and yet artistic manner. No favoritism was shown, as I knew well afterward, and the company of the Savoy Theatre itself was a model one. Artists of good reputation and fine voices were chosen in the first place, retained their positions for many years, and the company's work was consequently of the highest order.

As my turn drew near my nerves were on edge. I was not in the best vocal condition; but I was in for it and had to go through with it. No comment was made upon my singing. My name and address were taken down and I felt that perhaps I was not altogether hopeless.

Time passed and I did not hear from the Savoy Theatre, but continued with the concerts that came my way, upon one occasion appearing on the program with several artists of the Savoy Theatre and some well-known actors, thus seeming to be brought in touch with what after all I could not grasp, standing at the foot of a ladder which I feared I was not to be permitted to mount. Yet in about a month I was surprised by being asked to come again to the Savoy Theatre, where I was invited into the private office of Mr. Carte and found my friend Ford. Notwithstanding my former cold I had been accounted as one among the promising aspirants for stage honors, which in their own good time were coming around to me. I sang a number of things for Mr. Carte, who was noncommittal. I did not hear from him again until one wretched foggy day when I was suddenly summoned.

I arrived with galoshes, dripping umbrella, and mackintosh, and was presently shown upon the stage, lighted only by a little gas jet on an upright stand down by the footlights. Ford played the piano, Carte was in the topmost row of the gallery, Arthur Sullivan in the back row of the pit, and his friend and adviser, Mrs. Ronalds, in a box. From these points of vantage they took account of me at a disadvantage. I was asked to sing and to act, and chose the serenade of Mephistopheles from " Faust."

Though the part of Mephistopheles had long attracted me, I had never, of course, sung it upon the stage. Several years later, however, my manager did me the compliment to urge me to do so, and when I demurred, saying I was too short, he replied, " Oh, that is nothing; I have known plenty of little devils! "

I have since been told that I have a way of creating an atmosphere which causes my audience to forget that I am merely upon a concert platform; but on the occasion of my Savoy ordeal I had to convince three or four of the wisest heads in the world, for Alfred Cellier was present too. The scenery of the Savoy was wrong side before standing against the wall; there was no illusion and but little light. Strumming upon my wet umbrella as though it were a lute, and deporting myself as though I were indeed the Prince of Darkness in disguise, I trolled out my song.

To my amazement I was then and there engaged to

take the part of the Duke in " The Basoche " which went immediately into rehearsal. In this I made my professional début on the operatic stage on November 3, 1891, at the Royal English Opera House, Shaftesbury Avenue, now the Palace Theatre of Varieties. I was then almost thirty-five years of age, and should have been able to do this ten years before, at the very least.

During the rehearsals for " The Basoche " I found myself not getting along with Hugh Moss, who was putting on the piece. He was an actor of the old school, and I in my ignorance and inexperience found his orders irksome and was not doing myself justice. One morning at the midday recess, the conductor called me aside, invited me to lunch with him, and took the opportunity of giving me the best advice I had ever received.

Cellier said: " I see that you and Moss do not agree very well, and I must tell you that Mr. Carte and Sir Arthur have observed the same thing, and doubt whether you can carry through your part acceptably. I believe in you and so does Ernest Ford, and if you will take my advice, you will study stage deportment after our rehearsals here. Go quietly without saying anything about it to my friend Monsieur Marius, the comedian from Paris now playing at the Gaiety Theatre. He will be able to put you through this French part better than any one else, and will give you the lightness of touch which you lack and are not getting from our stage director. Furthermore," said Mr. Cellier, " as your part has a serious side, I would suggest that you go to some Shakespearean actor like Herman Vezin, and have lessons from him in a different school of dramatic art."

I followed Cellier's advice and immediately arranged for lessons with Marius, which I took every morning

upon the Gaiety stage before coming to rehearsal at the
Royal English Opera House. Every afternoon after
finishing my work there, I went to Vezin's chambers in
the top of the house at the north end of Waterloo Bridge,
where I studied such Shakespearean selections as the
quarrel scene of Brutus and Cassius from " Julius Cæsar."
The celebrated old tragedian acted these out with me in
the midst of a room filled with mementos of his long
career in Europe.

I learned much from Vezin the tragedian and Marius
the comedian, and kept my counsel at our own rehearsals, obeying every instruction to the letter, having discovered that another man was being prepared in my
part and that if a week's trial did not bring me up to ex-
pectations I should certainly be supplanted by a rival.
This put me on my mettle and I resolved not to lose my
job.

I had, of course, informed my mother of the great opportunity offered me of appearing under the best auspices
in a part which would undoubtedly suit me to perfection,
and I immediately received from her a letter in which she
withdrew all her earlier objections to my identifying myself with the operatic stage, adding that she felt my career
to be guided by Other Hands than hers, and bidding me
to strive always toward the highest ideals in my chosen
profession.

Moved by her noble self-denial — for what touched
me, her only child, was touching her very life — I resolved ever after to live up to the best that I knew
in my innermost soul and to hold high the banner of my
art.

I am reminded that her father, my grandfather Scull,
had during the time that I was in my uncle's office, ob-

served that I had musical tendencies and, as he lay on his death-bed, he had, with a generosity entirely unexpected, given me a check for fifty dollars, with which to begin the collection of my musical library. I treasure nothing more than the oratorios and good music which I acquired with that money, and still possess.

About this time I gave up smoking, which I found was somewhat irritating to my throat, preferring song to smoke, each of them evanescent enough in itself. If I were to make a career upon the stage, I was determined to put aside everything that might interfere with it. I had smoked for years; but, after four days of successful struggle, I abandoned the habit for ever, through the simple expedient of carrying about and putting to my lips when moved to smoke the stub of a lead pencil about the size and shape of a cigarette.

Meeting my friend Oliver Herford in London and telling him that I had stopped smoking because it irritated my mucous membrane, he said, " Why didn't you go on? Very soon you would have had no mucous membrane to bother about." As we talked, we spoke of London not yet having American " skyscrapers." " No," said Oliver as he peered into the pea-soup fog, " that's a pity, for I don't know any sky that needs scraping more."

At the time of which I speak I wore a pointed beard which was reddish — my hair had been a brick red as a boy and still had its golden tint, though I was early graying at the temples; but I fancied myself in my Vandyke beard and did not dispense with it until the last moment before the dress rehearsal. Calling that day shaven at the house of an intimate friend on my way to the theatre, I was announced by the servant, who knew me of old, as " the Reverend Mr. Bispham." Very lit-

tle serves to disguise me, and in my costume I came upon
the stage totally unrecognized by any member of the company for several minutes. I was in fine voice and by
reason of the private instruction I had been having in the
actor's art, I was at the first performance of the opera
enabled to carry it through to the satisfaction of my employers and of the public, and remained about six months
at that theatre — as long as the piece ran.

At the time of the production of " The Basoche " there
were a number of well-known American songstresses in
London, who had already come under the notice of
Arthur Sullivan, and from among these were chosen the
two beautiful and gifted sopranos, Esther Palliser, a Philadelphia girl, and Lucille Hill. These ladies with the
distinguished tenor, Ben Davies, and myself carried the
burden of the performance, which was well received, and
I found myself suddenly in the desired haven. My
voyage through life up to that time had not been tempes-
tuous, but, nevertheless, I knew not where to land and
settle down. This engagement so auspiciously begun, I
am thankful to say, gave me the right start, and I bent
every energy toward assuring myself and the public of
my standing in the musical world.

The designer of the resplendent costumes for " The
Basoche " was Percy Anderson, to whom I had confided
my desire to play my part, if possible, with a beard. I
still possess Mr. Anderson's sketch in water colors of
how I might be dressed as the Duc de Longueville while
retaining my precious hirsute appendage. Distinguished
looking as I appear in the sketch, it does not resemble
either of the costumes I wore, the principal one of which
turned out to be in every detail that which was described
to me by the old phrenologist as being worn by the person

he denominated as my guide. But the fact was not commented upon until some time later, when I was sitting for my portrait to Herman Herkomer, to whom for the first time I told the story.

CHAPTER XII

THE THRESHOLD CROSSED

Life is a great bundle of little things.   8
— *Holmes.*

AFTER the run of "The Basoche" was over, I filled
many minor concert engagements and was beginning to
make a little money.   Bearing in mind Mackenzie's injunction that it was the business of a singer to sing, I realized, too, that there was no business in it if the singer did
not get paid for his song or strive for his own advancement, and I let no stone remain unturned in my path up
the hill.   I sang wherever I was asked to sing, and took
a moderate fee rather than none at all.

I joined the Lyric Club where Randegger used to direct the Sunday evening concerts, in which many of the
foremost artists appeared, and I also belonged to The
Magpies, a club under the direction of Lionel Benson,
where were performed madrigals of the old school and
the best modern music for mixed voices, sending several
of the programs to New York for the information of
the newly founded Musical Art Society.   The member-
ship of The Magpies included the names of a number of
persons famous in England, not in music alone but in
painting, sculpture, literature, and political life, and of
the highest social station, including royalty itself.   One
of Queen Victoria's daughters, H. R. H. the Princess
Louise, Marchioness of Lorne, was an enthusiastic amateur.   Another daughter, H. R. H. the Princess Christian, was also an ardent lover of music, and sang well.

The Prince of Wales, afterward King Edward VII, was devoted to music, to which he listened at every opportunity, which included constant attendance at the opera. His brother, the Duke of Edinburgh, was no mean violinist and played at the first desk in the Royal Amateur Orchestral Association. Another of the Queen's sons, the late Prince Arthur, had a nice voice, for an amateur, and frequently offered to entertain his friends. A noble old lady of my acquaintance who had been speaking of his vocal performances in her drawing-room was asked by me how he sang. She archly replied, " Oh — like a Prince, I assure you ! "

It was at my first concert with The Magpies that I introduced to English audiences Richard Wagner's fine ballad " Les Deux Grenadiers," the words of which had been known only through the arrangement by Robert Schumann, famous for fifty years. It seems that Wagner, living, but almost at death's door, in Paris where for a mere pittance he was making piano transcriptions of the works of his rivals, happened upon Heine's own French version of his well-known poem " The Two Grenadiers," and by a coincidence set about composing music for it at the very time that Schumann was making his version, neither composer knowing that the other was thus at work.

To London Wagner's setting of the celebrated lines came as a novelty, and I frequently used the song which, notwithstanding its fine quality, is undoubtedly inferior in dramatic intensity to Schumann's setting. This latter, Georg Henschel used to render superbly. Once when he and I were singing in a large miscellaneous concert, Henschel had sent in Schumann's " The Two Grenadiers," while I had contributed Wagner's setting of the same ballad. Upon offering to change my selection, Henschel replied, " Oh, no, let us keep them both upon the program; it will be interesting to see how the two songs contrast "; and it was done, arousing renewed interest in both.

Some time afterward while being entertained in Bayreuth by Madame Wagner at the Villa Wahnfried, where I had been upon previous occasions, I was requested to sing her late husband's setting of " Les Deux Grenadiers," and was amazed to find that none of the Wagner family had ever heard the song before, though Madame Wagner told me that she knew of its existence. Indeed, not excepting the many celebrated German musicians present, it was a novelty to every one in the room, save the few who had heard me sing it in London.

Beyond knowledge of the music of Richard Wagner, the ladies of the Wagner family were, as a matter of fact, rather unmusical. Upon the very evening to which I refer, after Madame Lilli Lehmann had superbly sung Schubert's " Erl King," one of Madame Wagner's daughters turned to my informant beside her on the sofa and said, " Oh, how wonderfully she sings that great song by my grandfather Liszt! "

In consequence members of the Wagner family were not free from rather frequent raps from those who had a wider purview of the musical situation than they. For instance, Von Bülow, who had been Madame Wagner's first husband and continued his friendship with the family for many years, visited Bayreuth about the time to which I refer, not only to hear the master's music, but to pay his respects to his former family, so to speak. On taking his departure, a great crowd assembled at the station to see him off. After the daughters of the family had embraced him, he seated himself in the railway carriage. As the train was moving out, he arose, put his head out of the window, waved his hand to the crowd, and shouted out, " But there is one greater: Brahms! Brahms! Good-by! Good-by!" With that parting shot the brilliant and eccentric musician took his departure from Bayreuth, never again to return.

While singing in London I met many times the gifted but unfortunate Goring Thomas, who may be counted among England's most talented sons. His operas " Esmeralda "— why is it never given? — and " Nadeshda " had already made him famous, and he had just composed that exquisite cantata, " The Swan and the Skylark." Many songs added to his fame and he was never more productive than when the accident happened that gave him concussion of the brain. This lamentably resulted in fits of madness, in one of which he threw himself in front of an approaching train and was cut to pieces.

That most of Goring Thomas's operas have been produced at Covent Garden in Italian, that shortly after the opera " Signa," founded on the story by Ouida and composed by Frederick Cowen, was also performed in Italian at the Grand Opera, and that the works of Wagner were there performed in the same tongue, all before English-speaking audiences, caused me to reflect upon the futility of the decrees of fashion. Nothing but fashion and lack of reflection in following fashion's decrees could have brought about so ridiculous a state of affairs, whereby grand opera from English, German, and French sources should be sung only in Italian — and that before English-speaking audiences.

Notwithstanding the fact that English is a world language, that it has an enormous and precious literature of songs, that all the oratorios are sung in our language, that all newly composed cantatas for English festivals are written in English and in nothing else, that for these very festivals many foreign works have been translated into English, in which language they are sung as a matter of course, yet fashion had decreed that at the opera Italian should be the one and only language. The Royal English Opera was started with Sullivan's "Ivanhoe" and with plenty of money behind it, as a protest against this and as an effort to better conditions so calamitous that the Royal Carl Rosa English Grand Opera Company, though successful everywhere else, was year after year a failure in London.

Though a newcomer in the metropolis, the inconsistency of all this was so apparent that it occurred to me to speak about it to my friend Lionel Benson, conductor of The Magpies. I spoke also to Alberto Randegger, teacher and conductor, himself an Italian with a German name; to William Barclay Squire, now at the head of the musical department of the British Museum, and to J. A. Fuller-Maitland, music critic of the *London Times*. These gentlemen, with others influential in musical art, were invited to meet me at Mr. Squire's house, where I laid before them my idea that perhaps the time had now come for a change, seeing that Germany was a musical nation with a rich operatic literature and that France also had a long and growing list of operatic works for which performers could easily be brought twenty miles across the English Channel.

As a result the company present composed and sent a letter to Sir Augustus Harris, the well-known head of the Theatre Royal, Drury Lane, and of the opera at

Covent Garden, which he had revived and set upon its feet a short time before. In this Harris was asked to use his best endeavor to bring about such changes as would enable London audiences to hear French, German, and English operas performed in their respective languages. Harris replied that at the time he did not see his way to doing this, though as a matter of fact the idea made an immediate appeal to him, and it was not long before the Italian artist no longer had it all his own way. Germans were soon brought over from Germany to sing in operas of their own school; many French singers who had hitherto sung only in Paris were glad to have the opportunity of rendering French rôles in their own exquisite tongue; and operas by Englishmen were also heard in the vernacular of their composers: opera in Italian in short held sway in its proper place, as we hope it always will do. The back of the unilingual system was thus broken, though for some strange reason there still exists a prejudice against grand opera in English among many of the fashionable operatic set on both sides of the Atlantic.

Until the recent advent of Sir Thomas Beecham as an operatic conductor, who is well furnished with the wherewithal to do anything he pleases upon the stage, English opera had never fairly come into its own. Let us hope that the way now open is kept open and that British no less than American composers will be encouraged by the public at large to give us of their best without further fear of the unthinking attitude which has persuaded so many among us to regard the English language as unsingable.

All this time I was studying hard to increase my repertory, while tempering my character to meet any demands upon it. Almost equal to the possession of voice to a singer is the ability to do the work required quietly, systematically, accurately, and without giving trouble to the management, as my experience in "The Basoche" had taught me. Let me cite an example.

One of the most celebrated artists of the world, not an English-speaking person, by the way, after making a great reputation in Paris, London, and New York, was invited several years ago to sing in Berlin, where her demands and requirements on and off the stage were most exaggerated and exasperating. After her first performance at the Royal Opera, in Berlin, she was, notwithstanding the success she had made with the audience, requested to end her engagement immediately. From the moment of her appearance at the opera house she kept everything in a turmoil until she left it. As her manager once summed it up to me: "Confound these women, the older they get, and the worse they sing, the more the people want to see them, the more money they demand, the less they'll do, and the more trouble they make."

In all legitimate ways I was eagerly pursuing success in my professional life in London, after the conclusion of the run of "The Basoche." Besides numerous concerts, public and private, of greater or less importance, I was besought by several theatre managers to go into light opera, for which it seems they thought me well fitted, as I had made an undoubted comedy hit already.

But nothing seemed to suit me. Tschaikowsky's opera of "Eugene Onegin," which was offered me and which I studied, I gave up when I found the character did not fit my personality. I was declining so many things that I began to be in considerable doubt as to what course I should pursue in my professional life. The concert field, while interesting, seemed much overcrowded, and though I felt that I should continue in opera, the right thing did not seem to present itself. I had reached another crisis in my life.

CHAPTER XIII

PLANCHETTE AND PROPHECY

You would play upon me; you would seem to know my stops; you would pluck out the heart of the mystery.— Shakespeare.

AMONG others at a small dinner given at my house in London in March, 1892, was Baron Waleen, a Swede not identified with music, but interested in the investigation of psychic phenomena. He brought with him the toy called Planchette, by means of which automatic writing is assisted, and after dinner we tried a few experiments. They were on the point of becoming interesting when the conversation wandered from serious consideration of the subject into trifling questions, our experiments resulting in nothing.

A few evenings later I dined with Waleen and his friend Baron Rudbeck, the latter neither musician nor spiritist, but known to have manifested curious psychic powers. After dinner we three sat about a little table on which was spread a great blank sheet of white paper, upon which, under Rudbeck's hand, Planchette began at once to write rapidly and distinctly.

I was not touching the machine, nor had I propounded any questions to it; yet it soon wrote in large letters, "Opera, by all means." Neither of my companions knew to what this referred or saw any connection in it with anything that had gone before, until I explained. "It is an answer to a question I was about to ask," I told them: "Shall I continue in concert or make further endeavor toward opera?" Here was a direct answer to my un-spoken thought.

Needless to say, we three were interested, and grew excited as Planchette went on to reply without hesitation to every query I put to it. Rudbeck's right hand was resting upon it, his left hand covering his eyes, which he opened only when the instrument stopped. My first spoken question was, " What operas shall I study?" Let me here remind the reader that at this time I had no operatic repertory, " The Basoche " being the only opera I had ever learned. Planchette replied, " The operas of Verdi and Wagner." I realized instantly that the operas of the two composers named contained remarkably fine barytone parts. But, excepting the romance to the Eve-ning Star from " Tannhäuser," I knew not a note of any of them.

The next question I propounded to Planchette was, " Which of these operas shall I study?" The answer was, " Aïda," " Tannhäuser," " Tristan und Isolde," and " Die Meistersinger." We sat amazed. I was pleased as well, for no better parts exist than are to be found in these works, and my next question followed almost as a matter of course, " What parts shall I study?" There was a surprise for me at the end of the answer, which was " Amonasro, Wolfram, Kurwenal, and — Beckmes-ser."

This last disclosure puzzled me. I had heard " Die Meistersinger " sung more than once at Bayreuth, as well as in other places, and had laughed at Beckmesser, all the time so loving Hans Sachs that I was then trying to learn the noble music of that rôle, deeming Beckmesser too high, too unvocal, and too difficult for me to consider. I rather fancied myself as a vocalist, and therefore deliberately put away all thought of Beckmesser.   Now I was bidden to study it!

I could not account for it, but went on to ask my final question, " When shall I be engaged? "   To this the reply was, " In a couple of months you will know."   After this, try as we would, no single word came from Planchette, whose board I had not touched during the experiments.

I was so impressed by what had taken place that the next day I secured an accompanist and began work on the part of Beckmesser, the length and difficulty of which were appalling to me.   This labor was varied by study of the much easier rôles of Amonasro and Wolfram, while Kurwenal, so much shorter and more sympathetic, sank into my mind more readily than any of the others. For two months I worked like a slave on these, accepting, besides, an engagement to prepare the part of Alberich in the entire first scene of " The Rheingold " and the part of Wotan in the first scene of " The Valkyrie." These I worked up with Carl Armbruster, one of Wagner's assistant conductors at Bayreuth.

The concert at which I performed this music took place on the afternoon of May 22 at Ham House, Richmond, the residence of Lord Dysart, president of the Wagner Society, which was invited on the master's birthday to hear selections from his music.

As the company walked about the lawn after the affair, I observed among the guests the familiar face of Sir Augustus Harris, the impresario of the opera at Covent Garden, to whom I had been instrumental not long before in suggesting that the universal use of the Italian language should be discontinued in opera.

The next morning I had a message from my manager,

Daniel Mayer, to say that he had received from Harris a note asking if I knew the part of Beckmesser; as, if I did, I was to come at once to Covent Garden to rehearse it for performance with Jean de Reszke, Madame Albani, and Jean Lassalle, the barytone.

As I read I thought I should die of excitement, for now was the prophecy come true. " In a couple of months you will know," it said, and at that time I had been asked to do the least likely and most difficult of the parts I had been working on. Needless to say I accepted at once; but the rehearsals had not proceeded many days, when De Reszke caught a cold, because of which he asked to be excused temporarily from further preparation of so difficult a rôle as Walther, in view of his necessary appearances in other operas of the repertory. The rehearsals for " Die Meistersinger " were therefore postponed.

As I left the stage, much discouraged, I was accosted by Sir Augustus Harris, whom I had never met personally up to that moment, but who shook me cordially by the hand, saying: " I'm sorry that you can't sing the part of Beckmesser now, for it is going to suit you very well. Never mind, you shall have it when we do it. I like people who know things and are ready. By the way," added he, putting his hand into his breast pocket, " I have just had a letter from the German barytone who is here with the company from Hamburg to say that he has a bad cold and cannot sing the part of Kurwenal tomorrow night. I wonder if you know that part? "

I was standing on the stage of Covent Garden where the trap is that in the old version of " Faust " opened and let Mephistopheles through into another region. When Harris asked me the question I felt as if I should sink into the depths, such a failing was there of my heart at being asked to do the second one of the characters which Planchette had advised me to study. I remained on deck, however, and, pulling myself together, I answered, "Yes; I know that part." "Good!" said he. "Mahler is having a rehearsal of the orchestra at Drury Lane now. You had better go over there and take your book with you. Watch carefully; it is catchy stuff, you know."

I knew that it was "catchy stuff"; had I not for more than two months been caught in its toils? I went over and, sitting in a stage box with my book before me, paid every atom of attention of which I was capable to the music of my part as it came along. After the rehearsal I was taken by Gustav Mahler into the classic foyer of the theatre, where there was a piano at which he seated himself and took me through the whole rôle of Kurwenal, which I knew perfectly, leaving him satisfied that I could do it. It became mine on the following evening, June 25, 1892, without further rehearsal, except that Max Alvary, the greatest Tristan of his time, showed me the positions upon the stage before the curtain arose upon each successive act.

I may say without boasting, for it is merely a matter of record, that for a number of years I had no rival in the part of Kurwenal, nor in the part of Beckmesser. When this latter was finally produced I performed it so as to insure me the part, which, much as I enjoyed performing it, was so strenuous that had I not been blessed with what my mother called "the voice of a bull of Bashan" I should never have been able to live through it and the many other parts which immediately began to crowd upon me.

When people say to me, "What but foolishness did any one ever get out of Planchette or any other so-called

DAVID BISPHAM
as Kurwenal in Wagner's "Tristan and Isolde"

DAVID BISPHAM
as Alberich in Wagner's "Niebelungen Ring"

From Photographs by Aimé Dupont, New York

spiritistic advice?" I tell them the story just narrated. My action in taking the advice I received — whence it came, I know not — resulted at the time indicated in my being fully prepared for what I was asked to do.   In accepting this counsel and being ready with the parts I had been told to learn, I was undoubtedly enabled to accept the responsibilities whose execution straightway resulted in the foundation of my operatic career.

So I was engaged at Covent Garden, and was given opportunities by Harris to do anything and everything.   I was in no position to pick and choose, and was only too glad of the chance to obtain experience in my profession.

It is to be remembered that I had been advised to pay particular attention to the operas of Verdi and Wagner; that I had been told to study the rôles of Amonasro, Wolfram, Kurwenal, and Beckmesser; that "a couple of months" later I was actually engaged to sing Beckmesser, and that, upon the postponement of that part, I did in reality perform the rôle of Kurwenal.

Now occurred another curious thing.   One day as I was leaving Covent Garden after a rehearsal, I was accosted by Castelmary, the *régisseur* of the company, and asked whether I knew the part of Amonasro well enough to take it that evening in the place of Victor Maurel, who had notified the management of his sudden indisposition.   The state of internal panic that ensued — for the prophecy had now come true for the third time — left me outwardly calm and I accepted the responsibility with the understanding that I should have nothing to think of but my part, the costumes and make-up being supplied me. Castelmary in loyalty to his old friend Maurel requested me to wait a while, saying that he thought, after all, that the management should give the distinguished barytone another opportunity before letting a newcomer take his place. A messenger was accordingly sent in a hansom cab, and presently returned with word from the great barytone that he would sing. Though I did not perform it the part was offered to me, the third of the four characters I had been advised to study, and I was ready to sing it.

I have long intended to write to persons of standing in the investigation of such matters about this occurrence, which seems to have been almost beyond the possibility of mere chance. By some they may be set down in the class with the miracles of Lourdes; by others attributable to the phenomena of science; by Sir Oliver Lodge they may be attributed to spiritistic influence; and any one who has read Maeterlinck's marvelous story of The Elberfeld Horses may readily imagine that the power that enabled them instantly to solve abstruse mathematical problems is the same " psychic flash " that illumined for me the unborn future and showed me the path I should follow. But if you ask me my honest opinion, I am content to accept the facts as I found them, realizing that " there are more things in heaven and earth than are dreamt of in our philosophy."

CHAPTER XIV

Thither our path lies; wind we up the heights.
— *Browning.*

MY connection with the Royal Opera, following upon what I had done before, immediately increased my prestige in the eyes of the purveyors of music. As one result I made my first professional visit to Ireland, to take part in the Tercentenary celebrations of the University of Dublin, where I met Professor Max Müller; and before long I appeared again at Covent Garden during the autumn season, which was a sort of aftermath of the Royal Opera, due to the unprecedentedly busy summer season at the two historic theatres. It was then that I had the opportunity of singing several times as Kurwenal in " Tristan and Isolde " under the conductorship of Armbruster, with the tenor Oberlaender, the dramatic soprano Pauline Cramer, and with Esther Palliser as the admirable Brangäne, which she had, to the hurt of her voice, committed to memory in a marvelously short space of time.

I also began to have a share in the production of classical music at other universities besides Dublin under Robert Stewart: at Cambridge under Villiers Stanford, and at Oxford, where Ernest Walker and W. H. Haddow were leaders of the new movement.

There are several persons whom I have to thank for the encouragement they gave me at this period of my career, among them George Bernard Shaw, then a music critic and already widely known as a Fabian socialist, who had not at that time climbed far up the ladder of fame upon which he later mounted to such dizzy heights. I have always been treated well by the British Press, and have nothing but the kindest feeling toward all my critics, whether at that time or afterward they gave me helpful advice or chose to differ with me in respect to my interpretations.

J. A. Fuller-Maitland of the *London Times* I must acknowledge as having been from first to last a constant friend both personally and professionally. It was at his house one night in December, 1892, after an evening of music in which I had taken my share, that I sang, probably for the first time in London, the prologue from the new opera " I Pagliacci," the part which, when I sang it later upon the stage, I always rendered in evening clothes, making a quick change into the clown's costume after the address to the audience. I consider that the prologue had nothing to do with the story of the opera and could as well be sung by any person not taking part in the opera itself. It is the address of an actor to his audience, in which he bids them understand that we upon the stage are mere human beings, just as our auditors are, animated by the same feelings, made of the same flesh and blood, and partaking of the same joys and sorrows.

Among the conductors at Covent Garden was Armando Seppilli, from whom I have it that when Victor Maurel was about to create the part of Tonio in the city of Venice, he complained at the dress rehearsal that there was not enough in the part to give him the proper solo opportunity; and desired the composer to write an aria especially for him. It was obviously impossible thus to change an opera which had taken a prize, and upon this fact being called to Maurel's attention, he replied: " Very well; do not change the opera; write me a prologue which can be sung in front of the curtain before the opera begins at all." Leoncavallo immediately accepted the suggestion, went home, and that night wrote the words and music. These were rehearsed the next day, thus supplying Maurel, and every other barytone, with the finest opportunity to show his mettle.

Seppilli's story interested me, and I asked him how Maurel had dressed the part. He replied that the singer's original intention was to sing it in evening clothes, as the prologue had nothing to do with the subsequent story. On second thought, however, both Maurel and the management came to the conclusion that the plain black and white of conventional evening dress were not sufficiently effective, and the barytone sketched an exaggerated but conventional clown's costume, which he not only wore in the prologue but throughout the opera. With this I personally do not agree. I made the change into such a dress as the clown of a strolling company would be likely to wear along the road and in the villages when the company was drumming up its audience for the evening. But in the second act, the scene of the performance upon the miniature stage, I put on a real clown's costume with pointed hat, wig, and baggy trousers, and made up my face over again, red cheeks and all.

In the numerous concerts in which I appeared in London, wherever I had choice of my selections, I did not fail, while introducing the classics of song, to honor our American composers, George W. Chadwick, Horatio W. Parker and Arthur Foote among them.

I also performed the songs of many of my kind English colleagues, among them Arthur Somervell, the brilliant

Goring Thomas, Hubert Parry, Mackenzie, and Villiers Stanford. The latter was good enough to urge upon me the title rôle in his delightful Irish comedy opera " Shamus O'Brien," which I was unable to accept.

I kept up my studies with Shakespeare, also practicing the operas of Mozart and Rossini with Randegger, or working on the songs of Tosti with their distinguished little composer, who was *persona grata* with Queen Victoria and all the Court, as well as with the most distinguished operatic and other musical coteries of the metropolis. Valuable objects are done up in small packages, they say, and Tosti was no exception to the rule, being undoubtedly a valuable asset to his beautiful wife, who literally took him under her arm wherever she went. The story is told of her that at the conclusion of an afternoon drive with a handsome duchess she had her carriage halted in the jam of vehicles at Hyde Park Corner by an enormous policeman. Madame Tosti, looking admiringly at the representative of the law, said to the duchess in her charming French accent, " When Tosti die, I marry a policeman."

Among my associates in concert, classical and popular, I find the names of the violinists Tivadar Natchez, Johannes Wolff, Emil Sauret, and the great master Auguste Wilhelmj, who was then about to retire from public life, all of whom were encouraging to me. I have ever deemed it to be of the highest importance for a vocalist to associate as frequently and as intimately as possible with instrumentalists, who by reason of their training are generally broader-minded, better musicians, and possessed of much higher ideals than seem to be vouchsafed to most singers.

In the early days of 1893 I was asked by the distinguished conductor and pianist, Sir Charles Hallé, to take part in a series of his choral and orchestral concerts in Free Trade Hall, Manchester, where twenty-five years later, Woodrow Wilson, President of the United States, was to speak upon his much discussed plan for the League of Nations. In Hallé's concert presentation of Wagner's " The Flying Dutchman " I assumed the part of Daland to the Vanderdecken of Andrew Black, the Scotch barytone, who rightfully assumed for a period of years the mantle which was falling rapidly from the shoulders of Charles Santley.

Plunkett Greene also began to sail up breezily over the horizon, and immediately made an enviable name for himself; as a song singer he will always be remembered by those who heard them. His interpretation of Irish ditties was quite beyond compare, and men as well as women were at the feet of this typical Irish gentleman.

Edward Lloyd had become the legitimate successor of Sims Reeves, and was in the midst of a most successful and distinguished career. No other tenor upon the concert stage was his equal; all acknowledged his superiority; while among the contraltos the name of one who was to outrank all others was rapidly rising into prominence, that of Clara Butt, whose majestic figure was equaled by the glory of a voice which is now well known throughout the world.

I am proud to have been requested to go with Madame Melba upon a short concert tour in England and Ireland, about the time when Verdi's last opera, " Falstaff," that youthful emanation from the brain of an old man, was produced at La Scala Theatre, in Milan. Bearing in mind the advice of Planchette, I secured the first obtainable copy issued from the press of Ricordi, and had it with me studying the part of Falstaff as I traveled. Melba expressed curiosity about the music I was so intently poring over in the train one day and I told her of my strange experience with prophecies come true. This interested her so much that she strongly advised me to go to Milan as soon as our concerts were over and hear the performance of the title rôle by Maurel. This I did, and further studied the part with an accompanist there and with my old master Lamperti.

Returning to London by the end of February to appear in the concerts which had been arranged for me, I was surprised to receive a letter from Mackenzie saying that he intended to give three lectures upon Verdi and his latest opera, " Falstaff," at the Royal Institution, and inviting me to assume the title rôle in it! During the following year, 1894, I played this part more than twenty times upon the stage, surrounded by most of the company I had seen supporting Maurel in Milan.

CHAPTER XV

They have been at a great feast of languages.—*Shakespeare.*

ITALIAN, during my second season of opera at Covent Garden, despite the change that was obviously coming, was still the common denominator in languages. When I was given the promised opportunity at last to play the part of Beckmesser in " Die Meistersinger," it was with Madame Albani as Eva, Lassalle as Hans Sachs, and Jean de Reszke as Walther. Here were artists of four nationalities, and the opera, sung in Italian, was made still further interesting by the presence in the cast of Wiegand, a German, Guetary, a Spaniard, Hedmondt, an American, and several other Italian, German, and English-speaking men and women. Italian was the one ground upon which we could all meet with satisfaction, to ourselves, to the management, and to the audiences; these last, of course, not understanding a word that any of us sang.

I have ever held that if " Madame Butterfly " were secretly rehearsed and rendered in Japanese, no one would know the difference — except such of the Mikado's subjects as might chance to be present!

In 1893 I made my début as Alberich in " Siegfried," as well as in Mascagni's second opera, " I Rantzau," under the baton of the composer, and performed also the part of Hunding in " The Valkyrie," with Alvary.

The grand opera season of 1893 was not yet finished

when I was engaged to go on tour with the company
from Covent Garden, to which had been added most of
the members of the " Falstaff " cast from Milan.   During this tour of the British provinces, I was given my
chance of performing new rôles on which I had been assiduously working, in addition to my other duties.
Among them were Falstaff, Nevers in " Les Huguenots,"
Alfio in " Cavalleria Rusticana," and the Toreador in
" Carmen."   I gained a deal of experience on this tour,
the bright particular spot in which was the superb performance of Gluck's " Orfeo " by Julia Ravogli.   On its
conclusion I filled another engagement at Crystal Palace
at the Saturday orchestral concert under August Manns,
when Miss Emma Juch made her first appearance after
her brilliant operatic successes in Europe a few seasons
before.

In concerts I was a new quantity to the purveyors of
music, who declared that I almost invariably sang over
the heads of my audiences, selecting pieces which in their
opinion were " caviar to the general."   My concert repertory certainly included what I enjoyed singing: airs
by Handel, selections from Purcell, ballads by Loewe,
pieces by Schubert and Schumann, and advanced works by
contemporary Englishmen.   My reply, when somewhat
taken to task for the severity of my selections, was, " I
prefer breaking new ground to competition with every
other barytone in London in a repertory which is common property."   I believed then as now, that the artist
with courage to climb high upon the ladder gets into a
different atmosphere, and finds that people lift up their
heads and look after him, follow him as far as they can,
admire his progress, and attempt to breathe the rarer
atmosphere in which he lives.

DAVID BISPHAM
as Beckmesser, in Wagner's "Mastersingers."
From a Photograph by Dupont, New York

DAVID BISPHAM
as Schickaneder, in Mozart's "Impresario."
From a Photograph by Campbell, New York

The result was my immediate and frequent engagements thereafter at the Monday Popular Concerts at St. James's Hall with Lady Hallé (Madame Norman Neruda), Joachim, and the most notable musicians of the day.

By some power I have ever been led in the way of good; by the same power I believe myself to have been protected from evil. During the spring of 1893, I was approached by my friend, the late George Wilson, and asked to take part in Theodore Thomas's concerts at the World's Columbian Exposition in Chicago that year. Though the contract had been signed, the engagement was canceled by reason of Thomas's change of plans, and I remained in England to go upon the operatic tour I have mentioned. Had I left for America, I was to have met my mother and her brother at Lake Mohonk, and accompanied them to my uncle's country-place on the coast of Maine for a short visit before I went to Chicago; this was well understood, and the date fixed.

Picking up a London paper that day my eyes fell upon a head line telling of a railway disaster near Springfield, Massachusetts, resulting in many deaths. Although no names were mentioned, I felt a distinct pang at my heart and knew my mother had been one of the victims. On reaching my home I found a dispatch from my uncle, telling me of the instant death of my mother. I was inwardly aware that I had escaped a similar fate by reason of the change of plans that kept me in England. As soon as I had filled the engagements already made in London and elsewhere, I set sail for New York to attend to business connected with my mother's estate.

While there I had the opportunity of singing at one of Walter Damrosch's concerts at the newly erected Car-

negie Hall, when I assisted in the fiftieth anniversary
of the first production of Balfe's " The Bohemian Girl,"
by singing selections from that tuneful opera, one of my
numbers being " The Heart Bowed Down by Weight of
Woe," which upon a previous occasion I had unthink-
ingly rendered at a concert given at an asylum for pa-
tients suffering with melancholia with the alleged object
of cheering the inmates. The recollection of this came
over me as I sang the well-known air at Carnegie Hall,
and brought on a fit of hilarity which I had the utmost
difficulty in restraining, almost causing me to disgrace
myself by laughing aloud before the audience.

Many years afterward I undertook to give the musical
version by Henry Holden Huss of Shakespeare's Seven
Ages of Man at the Edwin Forrest Home for Aged
Actors, near Philadelphia. When I came to the Sixth
Age, with its mention of " the lean and slippered pantaloon . . . his youthful hose, well saved, a world too
wide for his shrunk shank; and his big manly voice, turning again toward childish treble, pipes and whistles," it
flashed upon me that I was performing before an audience
made up of octogenarians, whom I was only too aptly
describing to themselves. I was so embarrassed that I
fairly forgot the Seventh Age,—" last scene of all,"—
and would have stood there like a schoolboy who has lost
the thread of his declamation had not my good and trustworthy presence of mind come to my help. I tottered
to the footlights, spoke to the bewildered accompanist,
and said in an impromptu line which certainly is not
Shakespearean, " I am so old I can't recall what comes
next." To my surprise I was complimented on my " effective interpolation " by several of the eminent Shakespearean scholars who were present as guests, including

Doctor Furness and Professors Schelling and Jastrow. It is the only time I ever attempted any addition to Shakespeare, and I certainly never intend to make another.

As a result of " The Bohemian Girl," I was at once engaged with Madame Nordica to sing in " The Messiah " with the Oratorio Society of New York, the first of many occasions when the directors of this distinguished association did me the honor to ask me to appear before it. The pair of concerts at that time, in 1893, were so successful that an extra performance was given a few days later, and a good start made with the Oratorio Society. It is a matter of record in the annals of the society, that I have sung with it more frequently than any other living person.

I returned to London in time to fulfill my engagements with the Bach Choir as Amfortas in the first act of " Parsifal " under the direction of Professor Stanford, and thought then, as ever since when hearing " Parsifal," whether in Bayreuth or in New York, that Wagner's whole idea of effect in the stage setting and music pervading the Grail scene, must have been the result of his having heard in St. Peter's at Rome, Palestrina's greatest High Mass, than which nothing in musical literature is more impressive.

It was my good fortune when studying in Italy to receive through my friend Esmé Howard, at the time one of the secretaries of the British Embassy at Rome, a ticket which admitted me to St. Peter's on January 1, 1888, when Pope Leo XIII was allowed by the Italian Government to celebrate mass for the first time in the cathedral. The ceremony was conducted before a concourse of people so vast that it filled the enormous spaces of St. Peter's to their utmost capacity. The

Pope celebrated mass under the baldachino beneath the dome, while Palestrina's music was sung by the finest choristers of Rome, who for the occasion had been gathered in from the various churches to augment the choir of the Sistine Chapel. The day was cold and foggy and enormous icicles were hanging from every fountain in Rome. I was chilled to the bone, even in St. Peter's, into which the fog had penetrated — the mistiness there being augmented by the fumes from the censers swung by the acolytes. The moment for the elevation of the Host had come. The music arose in ecstatic strains, silver trumpets pealed from the dome, and from the utmost heights sounded the exquisite voices of a boy choir. The aged Pontiff raised the sacred Chalice, and at that moment the sun burst through the pall of cloud, sending a shaft of light through the windows of the south transept upon the white figure of Leo XIII, at the great moment, musically and dramatically, of the one supreme religious ceremony of our time. The throng fell upon its knees in adoration and in awe; it was as if God had touched with His finger His earthly representative and blessed him with the light of His countenance; indeed it was so accepted by the devout throughout the Roman Catholic world.

It is curious to note how in my life events have crowded one upon another; even though they matter little to anyone but myself, to me they are remarkable enough. I find that one of my early engagements was in Edinburgh with the Scottish Orchestra, which had come into being and which was well on its way to success under the directing hand of Georg Henschel; he who, when conductor of the Boston Symphony Orchestra, had advised me against going before the public as a professional singer. I was sufficiently successful at this concert, however, to have the honor of being engaged on many subsequent occasions by the man I so admired.

Mrs. Henschel used to tell with glee how, at their place in the Highlands, her husband, preparing during the summer for his forthcoming series of symphony concerts, would take his scores out to the lawn, where under a tree he spent hours in conducting an imaginary orchestra; even correcting imaginary mistakes, by tapping with his baton upon the stand and pointing to some phantom instrumentalist, saying, " F natural, not F sharp, Mr. Blank. Now we will go on, gentlemen, if you please."

Henschel's influence was enormous throughout Great Britain. As a conductor he was in the first rank; as a composer he stood high; he was admirable indeed as an exponent of bass parts in oratorio; but where to my mind he shone with the greatest brilliancy was in the series of concerts with his charming wife, which lasted through many years, and which were as well known in America as in England. Henschel was a master at the piano, and nothing short of a genius in the interpretation of classic songs, but he shared with his contemporaries, Max Heinrich and Doctor Ludwig Wüllner, the tonal peculiarities which seem almost invariably and inevitably to be impressed upon the Teutonic throat.

In this connection I am reminded of the visit which Madame Wagner made to Covent Garden in the early 'nineties, when she heard us in " Lohengrin." By " us " I mean Jean and Edouard de Reszke, Madame Schumann-Heink, Madame Nordica, and myself — two Poles, one German, and two Americans, all of whom had learned to sing in the best Italian manner. We were much pleased when Madame Wagner said of us on the stage after the performance, that for the first time in her life she had that evening heard the music of her husband rendered " from a melodious standpoint."

CHAPTER XVI

FESTIVAL AND UNIVERSITY

Let knowledge grow from more to more,
But more of reverence in us dwell;
That mind and soul, according well,
May make one music as before.
— *Tennyson.*

WITH me in 1894 all was going well. At the opening
of the year I was offered many engagements of increas-
ing interest. I appeared in London with Joachim and
his quartette, with the Spanish violinist Señor Arbos, and
with Leonard Borwick, one of England's finest pianists.
I traveled far and wide in the British Isles to sing in
oratorio and concert for my kind and increasingly appreciative clientele. I may thank God that the health
bequeathed me by my ancestors, the training received
from my mother, and my own artistic enthusiasm kept me
then, as they have ever kept me, fully and eagerly occupied, glad of my opportunities and grateful for the
approbation and trust that the public has bestowed upon
me. Engagements followed upon engagements: Bach's
" Passion Music " at Queen's Hall, with Joachim as the
solo violinist and Dolmetsch accompanying on the old-
time harpsichord; Gounod's " Redemption " at Crystal
Palace; and Mackenzie's fine oratorio " Bethlehem " at
the Royal Albert Hall.

Among women much in the public eye in those times
was Liza Lehmann, the admirable song writer and concert soprano, and a very beautiful contralto with an

equally beautiful voice — the lady shall be nameless — who failed after a few important engagements because of her poor musicianship. Loveliness may attract, a voice may charm, exquisite manners may captivate, influence may launch an individual; but musicianship is the only thing that can keep a singer going in a world of musicians.

How often have I not been ashamed of vocalists who, unable to render their parts correctly even in oratorio, where they may carry the music in their hands, are quietly laughed at by the clever instrumentalists behind them in the orchestra, who play for union wages, while the singers themselves are receiving princely fees and royal homage!

Among my colleagues at this time was an American tenor, now gone, whose stage name was Orlando Harley. I mention him to show what determination will do for an artist who sets out to win. This young man was the son of a banker in the Middle West, and had been educated at the United States Naval Academy at Annapolis, from which he was suspended for some slight breach of discipline. Considering himself unjustly used, he declined either to return to Annapolis or to accept a position in his father's bank, declaring that he intended to become a singer — a career which did not meet with the approbation of his parents.

He left home one night provided with such money as he could get together, and went to New York, where he lived at the Fifth Avenue Hotel for a few days, while he sought in vain for engagements at the Metropolitan Opera, in comic opera, upon the stage in Broadway shows, in church choirs, and in concerts. Finding his funds decreasing, he went to a second-rate hotel, then to a lodging house, and finally found himself with credit gone, all his clothes in pawn except the suit upon his back, and only five cents in his pocket. With this last nickel he bought himself a bag of biscuits, which he washed down with water from the fountain in Madison Square. Biscuits gone, he had nothing to eat for twenty-four hours and woke on a bench by the fountain in the morning, shivering, his sole protection against the cold a newspaper drawn over his knees after it had blown in his direction. Gazing blankly at it, his eyes fell upon an advertisement for a porter wanted in a business house down town; and, taking this as a good omen, he proceeded to the address indicated. Keeping his hands behind him he was interviewed by a kindly employer, who, shrewdly judging the young man to be a gentleman in trouble, invited him to tell his story and his name. Refusing to give his real name until he had made a name for himself, the young tenor told his tale and announced his intention to become known yet, despite his recent hard luck. He was taken into the office, his employer being also a musical enthusiast, received vocal lessons in part payment for his services, and was given a chance to show what he could do, with the result that before long he found himself making his way pleasantly in Europe, and on the threshold of a distinguished career, which was unfortunately cut short by death.

I was selected to be among the principals in all three of the Bach Festival concerts of 1895, a privilege that I highly appreciated, for it showed me the trust reposed in me by Stanford and his associates and led me straight into such oratorio work throughout the United Kingdom as otherwise would not have come to me. Opportunity is important, but still more important is the ability to embrace it.

It was about that time that I sang, too, under the baton of Frederic Cowen, who soon after became conductor of the Philharmonic Society. Many a time have I had the honor of working with that brilliant conductor and composer, who for a period after the death of Hallé conducted his orchestra till Richter was secured. I also sang in a series of performances in the Wagnerian concerts under Felix Mottl at Queen's Hall, London.

This series was also conducted — with his left hand — by Siegfried Wagner who, had it not been for the interest of his mother at Bayreuth, might never have been permitted to direct the music dramas there. Although he knew every note by heart and led without the score, and though the orchestra had the work so well in hand that it was nearly impossible for a mistake to be made, still all looked with distrust upon Siegfried's efforts as a conductor. He had composed an opera, which had been performed; but all his best friends thought he should have kept to his original profession of architecture. It was only natural, however, that he should be of assistance at Bayreuth, where his face and figure as he grew older were so strikingly like those of his distinguished father as to be positively uncanny as he went to and fro busying himself with the productions, or mingling with the notable society that thronged the little town for so many summers.

By this time, as it may be supposed, I was gathering together quite a repertory. I had been engaged to sing at Oxford for the University Musical Club, where I gave songs by Schubert, Schumann, Brahms and Wagner, with old Italian and modern English selections, and I was invited to appear later at one of the first of a long series of

Sunday night concerts, given in the great hall of Baliol College.

Thus I was enabled as I went along to live up to my mother's injunction to do the best that was in me in upholding the dignity of my art; but I never forgot that as " one star differeth from another star in glory " so does one audience differ from another in intelligent appreciation of music. It was possible to give on Sunday night at Oxford University what would have been quite out of place on Saturday afternoon at a Ballad Concert in St. James's Hall, where the audience would neither have expected nor enjoyed the music fitting for the classic precincts of one of the world's most distinguished seats of learning.

I had already begun giving concerts of my own in London. When engaged by others one defers to the opinion of one's employers; —" He who pays the piper calls the tune," and one must play in accordance with the wishes of one's patrons. It is different when one branches out for oneself in any art. Therefore, as I had long been partial to Schumann's music, I determined to give a concert devoted entirely to his works. I was assisted by Fanny Davies, pianist; the Americans, Mrs. Henschel, soprano, and Marguerite Hall, alto; with my master William Shakespeare as the tenor. Thus began on June 8, a series of recitals which have lasted until the present day, twenty-five years. During this time I have given about 800 concerts and recitals of my own.

The most important work of that season was that which occupied me at the Royal Opera, when it fell to my lot to sing Vulcan in Gounod's " Philemon and Baucis," besides other things which I had done before; and I played both at Drury Lane and Covent Garden, as Ottokar in " Der Freischütz," Pizarro in " Fidelio," and Wolfram in " Tannhäuser "— all for the first time. These made a total of fifteen appearances, which in addition to the concert work of which I have spoken, and the preparation for " Falstaff," soon to be performed on tour, gave me indeed busy days and nights.

Looking back upon this and many similar years, I wonder how I ever got through them.   Even so have I wondered, when climbing in the Alps and looking back from the distance of miles at the scene of some perilous descent, how I could ever have negotiated those precipices and come out alive!

Among the artists who performed the Wagnerian operas, besides Max Alvary and others of whom I have already spoken, was the brilliant soprano Katharina Klafsky, then in the prime of her art both as a singer and as an actress.   Histrionically she was the equal of Alvary, which is saying a great deal, for he had as fine a dramatic talent as I have ever met in a vocalist.

It was only a few years later that the voice of Madame Klafsky was hushed in death.   So greatly beloved was she in Hamburg, where she had sung for many years, that her dead body was borne through the streets on an open bier, Elizabeth-like, and followed by thousands whose streaming eyes bade a last farewell as they gazed upon the waxen features of the beautiful face they had loved and admired so often on the stage as it passed for ever from their sight.

Max Alvary, too, has gone, after a meteoric career cut all too short.   He was the son of the painter Andreas Achenbach, and his father and sisters, who had social aspirations, felt the singer had disgraced the family name by singing in opera, heedless of the fact that he had made a great name for himself, while his manly beauty gave his audiences many a picture better worth the seeing than any painting of them all.

In 1894 we were still giving " I Maestri Cantori " in Italian at Covent Garden. That year, the beautiful Madame Emma Eames, one of the prides of American vocal art, made her début as Eva to the Walther of Jean de Reszke. Plançon was Pogner and Ancona was Hans Sachs, a part as difficult for him to study as it was for me to have committed the part of Beckmesser to memory.

As I drove from my house in Kensington Gore to Covent Garden in a hansom cab I frequently had the score in my lap studying it along the crowded thoroughfares. On one occasion I remember looking up and catching the eye of Villiers Stanford, who greeted me from the sidewalk as I passed. Meeting him that evening at a private party, he hailed me with a laugh, saying: " As you drove along there to-day you looked exactly like Beckmesser sitting in his box." I said: " How remarkable! I was studying the part of Beckmesser at the time."

So it is; I seem to realize the part I am learning to the extent of becoming almost the living embodiment of whatever fictitious or historical character I am called upon to represent. I have been so carried away by the spirit of my own impersonations that I have lost myself completely and for hours together have not had a thought of my own, the actualities of the evening being the dream, the artistic dream the actuality. This completeness of identification is not arrived at with ease or without long study, or even then by any effort of will. It begins with

my preliminary view of the part I am to assume and proceeds step by step with my understanding of it from every
bearing upon which I can adjust my vision.

To me " All the world's a stage, and all the men and
women merely players." I carry this from the human
beings who are on the scene with me, every one as real
in his assumption of a character as mine is to me, to the
very stage interior in which the scene is enacted, which
becomes as much a reality as any hall in any building
made of perdurable stone.   It is a matter of amazement
to me that the principal characters of drama, and of fic-
tion, are far more real than almost any out of the millions
on millions of human beings who have lived and gone,
leaving no memory behind.   This feeling is more general
than may be at first believed, but many a part acted
by us players upon the stage is more vividly remembered
by our auditors than the actual persons they meet in
private life.

CHAPTER XVII

THE FAT KNIGHT

Falstaff sweats to death,
And lards the lean earth as he walks along.
— *Shakespeare.*

IN a month the company from Covent Garden went on tour.   Consulting my records I find that I was put down for Wolfram in Italian, in which language I had first studied the opera, though for the performances with Alvary I had to work it over again in the original German; for Nevers in " Les Huguenots," for the Toreador in " Carmen "; for Vulcan in " Philemon and Baucis " in French; for Tonio in " I Pagliacci," and for Alfio in " Cavalleria Rusticana."   I was also expected to do both Mephistopheles and Valentine in " Faust " and had to be ready to sing both Hans Sachs and Beckmesser in Italian in " Die Meistersinger."   That was my repertory, and I prepared myself to perform any or all of these characters as called upon.

The company being large, however, and the susceptible feelings of its foreign members having to be taken into consideration, I was asked to relinquish the part of Sachs, and Falstaff was given me instead.   Much as I have longed to perform Hans Sachs, I have never been permitted to do so in opera; and upon this tour, even the part of Beckmesser was given to Pini Corsi, than whom there never was a finer buffo singer.   As Ford in " Falstaff " he and I, with Julia Ravogli as Dame Quickly, had

great fun, and eagerly looked forward to our performances.

Our tour opened at Blackpool in Lancashire, with which
county my family name had been associated for so many
centuries, and the week we played at the Opera House
Beerbohm Tree was also acting in Blackpool.   I had been
a great admirer of his amazing performance of Falstaff
on the stage of the Haymarket Theatre, London, of
which he was for years the manager, and had previously
consulted him as to my costume and make-up.   The interest he took in my performance was such that he came
to my dressing room and gave me valuable hints, even
painting my face with his own master hand, laying on
the high lights and counseling me from the wealth of
his own experience in this character how to make the
audience feel that I was the great, gray, gross, greasy
glutton I should appear to be.   Tree went off to his
own theatre while I in nervous agony proceeded with my
own difficult part.

In this character, not more than a few square inches
of my actual self were visible to the audience; all they
saw was what surrounded the poor little entity of me
inside.   On my legs were enormous pads made of sheep's
wool, sewed inside of stockinette and so shaped as to
resemble, when drawn on, what, of course, they should
resemble, the legs of a fat man.   In the first act I wore
great boots that came above my knees; these, too, looked
fat.   About my body I had a sort of mattress into the
padded arms of which I thrust my own arms while my
dresser tied the whole contrivance up the back with many
strings.   Over this was a great leather jerkin, and over
that again a cape.   But all this was easy to put on and
take off; the difficult and time-consuming element in the

assumption of the fat knight's character was the make-up of the face and head.

The beard had been especially constructed so that what seemed to be a pink skin, a triple chin, and a pair of fat jowls showed through a rather thin blond beard beginning to gray. This was held in place by a stout elastic band over my head, but, for safety's sake, it was also gummed to my skin. Below the chin a long flap of skin-like material hung down upon my breast and was tied under my arms behind. From the right side and from the left a fat neck seemed to descend into my clothing, and when the wig was put on a flap at the back resembling the many folds of a fat man's neck ran under my costume down my back and was tied around in front of me by tapes. The nose, pimpled, purple, and groggy, I fashioned out of a sort of putty which comes for the purpose and is supposed to stick to the flesh.

When at last I was fully made up and costumed, and was getting along well into the middle of the opera, I found myself in such a bath of perspiration, descending like the precious ointment even unto Aaron's beard, that my heavy clothing was soaking wet, and my head and face were reeking with sweat that ran down inside of my whiskers. Unfortunately it also ran down my forehead and under the false nose, which was seen by the audience to loosen and elongate. At last, amid the shrieks of the spectators, the nose quietly slid from my face, down my " fair round belly," and dropped upon the stage under my feet. I could not see it over my huge front and, with my next step, accidentally trod upon the slippery mass and was thrown flat upon the floor. The audience, already in a state of merriment over the comedy, went almost hysterical with laughter, but I had to go bravely on with my

part after being picked up, and glad enough was I that
my disguise was thick enough to conceal my mortification.

Tree had invited me to supper with him after the performance, and I recounted my uncomfortable experience
to him and Haddon Chambers, whose play he was acting.
We all had another good laugh when Tree told us of
his own experience the first time he played Falstaff, when
the string which tied his trunks on broke and the trousers slipped down around his heels until he could not move
his feet at all, but had to hop off the stage to have his
costume readjusted, while his audience enjoyed his mishap
as heartily as mine had reveled in my misfortune.

Such things as these help to carry us merrily through
the arduous duties of our profession, where every night
we live a life within a life. True indeed it is as Shakespeare says, " One man in his time plays many parts ";
yet not all the plays ever devised can match the experiences of actual life.

I played Falstaff more than twenty times that season
and lost as many pounds in weight by the experience, losing also my temper nightly while getting into that miserable, uncomfortable costume; but my dresser knew how to
take me, and a good tip would salve his wounded feelings
as quickly as cocoa butter would obliterate my own disguise and bring me to myself once more.

Almost as many stories are told of Beerbohm Tree
as used to be circulated about Sir Henry Irving. Both
these extraordinary actors are said to have taken all such
tales as tributes to their popularity and with the best of
grace, even to the enjoyment of seeing their peculiarities
imitated by others. But Tree never quite relished the
caustic wit of W. S. Gilbert, whom I heard make his famous commentary on Tree's performance of Hamlet. A

DAVID BISPHAM
as The Vicar, in Lehmann's "Vicar of Wakefield."
From a Photograph by Bacon & Sons, Newcastle-on-Tyne.

DAVID BISPHAM
as Falstaff, in Verdi's "Falstaff."
From a Photograph by Crookes, Edinborough

number of the actor-manager's friends came on the stage
at the Haymarket Theatre after his first appearance in
that difficult rôle and Tree asked Gilbert frankly how he
liked his impersonation of the melancholy Dane. Gilbert with a look of ingenuous innocence replied: "My
dear fellow, I never saw anything so funny in my life,
and yet it was not in the least vulgar."

In further conversation Gilbert contributed his bit
to the solution of the Shakespearean enigma by saying:
"Hamlet, you know, was a man idiotically sane, with
lucid intervals of lunacy."

During this tour I was interested in making a translation of "Falstaff" which should if possible better that
of Beatty Kingston, parts of which he had acknowledged
to me not to be to his satisfaction. Knowing my Shakespeare well I made memoranda throughout the vocal score
for lines which, in the event of my ever performing it in
English, could be used by myself at least, adapting from
other plays of Shakespeare such actual phrases as fitted
Verdi's notes. It has unfortunately never fallen to my
lot to sing the opera in English, but the version follows
which I have used on countless occasions in my concerts
when rendering the delightful song in which the fat
Knight endeavors to commend his vast bulk to his lady-
love by telling her how thin and slender he used to be
when he was young; thus —

> When I was page in the old Duke's house,
> Comely of figure and quick as a mouse,
>   I was a vision supple and tender,
>   Nimble and slender — so slender!
> That was a gay and a merry time, forsooth;
> The May-day and heyday of my happy youth;
>   I was able to ogle, to coax, and to wheedle,

Slim enough to slip through the eye of a needle,
When I was page so comely and tender,
Nimble and slender!
I was a vision supple and tender,
Nimble and slender — so slender!

When I was page to the old Duke's Grace,
Matrons and maids of illustrious race
Rewarded my service and homage with many
And many a loving embrace.
Then was I courted, favored by the fair,
Heart-whole and happy, knowing not a care;
Merely to live was ineffable pleasure,
Endless enjoyment and bliss without measure.
When I was page so comely and tender, *etc.*

Our tour took us to the principal cities of England, Scotland, and Ireland. It was while in the capital where "old Scotia's grandeur springs" that an Italian soprano and I visited the ancient cathedral of St. Giles. Under a bleak and lowering sky in a Scotch mist we came upon the gray and forbidding-looking edifice, and the child of the sunny south asked me, with a real desire to be informed on so grave a subject, "Do they have the same God here that we do in Italy?"

Our journey over, I resumed my concerts, singing that autumn selection from "The Mastersingers" and "The Valkyrie" with the best of all Wagnerian interpreters, Hans Richter, with whom it was my privilege to work many a time afterward, deriving the greatest benefit from association with him. Taking it all in all, and looking back upon a long line of orchestral conductors, I consider him to be the chiefest of them all. It is much to be regretted that he never came to America, for Richter said he would come if Joachim came; and Joachim said he would attempt the journey if Richter did, but as a matter of fact neither of them wanted to cross the ocean, even to visit the New World.

Deeply impressed as are all these experiences upon my memory, nothing can ever obliterate from it Tristan's death scene, when for the first time I played Kurwenal with Max Alvary. I seemed not only to be living the character, but to be dying it no less. After my fashion of merging myself in my part I seemed then, as always since, actually to be the old servitor dying by the side of his friend for whom he had fought, like some faithful dog kissing the hand of his master as the last act of a devoted life.

During the season of 1894 I sang for the first time in Berlioz's " Damnation of Faust " as Mephistopheles, a part in which on many subsequent occasions I reveled, and was also concerned with Arnold Dolmetsch, the expert in old instruments, in the revival of the comedy by Bach called " The Peasant's (Bauern) Cantata," which was given at Staple Inn in the very room where it had been performed nearly a century and a half before and with instruments of the kind actually then in use.

Saint-Saëns' beautiful opera, " Samson and Delilah," was another work new to me which I performed with Santley soon after. It is a great favorite upon the English concert platform, offering fine opportunities for both principals and chorus, yet it may not be heard as an opera by reason of the existence of a law forbidding the stage presentation of any scriptural episodes. Still within my recollection Massenet's " Hérodiade " has been performed at Covent Garden, but under another title and with the familiar biblical names duly changed. So goes on the merry game of " beating the devil about the bush."

CHAPTER XVIII

ARTS AND LETTERS

The very knowledge of many arts, however we may follow another, helps to equip us for our own.— Tacitus.

I LIVED for ten years at No. 19, Kensington Gore, close by the Royal Albert Hall and opposite Kensington Palace Gardens. In that little house I entertained many a celebrity of the day, with many evidences of the friendship of persons in the musical, artistic, and literary worlds. The great painters, Watts, Millais, Leighton, Poynter, Alma-Tadema, Dicksee, Burne-Jones, were my friends, with the Americans, Whistler and John S. Sargent.

Sargent was not only fond of music, but played the piano remarkably well, and I often sang to his admirable accompaniments. One Sunday he and I were bicycling to a luncheon party at the house of Madame Liza Lehmann, a few miles out of town, when it came on to rain, leaving the roads so slippery that our wheels skidded and threw both the painter and me into the mud and water at the roadside. We picked ourselves out in a dreadful mess, arriving at our destination in such a state of unsightliness that we had to be supplied with fresh clothing. Madame Lehmann's husband, Herbert Bedford, was of middle height and slender, Sargent was tall and stout, I was short and thick; and the effects of the borrowed clothing were ridiculous. Sargent put his host's trousers on wrong side before and concealed the open deficiency with a frock coat, while I had to turn up both

146

coat sleeves and trousers. We arrived in the dining-
room an hour late, such scarecrows in appearance that
the uproarious merriment greeting us fairly stopped the
show.

I was visiting cousins of Mendelssohn, the Alfred
Beneckes, who lived at Dorking, neighbors to George
Meredith, poet and novelist, in whose honor a dinner
party was given. Grant Allen, also a neighbor, was
among the guests, and proved to be the first man I had
ever known who used the typewriter in composing his numerous books, including his biography of Herbert Spencer.
This noted philosopher, like Allen himself, was keenly
sensitive to the beauty of the speaking voice, yet neither
could tell one note of music from another or had any appreciation of the art. This I learned while we were waiting for our guest of honor, wondering why he should be
so late.

After what seemed an interminable time George Meredith came in, or rather stumbled in, after walking across
the half mile of meadowland between the two houses.
He apologized for his tardiness, speaking very fast and
very loud, and holding himself steady by means of a chair,
a table, the mantelpiece, or whatever he chanced to be
near. With all his reputation for abstemiousness I
feared the eminent author was under the influence of
liquor, especially when he failed to regain either poise
or manner until we were seated at the dinner table. The
poor man had, it proved, suffered a slight stroke of pa-
ralysis not long before, which he was doing his best to
conceal from his friends, though knowing that it would
increase upon him and might end his life at any moment.

I saw Meredith many times after that and was often
with him in the little workroom he had built on Box Hill

near his house.   After he became too ill to go even so
far from home, I used to sit in his little cottage and listen
to his most interesting talk.   He was keenly sympathetic
and drew me out about my aspirations in my work and
the manner in which I came to be a singer.   He expressed
his open regret to me about his own failure to make his
delicate and delightful work more widely known, for it
was only toward the end of his life that he began to
reap the rewards of fame in the increased circulation of
his novels and poems.   Then it was that the people began to make pilgrimages from far and near, from Europe
and America, to the simple abode of this great literary
artist, and yet he said to me:

"How fortunate you are, my dear fellow, to find
yourself appreciated while you are still in the prime of
manhood, and can enjoy it.   Here I am hanging on to
my chair, and only in my declining years am I known to
exist by the world at large."

Not long after this brave old soul joined the company of his fellow immortals.   Fortunate indeed are we
as heirs of the fruits of such genius!

It was Meredith who told me of the first marriage
of the painter, Frederick G. Watts, and its unhappy ter-
mination.   We had been speaking of a recent visit to his
friend's studio, and he began, "That reminds me" and
went on with the curious story.   Years before, when
Watts was painting the portrait of the exquisite girl who
was to become so widely known to fame as Ellen Terry,
he was disappointed in one of the sittings.   Her elder
sister, who had been her constant companion, came to
him alone to say that Ellen would not return.   Expressing his surprise and his fear lest he had given offense,
he was told that the girl had fallen in love with him,

though knowing he was old enough to be her father, and would not see him again, understanding the hopelessness of her passion.

The famous painter, possibly flattered at having engaged the regard of a woman so young and so charming, considered it his duty, perhaps, as well as his privilege, to offer her his hand and heart. This he did in all chivalry through the sister. Departing with the tender message, she returned presently with the radiant Ellen, who threw herself into the arms of him who soon became her husband. Meredith went on to tell me of a dinner party given in the studio after the wedding, the guests being the most eminent men of the day in art and letters. The fair young hostess was not expected to be present after she had greeted her husband's friends in the drawing-room. But she went quietly to her own apartment, arrayed herself in the costume of Ariel she had provided, let herself through the skylight into the studio with a rope ladder, and landed without warning in the center of the dinner table, where she posed and danced before the astonished assemblage.

" Imagine," said Meredith, " the surprise of the guests, and imagine the chagrin of poor Watts, who chid his young wife and bade her leave the room, mortified and cut to the heart. She not only left the room, but she left her husband's house that night and never went back to him. And both of them, after the divorce, married again and married happily."

At the country house of Lady Palmer, where I was a frequent guest, I met the ill-omened genius, Oscar Wilde, still at the height of his fame and a prime favorite in London society. Few men have been more brilliant in conversation, as he knew very well, for he knew his own

value in the world of letters and of the theatre.   He had
given up his earlier eccentricities after his marriage, settled himself in Tite Street, Chelsea, and was devoting
himself to the poems and plays upon which his better
reputation will rest.   I have always thought it a symptom
of his oncoming madness that he should have made such
a confession as that contained in his brilliant novel, " The
Portrait of Dorian Gray " ; apropos of which his unsus-
pecting wife once complained to a friend of mine, " Since
Oscar wrote ' Dorian Gray ' no one will speak to us."
With his downfall came the instant withdrawal of his
sparkling comedies from the stage of the St. James's Theatre, and for years the disgrace he had inflicted upon
English society was so deeply felt that his name was never
mentioned.

George Alexander was wise to have produced such
plays, as he was wise in giving his stage to the delightful work of Arthur Pinero, and few were the failures
laid up against him and his management, his shrewd and
charming little wife proving herself the most competent
of advisers.   But they made one serious mistake, which
could hardly have been guarded against, in bringing out
the dramatization of Henry James's novel, " The American," the premier of which I attended.   I had admired
the book from the time of its publication and went to the
theatre with eager anticipation thinking the story would
attract London society.   I thought the play admirably constructed and of marked literary interest.   It was admirably acted, too, with the exception of the protagonist, assumed by Alexander himself, who was quite un-American.

I had known Henry James for years in London, where
his works were greatly admired by persons of discern-
ment, though little more calculated than Meredith's to

gain the plaudits of the populace, and he was not known at all as a writer of plays. The first night the house was divided against itself, the connoisseurs in the stalls enjoying it as frankly as the pit and gallery disliked it. At the fall of the curtain rapturous applause burst out from one, and an unmerciful hissing and booing from the other. Mr. Alexander thought to quiet the disturbance by bringing on the author, for whom the stalls were shouting, but the rest of the house showed its disapproval so vehemently that Mr. James retired in confusion, to be called on again by the better element and booed off once more by the other persons in the house. The play was withdrawn forthwith, and the great novelist sought no more for dramatic laurels.

George Moore frequented my house for the sake of the musical company to be found there, and the novel he produced, hardly, I venture to hope, as the result of his visits, was the shocking " Evelyn Innes." In those days he had fair straight hair, his eyes were pale blue, and his complexion light in hue. He always looked to me like a living water color. One may note, in studying Walter Sickert's portrait of him, the feeling that one is looking right through his head into a sky behind. But one forgot his personal appearance when under the charm of his vivid conversation.

Morton Fullerton, who took Blowitz's place on the *London Times,* told me a humorous story of Lord Tennyson which deserves recording. He was walking with the Poet Laureate near his place in the Isle of Wight, when they saw at a distance what appeared to be two wandering tourists. The famous man showed and spoke with every sign of perturbation, palpably annoyed by the approach of mere curiosity seekers. The intruders

passed without the least recognition of the presence of
genius, when the poet broke out in even stronger accents
of annoyance, " Why, they didn't even look at me! "

I have visited the quaint and ancient house of Coventry
Patmore at Lymington, some little way south of Southampton, a very old brick structure furnished with a beautiful and striking simplicity in perfect keeping with the
dress and characters of its inmates. The Angel of the
House, to whom the poet addressed so many of his verses,
had gone some time before, leaving behind her two daughters whose apparel in both cut and texture reminded me
always of the clothes of my own Quaker people —
more so than of any other persons I have ever met,
though the Patmores were devout Roman Catholics. It
is interesting to speculate upon the tenuous laurels of one
so devoted to work of the sincerest and most artistic
character, whose present fame seems so largely to rest
on the beautiful and touching lines of " The Toys," a
single poem out of several volumes.

Sir Richard Burton is a man I am proud to have numbered among my acquaintances, and a man of more striking appearance and assured greatness I have never seen.
He was a large man, and looked like nothing so much as
an old lion — short gray hair and a bronzed skin seamed
with scars, and a manner that bespoke the independence
that so marked his striking career. His knowledge of
Arabic and his miraculous escape from the perils of his
self-imposed pilgrimage to Mecca with all the qualities
of heart and mind that this bespoke, entitled him to almost any gift at the hands of Government, but his im-
patience of control made it impossible for him to work
with others. His beautiful and almost too pious wife

was a fit mate for him in personality, making them a wonderful couple merely to sit and watch.

One of the delectable old English country houses where
I was often welcomed was that of Sir Lawrence Jones,
where I shall never forget the little play, quite in the
manner of the Pyramus and Thisbe episode in " A Midsummer Night's Dream," which was given one evening
by the peasants of the neighborhood for the edification
of the quality. It was redolent with the same unconscious
humor which Shakespeare made immortal, and provided
us with laughter and delicious phrases from an older
time, which lasted many a day. Sir Lawrence inherited
a trunkful of documents and old letters from his grandparents' time, through which he went one day with the
intention of proving the general worthlessness of them
all before condemning them to destruction. Among
much that had lost all value he discovered an envelope
superscribed in his grandmother's handwriting with a
note that stated the lock of hair it contained to be that
of the great Napoleon, cut from his head just after his
death by General Montholon, who was one of the former
emperor's suite at St. Helena, and given by him to Sir
Lawrence's grandfather. He was generous enough to
share this with me, and I have it still, with the authenti-
cation, " Cut from Napoleon's head immediately after
his death," and signed with my friend's name.

My early friendship with that shy and retiring woman
of many gifts, Mrs. Frances Hodgson Burnett, has been
mentioned, and it was to her that I sent that unfortunate child of genius, the sculptor John Donoghue, who
made an admirable portrait bust of her little son Lionel
after his untimely death. Donoghue was discovered by

Oscar Wilde in Chicago, where he was working on tomb-stones and memorials of that nature. His ability was so marked that one of the rich men of that city sent him to Rome, and there as the climax of his artistic career he modeled not only his beautiful " Sophocles," but a heroic figure called " The Spirit," a conception so huge that nothing less than the dome of the ancient Baths of Dio-cletian would suffice for its production. I have a photo-graph of it, showing the sculptor not reaching to the knee of the seated figure.

It was intended to exhibit it at the Columbian Exposi-tion in 1893, and the gigantic plaster mass was cut into sections and shipped to New York from Rome for that purpose. But the size of these fragments was so great that they could not be transported by railway to their destination. The steamship company by which they had been sent demanded their removal and I was noti-fied to that effect as the friend of Donoghue. I went to the Commissioner of Parks in New York, and offered him the statue, which he would have placed overlooking one of the lagoons — provided I defrayed the expense. This was greater than I could afford, and this mas-terpiece was broken into small bits and scattered over the surface of empty lots near the docks. Donoghue's disappointments proved too much for him after he re-turned to America, and he died by his own act.

It was with John Sargent again that I saw the " Aga-memnon " given at Radleigh College, Oxford, and once more we were doomed to a thorough drenching from the rain. But he escaped another downpour when the same play was given in the Harvard Stadium, escaping also one of the most laughable spectacles that great tragedies sometimes lend themselves to in the most unexpected manner. Part of the orchestra was delayed, and the performance began without that knowledge having been conveyed to the stage management. The play was prematurely opened by the appearance of the Herald on the battlements when, word being given him, he did not deliver his lines, but sat down on the parapet and dangled long legs over them in spite of the rain. Presently the belated instrumentalists arrived, running to escape being soaked, and ducking down to their quarters under the altar like frightened rabbits. This altar had practicable steps on one side only, and when George Riddle appeared as Tiresias followed by his attendants, as he stalked serenely in front the bearer of the libation tripped and spilled it all over the platform, and the bearer of the sacred flame stepped on the wrong side, with the result that the frightened violinists below were abruptly stopped by another pair of long legs falling through the approach to the altar, while the sacred fire never was lighted.

I was present at a gathering in the old Press Club in Chicago during the closing days of Sir Henry Irving's last engagement in that city. The great tragedian was suffering then from what eventually brought about his death. When he was called upon to respond to the encomiums which had just been pronounced upon his work, he rose and stood silent before that gathering of the representatives of all the newspapers there vainly trying through the space of minutes to gather his thoughts. I cannot forget the anxious face of his son Laurence, or the suspense that hung like a threat above the assemblage. But men of the stage long since learned self-command, and he spoke at last, slowly and impressively, gathering strength as he proceeded, until he closed with a ring of himself in his best days.

One of the compensations for the arduous life that must be led by one who seeks a career as a public performer, whether actor or singer, may be found in the records of this chapter, which recount only a few of the interesting events that have befallen me outside the strict limits of my profession, and but few of the host of men and women of note whom I have met and known in Europe and America. It is hardly too much to say that there are few bearers of distinguished names in the world which takes beauty, in sound, in form, in color, or in word, for its daily worship, whom I have not numbered among my friends in my own day and generation.

CHAPTER XIX

PHANTOMS OF HARMONY

Was it a vision, or a waking dream?
Fled is that music: — Do I wake or sleep?

EMIL SAUER, the pianist, was among my valued friends in London at this stage of my progress, and it is to him that I owe later one of the charming experiences of my life. He played his own beautiful piano concerto with the Philharmonic Orchestra in New York, and its performance gave me a vision of pure music, much as I am able to visualize the characters I assume on the stage. I was in a box at Carnegie Hall, and as Sauer played his delightful strains, I was wholly detached from my surroundings. I became aware that it was a summer morning, with the weather fine but hot. Toward noon the heat grew oppressive, and the engaging landscape spread before me was of no importance in comparison with the need for the refreshing shade of a great tree. A storm was brewing, and finally broke; and after it came a superb sunset. A splendid cool and purple night followed; the dawn approached, and the sun arose in a blaze of glory. This in brief was the distinct story of a poet's long day; no words can describe it, music only could voice the composer's vision.

Seeking out Sauer after the concert, I was delighted to learn that, though his concerto had not been programed in any such way, these were actually the thoughts and experiences which he had in mind while writing this noble piece, which is far too little known and should be sought out by pianists and added to their repertories.

The singer of songs has the advantage of the words, which have been the source of inspiration for the music. But an instrumental writer appeals directly through music alone to the emotions of his audience. In most cases the audience enjoys what is written without comprehending what the composer has intended. The voices of his instruments are the only ones at his command, and in a symphony words are out of place. The world must gather from songs without words such comfort as it may.

I have always felt that for songs of a certain character some accompaniment should be devised midway between that of the piano and that of a full orchestra. A number of pieces have been written for me in the endeavor to illustrate more richly than is possible with the sound of the piano the meaning of the poet's word. A beautiful piece was composed for me by Ernest Walker of Oxford to William Morris's poem " From the Upland to the Sea " in which the voice has the advantage of declaiming the words and takes an equal place with the pianoforte and the voices of a string quartette. Walford Davies was kind enough to set Browning's " Prospice " to music for me, in which the voice is heard with a quintette of piano and strings. As an ample suggestion of orchestral music and much less expensive, I suggest to present-day composers that they consider this means for expressing themselves, as any new mode for making known one's artistic thoughts should be of value.

At this time of my career I became particularly interested in the ballads of Loewe, the clerical contemporary of Schubert, who left the church to devote himself to the composition of songs. I commend his splendid ballads to all singers, for they are among the best and most comprehensible of music stories, so to speak, that exist in all song literature. What can be finer than the Scotch ballads of " Archibald Douglas," and the gruesome " Edward," or the fantastic fairy tale of " Tom the Rhymer "? Loewe's setting of " The Erl King," which Schubert had done before him, is by many considered equally fine, and nothing in the whole range of comedy can excel his delightful " Wedding Song." There is no mystery about these ballads, and yet they are exemplifications of the highest form of their art. Flowers of music are indeed as beautiful and as amazing in their variety as natural blossoms.

Besides giving many recitals and appearing in works which I have already mentioned, I sang in Sullivan's oratorio " The Martyr of Antioch " and his cantata " The Golden Legend "; in Hofmann's " Melusine "; in Mendelssohn's " Walpurgis Night," and in Rossini's " Moses in Egypt." I had also the opportunity in the spring of 1895 of taking part at Crystal Palace under the conductorship of Hubert Parry in his remarkable oratorio " Job," which should be more frequently heard in America. Notwithstanding the somberness of the subject, it is a composition of great musical value and affords, to the barytone part in particular, one of the finest modern pieces of musical declamation. The title rôle was originally written for Plunkett Greene, who created the part and rendered it many times with superb dramatic feeling.

Tinel's " St. Francis " was performed by me soon after this under the conductorship of Hallé, with Prout's " Hereward," and Goring Thomas's posthumous work, " The Swan and the Skylark," while Berlioz's " Te Deum " and Verdi's " Requiem " followed in quick suc-

cession. Gounod's " Redemption " and Mendelssohn's
" Elijah " I also sang before the opera season of 1895.

" Elijah " is almost sufficiently dramatic to be included
in the operatic repertory. The experiment was tried in
England of putting that oratorio on the stage, and Erickson Bushnell, the well-known American singer, a man of
considerable private means, was also smitten with the
idea and attempted to give " Elijah " in operatic form.

Many years afterward, when I myself had frequently
sung " Elijah " in New York, I was seriously urged to
render it on the stage in a series of performances. I
deliberated upon this, realizing the extreme difficulty of
mounting a masterpiece of oratorio so that even to enthusiasts it would be in the least acceptable as an opera.
The spirit of the work, to be retained at all, would have
to be communicated to the actors and singers by an artistic director, to whom literature, religion, and poetry
were of paramount importance and of equal value. No
mere stage manager could do anything with " Elijah "
as an opera. The only person whom I have heard speak
with real poetic and lofty religious insight into the possibilities of such a production is that admirable Welsh enthusiast, the choral director Tali Esen Morgan. But
such are the difficulties that would attend a production
of this kind, that it is better to live in the hope and expectation of the future possibility of some such artistic
wonder, rather than to have in the retrospect blasted
hopes. Mendelssohn in writing the " Elijah " had a
veritable inspiration, and had he intended that work to be
produced other than as it was originally produced as an
oratorio at the Birmingham Festival in 1846, he would
have elaborated it accordingly; as it stands so it should
be performed, and then every spiritual member of the

audience can visualize to his heart's content and come away satisfied.

I remember once hearing William Stoll, Jr., a Philadelphia conductor of orchestra and an excellent violinist, declare that he had the gift of auralizing music; he knew the symphonies so well, he assured me, that if he desired to hear one of them as he was about to go to sleep, all he had to do was to start it in his mind and he would hear a perfect performance, as if played by master instrumentalists, from the first note to the closing bar.

This reminds me of what I have read of Goethe, who, if he wished to see again a statue or a picture from some gallery in Europe, would sit quietly facing a dark corner in his study, concentrate his thoughts upon the Venus de Milo or some other work of art, when it would immediately seem to form itself and to stand out, so that it appeared to his mind's eye as if he were looking at the actuality.

A Philadelphian named Waters has told me that he once had a distinct vision upon waking in the morning. As he lay looking into the room from his bed he saw a pair of hands playing upon a curved keyboard, unlike that of any piano or organ of which he knew. Years afterward such keyboards and organ appliances came into existence and are now used. The strangest part of my friend's narrative was that, at the time he had this prophetic vision of the new keyboard, he also heard from the instrument music of the most extraordinary kind, quite unlike anything he had ever listened to.

The subject is one of such interest that I may be pardoned if I quote here a letter written in 1874 by the late Frances Ridley Havergal, the English poetess and writer of hymns, to her mother, in which she says:

" In the train I had one of those curious musical visions, which only very rarely visit me.   I hear strange and very beautiful chords, generally full, slow, and grand, succeeding each other in most interesting sequences.   I do not invent them, I could not — they pass before my mind and I only listen.   Now and then my will seems aroused when I see ahead how some fine resolution might follow, and I seem to *will* that certain chords should come, and then they do come; but then my will seems suspended again, and they go on quite independently.

" It is so interesting: the chords seem to fold over each other and die away down into music of infinite softness, and then they unfold and open out, as if great curtains were being withdrawn one after another widening the view, till, with a gathering power and fullness, it seems as if the very skies were being opened out before one, and a sheet or great blaze and glory of music, such as my outward ears never heard, gradually swells out in perfectly sublime splendor.

" This time there was an added feature: I seemed to hear depths and heights of sound beyond the scale which human ears can receive, keen, far-up octaves, like vividly twinkling starlight of music, and mighty, slow vibrations of gigantic strings going down into grand thunders of depths, octaves below anything otherwise appreciable as musical notes.

" Then, all at once, it seemed as if my soul had got a new sense, and I could see this inner music as well as hear it; and then it was like gazing down into marvelous abysses of sound, and up into dazzling regions of what, to the eye, would have been light and color, but to the new sense was sound.   It lasted perhaps half an hour."

One is compelled either to accept the statements of

Mr. Stoll, Mr. Waters, and Miss Havergal, or to brand them as insane, or mendacious, or both; yet, if men do not hear and see these visions, whence come the inspirations that lead to the productions of great works of art? We who perform what has been written and those who listen to our performances are the living witnesses of the fact that such inspiration has been vouchsafed to mankind.

In no other way than through his extemporization and his written work could Beethoven have given proof to the world that he was the chosen instrument to communicate a Heaven-sent message. Truly, the poet is born and not made, and just as truly will he speak to the world in the language of the Infinite, regardless of whether the world at the time understands it or not.

Several appearances at the Monday " Pops " with Joachim, Sauer, Borwick and others in fine chamber music followed " Elijah," but I took the greatest pleasure that season in the Bach Festival, in all three performances of which I had the distinction of being engaged, singing in the " Passion Music," and in the cantatas " Wachet Auf " and " O Ewigkeit," Joachim playing the violin obbligato, all being under the leadership of Villiers Stanford, who had brought the chorus to a high pitch of perfection. It was during the previous season of the Bach Choir that John Runciman, who had taken Bernard Shaw's place on the *Saturday Review,* impertinently said of the chorus that " the altos were evidently selected from among those ladies who could no longer sing soprano." This season any such defect was remedied, and I look back upon the performances with the greatest interest and artistic pleasure.

I had advanced so far in my profession that I was that

year, 1895, first engaged to sing at the concerts of the
time-honored Philharmonic Society, when I revived what
was almost a novelty to London, so seldom was it performed, the fine scene for Lysiart from Weber's " Euryanthe," under the conductorship of Mackenzie.

By way of filling in the time, I gave the second of my
own concerts that year at St. James's Hall, consisting
of music by Brahms, in which I was aided by Fanny Davies
at the piano, Signor Arbos, the Spanish violinist, Mrs.
Henschel, Miss Agnes Janson, and William Shakespeare,
in the quartettes of the master's Opus No. 112, which
includes the delightful and seldom heard " Love Songs."

One of the noted figures in the musical life of London
at that time was Franz Korbay, whose Hungarian gypsy
tunes were being sung by every one able to cope with them.
Korbay was as well known in New York as in the British
metropolis.   One of the most remarkable exhibitions of
Hungarian enthusiasm I have ever seen was given at a
fashionable *soirée* in London, where there was dancing
toward the end of the evening.   Korbay caught the eye
of the conductor of the orchestra, which was entirely
composed of his own countrymen.   The conductor
seemed to read the thought of his compatriot; signaling
to his men, they at once struck into one of the character-
istic dances of their people.   Madame Korbay broke off
the conversation she was having in another part of the
room, turned, and made her way immediately to her
husband near the orchestra.   As if realizing that something remarkable was about to happen, every one fell
silent and cleared a space in which Mr. and Mrs. Korbay, though not on speaking terms and about to be di-
vorced, entered with the utmost spirit into one of the
gypsy dances, which they carried through in the most

amorous fashion. The result was that court proceedings were almost stopped and courtship resumed, for the spirited couple were on the point of making up for good and all. The effect produced on that smart London drawing-room was indescribable, but it set things going.

The Irish-American singer Dennis O'Sullivan was one of a house party in an ancient English country mansion, where I, too, was a guest. A stately dinner was being given at which were present a duchess, a famous dowager, a celebrated general, a noted parliamentarian, and other persons of distinction. The conversation lagging, O'Sullivan pulled from his hip pocket his inseparable companion, a tin penny whistle, in the manipulation of which he was an adept, and played, to the amazement of the guests and the chagrin of his amiable hostess. Yet she thanked him afterward, for from that moment her dinner party was a success, where previously failure had stared her in the face. He, too, had set things going.

The operatic activities of 1895 included several performances of Auber's " Fra Diavolo," which was given at the particular request of that operatic enthusiast, the Prince of Wales. Unless duties kept him from Covent Garden, he occupied his seat in the corner of the club box, where he was joined by his intimates. He sometimes came upon the stage through the narrow private passage made in the thickness of the wall of that old theatre many years before, to congratulate the artists, many of whom he knew.

In " Fra Diavolo " I took the part of Lord Allcash, and with Madame Amadi, an Englishwoman, as Lady Allcash, we performed our parts in English when we spoke together, and in assumed broken Italian when we were speaking or singing with the others. De Lucia was admirable in the title rôle and Zerlina fascinatingly performed by the beautiful American soprano Marie Engle, while my old associates of " Falstaff " days, Pini Corsi and Arimondi, were irresistibly funny as the two brigands.

In this opera I altered the style of dress that had up to that time prevailed upon the stage, and instead of furnishing the English lord with a pair of " Piccadilly weepers " and an exaggerated checked suit, à la Lord Dundreary, I made my character a veritable John Bull, for that worthy as he is known to the world to-day came into being about 1830, at the time " Fra Diavolo " was written.   I went back to the top boots, the blue swallow-tailed coat with gold buttons, the frilled shirt front and choker collar, and the mutton-chop whiskers, and enjoyed masquerading in the part to my heart's content.

Another novelty of the season of 1895 was Frederic Cowen's grand opera " Harold," a story of the time of William the Conqueror, which character I assumed, with Madame Albani and the Russian tenor Philip Brozel; the principals and chorus in this sumptuous production all using the English language in which the opera was originally written.   Nobody seemed to think of it as an innovation, for every one could understand the words as we sang them, which was a rarity in the classic precincts of Covent Garden.

I had that season the interesting experience of singing both with Calvé and Madame Gemma Bellincioni in " Cavalleria Rusticana," and in noticing the difference in their handling of the rôle of Santuzza and in comparing them with the great Italian actress Eleonora Duse, who had frequently performed the same part on the London stage.   Duse was all intelligence, Calvé was all fire, and

Bellincioni was all superbly controlled emotion. I have
rarely been more affected by any one with whom I have
acted than by Bellincioni, who apparently did not think
of herself as a singer, indeed her voice was not of the
best quality and at the time it was in its decline; yet she
possessed that indefinable personality and magnetism
which excited the deepest emotion in the minds of her
auditors.

I always had been able to arrange with my managers
that I should be allowed to accept other work between
my operatic performances; and this season, under Richter,
I sang Wotan's Farewell from " The Valkyrie "; under
Mottl, Hans Sachs's monologue and duet from the third
act of " The Mastersingers " and the Lament of Amfortas from the first act of " Parsifal "; also, with the
same conductor in the second act of " The Flying Dutchman " as Daland, and as Hagen in the third act of " Die
Götterdämmerung." I also sang in the third act of
" Parsifal " with Van Dyck, who was then in the height
of his fame because of his wonderful impersonation of
the title rôle at Bayreuth, and under Siegfried Wagner as
Alberich in the first scene from his father's " Rheingold,"
a part I was to do later upon the stage on many occasions.

The willing horse was being driven pretty hard, but
he was in double harness with Song and did not mind it.
He enjoyed all that came his way and entered then, as
ever since, into the spirit of everything he has undertaken,
for the reason that he has undertaken nothing that he
did not enjoy.

CHAPTER XX

FROM GRAVE TO GAY

Wherein I spake of most disastrous chances,
Of moving accidents.— *Shakespeare*.

DURING the autumn and winter of 1895 I gave a
number of concerts of old English music with Arnold
Dolmetsch, accompanied by the old-fashioned instruments, the harpsichord, the lute, and the viola da gamba.
Mr. Dolmetsch was a distinguished authority on the subject of old musical instruments and there was scarcely a
great old house in England that did not yield up to him
its clavichords, spinets, and virginals, which were restored
under his direction; their intimate and refined sounds
afforded a distinct sense of relief after the stress of so
much modern music. Personally, it gave me the greatest
pleasure to hear and take part in the quaint music of
Jenkins, Laniere, Purcell, and William and Henry Lawes.

It happened that once while Dolmetsch was accompanying me on the harpsichord, as I sang Henry Purcell's
remarkable " Let the Dreadful Engines," I observed a
cat quietly walking across the back of the hall. He
glanced up the middle aisle and caught sight of me, in
whom he doubtless recognized a sympathetic friend, for
I am fond of animals. A dog has come upon the stage
to me, two rats have played at my feet for a considerable
time in the glare of the footlights; and at a concert a bat
kept flying about my head — much to my discomfiture,
for to that sort of creature I am not partial. But at

this concert the cat walked up the aisle, leaped upon the stage, arched his back, rubbed his fur against my leg, elevated his tail, and purred with great satisfaction as he made a series of figures of eight between my feet.

Dolmetsch, seated with his back to me, saw nothing of what was going on. I had to continue with my song, but when a young girl burst into a giggle of merriment, the whole audience went into shrieks of delight.

Presently the distinguished Belgian harpsichordist, turning to see the cause of the disturbance and catching sight of the cat, hastily snatched from the piano desk the whole volume of music and hurled it at the beast, which with a savage yowl sprang into the air, almost into my face, and dashed away. The laughter of the audience continued so long and loud that we performers were obliged to leave the stage, not to return for many minutes, when some semblance of order had been restored. This incident happened near the end of the concert and provided an anticlimax as unexpected as it would have been effective if it had happened in the proper place.

That season I also had the great and interesting pleasure of making my appearance by Royal command at the State Concerts in Buckingham Palace, an honor afforded me several times later on.

Upon this first occasion the late Adelina Patti was the principal singer, and though she was past her prime she was idolized by the British public and acclaimed by the Prince of Wales, and by as distinguished a noble and diplomatic assemblage as any country could boast of.

Mme. Patti, while not being a great actress, was always adequate in the histrionic side of her parts, though, after the fashion of her day, she invariably came to the footlights to sing her great arias regardless of the business of the stage; its occupants might do as they pleased as long as she had the undivided attention of the audience. She was indeed a song bird, *par excellence,* and never allowed anything to upset either her equanimity or her comfort. I shall never forget her closing scene in "Aïda," where she and the tenor are supposed to be immured in a tomb of stone. At the close of the duet Patti, who had instructed the stage manager to make her comfortable, would carefully adjust a sofa cushion which had been placed conveniently at hand, would kick with one high-heeled Parisian slipper a train around behind her and assisted by the tenor would compose herself in graceful position — and die.

The last time I ever saw Mme. Patti upon the stage was at Covent Garden Theatre, at a gala performance at the time of Queen Victoria's Diamond Jubilee, when the attention of the audience was attracted even more to the splendor of her dress than to the brilliancy of her voice. Upon her corsage there blazed a solid front of diamonds, and I was told that every gem in her possession had been carefully sewed upon the bodice of her dress, ropes of pearls hung from her neck, her hands were covered with jewels, and a diamond tiara sat upon her graceful head. So valuable was the world-renowned prima donna that, besides her husband, she was guarded by several detectives, one of whom was with her in the carriage upon her way to the opera house, while another sat upon the box. One of these remained outside the door of her dressing room throughout the evening, while the other, with a companion, escorted her to the stage, remaining at her entrance and exit, guarding her as she returned to her dressing room and later to her hotel.

The manner of one's bidding to participate in any

royal musical function began with a polite note from Sir Walter Parratt, who had the title of Master of the Queen's Musick, written from his house in the thickness of the wall of Windsor Castle, signifying the pleasure of her Majesty Queen Victoria that one should take part in the State Concert held at Buckingham Palace on such and such an evening in conjunction with such and such artists.

The Queen herself had never listened to any music in public after the death of her husband, the Prince Consort, many years before. At these State Concerts, though no fee was offered, each artist, even Patti, who received a thousand guineas a night under ordinary circumstances, was given by the bearer of the Queen's purse an honorarium of ten guineas by way of covering the incidental expenses to which an artist might be put. Any appearance before the Queen herself was recompensed by exquisite courtesy and a personal gift from her Majesty, several of which I have the honor to have received.

As I have indicated, we were singing in four languages upon the stage at Covent Garden, though the institution was still officially known as The Royal Italian Opera, but notwithstanding this Hans Richter suggested that he would like me to assist him in performances in English of Wagner's "Niebelungen Ring," for, as he told me, no one was more keenly alive than the master himself to the value, to the audience, of the meaning of his text; and he wished that, in whatever country sung, it should be rendered in the language "understanded of the people."

At last English was being used upon many occasions at Covent Garden. The tenor, E. C. Hedmondt, who had for so long been the leading spirit of the Carl Rosa Company, produced on October 19, 1895, on the fiftieth

anniversary of its first production, Wagner's "Tannhäuser" in English on that classic stage. Hedmondt
himself appeared as Tannhäuser, I as Wolfram, Miss
Margaret MacIntyre as Elizabeth, Madame Recoschewitz
as Venus, with Mr. Bevan as the Landgrave. The conductor was Mr. Feld.

It was while Tannhäuser was being given during that
short season that an accident happened which amused us
as much as it annoyed the management. The opening
scene of the opera takes place in the Venusberg, where
Tannhäuser is made to witness several beautiful episodes
from the classic myths through the wiles of the goddess.
During this powerful arc lights were used, one of which
was mounted for the moment upon a stepladder twenty
feet high. In the sudden change to the valley of the
Wartburg, Venus and the couch upon which she lies were
successfully removed; the dancing nymphs and fauns disappeared from the stage, and the scenery as by magic
arose, descended, or was drawn to either side. But the
nineteenth century stepladder was left peacefully standing in the middle of the stage toward the back, so situated
that any one who climbed it would find himself at the door
of the ancient castle upon the hill. When Tannhäuser, in
the person of Mr. Hedmondt, turned to greet the Landgrave and his friends, he found this unsightly object, the
harmless but necessary stepladder, just where he did not
need it as an approach to the castle where dwelt the saintly
Elizabeth.

It was during this season that I not only made my first
appearance as "The Flying Dutchman" but as Wotan in
"The Valkyrie."

The autumn of 1895 introduced me to festival work
in England, where functions of this kind are really carried

on in festal state. My first experience was at the ancient town of Gloucester, in the superb Gothic cathedral under the auspices of the most distinguished citizens of the town and of the neighborhood, and under the patronage of the Queen and Prince and Princess of Wales. The cathedral choir sang, greatly augmented by the voices of musical amateurs of the city, and assisted by the choirs and choral bodies of the neighboring towns of Worcester and Hereford, with the sanction and under the eye of the bishops and clergy of these ancient dioceses. Splendid music was performed under the most impressive circumstances I had ever experienced. Strains of melody, miracles of harmony, rose and mingled with the frozen music of the Gothic nave of the ancient sanctuary, past the old Saxon pillars into delicate masonry that was itself the melody for the mounting harmonies below. Outside the city was *en fête,* flags and banners everywhere, and a gorgeous old-world civic pageant to mark the importance of the celebration. Just so the elder burghers of Nuremburg made St. John's Day glorious as shown in the mimic representations of " The Mastersingers."

In the cathedral no applause is ever permitted, and the impressiveness of the music is thereby greatly enhanced. An American contralto, in telling me her experience at one of these cathedral festivals, said she had not been informed of this unwritten rule and had not observed that there had been no applause prior to her own solo. When she sat down after its rendering, in perfect silence, having naturally expected from many previous experiences elsewhere evidences of approval, she was so taken a-back that she was scarcely able to finish the performance at all. She thought that she had made a lamentable failure, and that she would never be heard again in England, when as a matter of fact she had made such a success that the committee warmly congratulated her at the conclusion of the performance.

The surroundings of such an occasion as an English festival in a mediæval cathedral are so impressive beyond any words of mine to express that one scarcely wishes afterward to hear music of that character anywhere else. This was the first of a number of such engagements for me, and I am thankful indeed to have had such notable privileges.

The day before the Gloucester festival opened, being in the cathedral alone after a rehearsal, I observed some scaffolding in the neighborhood of the organ and judged that repairs were being made. An ancient verger clad in his antique cap and gown, seeing me looking at the boarding, volunteered the statement, " They've been doin' summat with the horgan, sir; they've took out the old mattics and 'ave put the new mattics in."

It was only two weeks later that I sang for the first time at the festival at Leeds, where the chorus consisted of about 350 voices carefully chosen, not only from the Leeds Choral Society, but from the choral bodies of Bradford, Huddersfield, Halifax, Dewsbury, and Batley, in all of which towns the work to be performed has previously been carefully prepared. The result, as may be imagined, was a glory of vocal sound.

The conductor was Sir Arthur Sullivan. At the desk his demeanor was quite different from that of any other leader under whom it has been my good fortune to sing. Sullivan had thick dark hair, a swarthy skin, and wore glasses. He invariably sat in the usual high chair and seemed to keep his eyes always on the score in front of him. His beat was restrained and rather cramped, his baton moving across the top or up and down the sides of the score; yet nothing in the world escaped the attention of this quiet, reserved little man, the fingers of whose well-manicured right hand were invariably stained with cigarette smoke.

To show young artists what I did, and what they may have to do, I may say that I made more than 130 appearances in that twelvemonth, and that during this period my repertory of songs numbered about 120 pieces, including duets and quartettes, over 30 selections sung with orchestra, about 15 oratorios given, 10 appearances in 5 operas in concert form, and 25 performances of 9 operas actually sung upon the operatic stage.

I do not hesitate to say that I look back with considerable pride upon this season, and I find, upon consulting my bound volume of programs, in which everything is numbered, 737 separate pieces in which at one time or another in my life I had appeared up to December 31, 1895.

Let it be understood that the reason I mention these things is that students who intend taking up an artistic career may grasp the character and the difficulties of the work that lies before them. Those content to do a few things will not go far upon the way; but those who really have ambition and a will to study will find their work pleasurable, of course, yet anything but easy. The loftiest heights and rewards are attained by few in any walk of life, and, taking one consideration with another and balancing the matter sensibly, it will be found that the artistic career is much the same as any other profession. It may be said of it, as of worldly pleasure, that it is often of short duration and highly overrated; so we must begin betimes and work intelligently. We can not reasonably expect to accomplish anything worth while unless we work *con amore*. We must strive in music for the love of music, and with no expectation of great gain until we have reached the point, in practice and in authority, where we may justly demand a considerable fee for what we do. Even then a great deal has to be learned and performed for charity or by way of education, or in the necessary pleasure of helping others to achieve the success which one hopes for oneself. Indeed, had it not been for the enthusiasm I felt for my work I should never have been asked to return to my native country, there to continue the artistic journey which had been so auspiciously begun in the Old World.

CHAPTER XXI

SWIMMING WITH THE TIDE

*Progress is not an accident, but a necessity. It is a part of nature.—
Herbert Spencer.*

THE year 1896 opened as busily as its predecessor had closed, and I found myself immersed but comfortably swimming in the stream of art in which I had already begun to support myself without undue effort, though effort there must always be. But I was going with the tide and not against it, and that makes all the difference in the world.

Another of my own London concerts took place in the early days of January, when the program was devoted entirely to compositions by British composers, mostly of that day.

Fond as I was of the classics of other countries, I was keenly alive to the value of contemporaneous English music. Of music by Americans I knew but little as yet, excepting the comparatively few songs then making their way in London, which I never ceased to bring before the notice of the public, placing the works of my countrymen upon the same program with those of the acknowledged masters of other times and other nations; for in what way better than by contrast can one judge the merit of one's fellows?

It was my pleasure to sing on more than one occasion with a body of amateurs called the Liverpool Orchestral Society, which had gradually been gathered together by a very musicianly cotton factor of Liverpool, one of the most cultured and enthusiastic amateurs I have ever known. He had rare taste, was himself no mean performer upon the piano and violin, and ere long from small beginnings an excellent orchestra was formed from which the best members were graduated into the Liverpool Philharmonic, then under Richter. Many of these men are alive and of great value to the musical growth of England, blessing the name of Alfred Rodewald, their benefactor, for his interest in them and their beloved art.

It is easier to encourage the growth of orchestral music in this manner than it is to find millionaires willing to put their hands in their pockets after the manner of Colonel Higginson of Boston, to support what is nearly always a losing venture. As it is with music so it is with the theatre; it should come into existence after its own fashion. For few indeed and far between are those who can say, " Let there be," and " there was." Neither of these arts has of its own accord a way of springing " full panoplied from the front of Jove." These along with the rest of nature must follow nature's course. The seed must be planted in good ground, it must be watered and nourished, it must be helped to grow, and in all cases fruition must be waited for. Sir Henry Irving said in one of his addresses at Oxford University, " The stage, to succeed as a fine art, must succeed as a commercial undertaking." And neither music nor the drama can get along at all without enthusiasm within and without.

Many concerts followed up and down the country under excellent circumstances and with the best artists, but at a concert in Southport I had my first experience of the disrespect shown to artists by persons of a certain stamp. During the afternoon I had been rehearsing a duet with

Miss Clara Butt in her hotel apartment and after I left she went on practicing for that evening. Later in the reading room of the hotel I overheard two men speaking with a broad Lancashire dialect. " I say, Harry, did thou hear that row going on upstairs? " " Aye! " replied Harry; " I heard somebody a-singing." " Well," said the other, " she were in the room next to mine and I beat upon the door, and told her to shut up, for I wanted to take a nap." " Oh! " said Harry in amazement, " did thou know who that were? That were Clara Butt! " " Well! " said the other, " I don't care who it were, she'd no business to be shoutin' and 'ollerin' when I wanted to go to sleep." As I heard the man speaking I thought, " Alas! for the chivalry of my ancestral county! "

Arthur Chappell, director of the Saturday and Monday " Pops " at St. James's Hall, continued to honor me with engagements at his remarkable offerings of classical music, when it was my constant endeavor to keep the vocal selections up to the mark set by Joachim, Lady Hallé, and the others in their instrumental numbers. There had been much comment the season before upon the inferior character of many of the songs. I, therefore, with great interest to myself and, I believe, to my audiences, though against the wish of Mr. Chappell, who, strangely enough, did not care for good songs, invariably brought forward certain vocal gems such as are to be found in great numbers by whoever cares to delve even but a short way beneath the surface. Early in 1896, in a program otherwise devoted to Beethoven's instrumental pieces, I revived that master's song cycle, " To the Distant Beloved." Upon previous occasions I had indulged in similar revivals of almost unknown works by Schubert and others. But public opinion is hard to move in London,

and where vocal music is concerned, a more obvious form
of song than that which properly consorts with classical
instrumental music is more readily appreciated, even by
the highly cultured musical amateur. On the contrary,
the prevailing taste for choral music is of the most advanced character and I had the opportunity of singing
within a few days, though in different cities, not only
Bach's " Passion Music according to St. Matthew," but
also his rarely given " Passion according to St. John."

With the early spring of 1896 there began at Drury
Lane a preliminary season of grand opera in English
under the baton of Luigi Mancinelli, and during this
season I sang in " I Pagliacci," wearing, as before, evening clothes while rendering the prologue, and repeated
Wolfram and Wotan, adding to my repertory the part
of Telramund in " Lohengrin."   I also appeared for the
second time at the London Philharmonic Society, when
I gave with orchestra Wagner's seldom heard " Les deux
Grenadiers " and Mozart's even less known but very fine
bass aria " Per questa bella mano."

That spring in London I gave two more concerts of
my own before the grand opera season began, enlisting
the assistance of Piatti, the fine 'cellist, Fanny Davies, the
pianist, and Signorina Landi, the Italian alto, with Gabriel
Fauré, the French song writer. But what stands out
more particularly in my mind in regard to that occasion
is, that I was further assisted by an old friend and preceptor, the distinguished actor, Herman Vezin, whom I
had requested to recite, to the music of Schumann, Hebbel's ballad " Fair Hedwig " and " The Fugitives " by
Shelley.

I have always been interested in recitations to music,
and though some of these pieces are undeniably better

than others, the same can be said of every other style of composition, vocal or instrumental. Though I was myself not yet ready to adventure upon an experiment in which I subsequently had so wide an experience, I was desirous of seeing what a fine actor could do with such pieces. As a matter of fact, Mr. Vezin was not a musician and consequently failed to produce the full effect I had expected; but that did not in the least dash my enthusiasm for this form of art, nor deter me later from experimenting to my heart's content.

No survey of London concerts however brief would be complete without a tribute to the superb musicianship of that great pianist and distinguished musician, Mr. Henry Bird, who has so often been a very present help to me in time of artistic trouble, and upon whom I always relied for his masterly handling of the piano at my own recitals. His ability was such that he became an institution, and much of my success is due to his coöperation.

It is very interesting to me to glance over my collection of hundreds of programs at this time of my career, and to note how, in the short period of less than four years since my appearance as a mere tyro at Covent Garden, my artistic stature had grown. It may have been, and probably was, that I just happened to come in time to fill a niche that was temporarily vacant in English musical life; but sure it is that I neglected nothing that presented itself, and had my hands full in doing what came to me to the best of my ability.

The season of grand opera that began in June at Covent Garden enlisted the usual number of vocal celebrities from all parts of Europe and America, and it fell to my lot to sing twenty-five times beginning with Humperdinck's " Hänsel and Gretel," in which Peter, the father, was assigned to me, to my great delight, for any one with a sense of humor must revel in such a " fat " part.   Then followed Lord Allcash in " Fra Diavolo " and our performances of " The Mastersingers " attracted renewed attention.

In the performances of " Lohengrin " that year at Covent Garden we began first to sing Wagner in German. Jean and Edouard de Reszke, both Poles, accustomed to Italian or French, Madame Albani, a French Canadian, as Elsa, and myself, an American, as Telramund, all singing in German; Fräulein Meisslinger, the only German of the cast, sang Ortrud, and extremely well she did it.

It was at the dress rehearsal for our first performance of " Lohengrin " that I suggested to Jean de Reszke that our contest should look more like a fight, and less of a foregone conclusion for the divinely endowed Knight of the Swan.   He readily fell in with my wishes and from that time on there was given — what was in my experience lacking in all previous performances — a significant reason for the overthrow of the malevolent Telramund. This is a character which, by the way, I invariably associate with Macbeth, for he is as certainly under the domination of a strong and evil-minded woman as ever Macbeth was, and each is ready to commit any deed at the behest of the more powerful will.

That season Jean de Reszke assumed for the first time the part, perhaps his greatest, of Tristan, with his brother Edouard as the King; and with Madame Albani as Isolde.   I once more assumed, as I was to do many times thereafter, my beloved part of the faithful, dog-like Kurwenal.

In the preparation of this opera I suggested again that

some reasonable pretext should be afforded for Kurwenal's death. The management of the fight at the
castle gate was turned over to me, and I instructed two
of the supernumeraries to work their way around behind
me, and as I was engaged in defending my master, to
stab me in the back with their spears. This was done
and, as Quince says, I " died most gallant for love." In
doing so I almost caused the death of one of my oppo-
nents in the chorus. Though the action was clearly understood, in the excitement of a rehearsal he unexpectedly lowered the shield upon which my heavy blow aimed
at his head was to have fallen, and he felt the full power
of my strong right arm as my weighty sword, no stage
makeshift on this occasion, cut deep into his cheek bone.
There was almost a riot among the chorus and supers,
but it was soon realized — and no one realized any more
quickly than the injured man himself — that he alone
was to blame for the accident. I saw that his wound
received careful attention and the distribution of a little
pourboire at the luncheon interval helped to calm the
indignant multitude; but though the fight always went
very well in subsequent performances, I managed to die
thereafter without bringing any one else down with me.

In the revival of " Les Huguenots " that season
Madame Melba sang the part of Marguerite de Valois,
and Madame Albani was truly superb as Valentina.
She sang it as well as any one in Europe, and in such a
part was more at home than as Isolde which she had but
recently studied. Among the men there was a shifting
of parts. My former rôle of de Nevers was sung by
Ancona, while I assumed the part of San Bris, and Pol
Plançon took the grateful part of Marcello.

This great basso, though he had sung in London for

many seasons and continued to be a favorite both there and in America, never accomplished anything in the English language beyond the few words that sufficed to procure the necessities of life.

Looking over my programs, it is amusing to recall the State Concert that year at Buckingham Palace, when Madame Eames, an American, sang in French; I sang in Italian; Madame Mantelli, an Italian, sang in French; Alvarez, a Spaniard, sang a German love song in French; while at the request of the Prince of Wales, Plançon, Frenchman, sang " The Lost Chord " in English.

This was written down for him so that he could sing the equivalent syllables, which meant less than nothing, from an amazing page of script that would have puzzled the most accomplished comparative philologist. The Prince, who had seen the words as transcribed, went into convulsions of laughter behind his program, while the whole Court wondered what was provoking such royal mirth.   It was this:

> Si-ted ouan dei at dhi or-ganne
> Ai ouaz oui-ri an dil ah tiz
> Ahnd mai fin-gerz ouann-der daid-li
> O-vaire dhi no-izi kiz, *etc., etc.,*

CHAPTER XXII

MY AIN COUNTRIE

God sent His singers upon earth
With songs of sadness and of mirth.
— *Longfellow.*

IN the autumn of 1896 with a light heart I gave my
farewell London concert for that season at St. James's
Hall and before long found myself on my way to my
native land, filled with artistic hope and an enthusiasm
which had never forsaken me. It was the tenth time
that I had crossed the Atlantic Ocean, frequently in
storms or disagreeable weather, but upon this occasion
everything was bright, and the sea almost as calm as a
millpond from shore to shore. As I stood in the prow
of the vessel one day alone, trying to peer beyond the
rounded edge of the world, my imagination outran the
swiftly moving ship and I seemed to see the vast expanse
of North America and to realize in some measure for
the first time the responsibility before me.

I was then the only American man singing upon the
stage of either continent in grand opera. I felt that my
position was unique and must be upheld as worthily as
lay in my power. And I earnestly hoped that I might
be enabled to maintain my standing with dignity, whatever I did, and to be the influence for good in American
musical art that my mother would have wished had she
been alive to greet me.

I owe it, I am sure, to Jean de Reszke, who always took

an interest in my work and for whom I felt the warmest friendship, that Maurice Grau, who for some time had been directing the fortunes of the Covent Garden Opera after the death of Sir Augustus Harris, invited me to go to America to become a member of the Metropolitan Opera Company in New York, where all my *confrères* had for at least two years before been delighting the public. At last I had sufficiently made myself one of them, artistically speaking, to be considered able to hold my own on the operatic boards of fastidious New York.

In making my contract with Mr. Grau, I naturally tried to do as well for myself as possible, for I may say that by this time my earning capacity had advanced to considerably more than the small sum I had received in my uncle's office at home. Grau was a close calculator, but an agreement once made he stuck to it whatever it was, but would do no more than he had undertaken to do in writing. It was said of him that though he would give a man a fine cigar, he would not offer him a match to light it with unless such generosity had been nominated in the bond. But, as I was holding out for an emolument greater than that which he had suggested, I gained my point in a way that I had not looked for. Though Grau was willing that I should take as many concerts as I could fit in between the operas which he guaranteed me, he was inclined to be rather close as to my salary until I urged the extent and variety of my repertory and my willingness to appear frequently, and often unexpectedly. He suddenly turned to me and said: " Very well, let it be as you say. I will give you what you ask, for in all my experience as a manager I have never had an artist so reliable as yourself. I wish you every good fortune in your native country and I predict success for you.

You will open at the Metropolitan Opera House, New York, November 18, as Beckmesser in ' Die Meistersinger,' with the de Reszkes, Mr. Plançon, and Madame Eames."

The New York season of the autumn of 1896 opened in a blaze of glory, with Mesdames Calvé, Melba, Eames, and Litvinne, all in the fullness of their powers, heading the sopranos, while Madame Mantelli and Rosa Olitzka led the altos.   Jean de Reszke, in the height of his fame, set a noble pace for the other tenors, Salignac and Cremonini.   Ancona, Campanari, Lassalle, and myself were among the barytones, while Edouard de Reszke, Plançon, and Castelmary formed a basic foundation strong enough to uphold any artistic superstructure.

This galaxy of stars performed that season a repertory of twenty-four operas as follows: " Romeo and Juliet," " Faust," " Philemon and Baucis," " Carmen," " Le Cid," " Cavalleria Rusticana," " Les Huguenots," " L'Africaine," " Don Giovanni," " The Marriage of Figaro," " La Traviata," " Il Trovatore," " Rigoletto," " Aïda," " Lucia," " Hamlet," " Mefistofele," and " Werther," Wagner being represented by " Tannhäuser," " Lohengrin," " Siegfried," " Tristan und Isolde," and " Die Meistersinger." The German operas were conducted by Anton Seidl; Mancinelli and Bevignani accounted for the rest of the repertory.

It is useless to institute comparisons between the casts of those times and casts of the present day; it is sufficient to say, however, that the aggregation of artists gathered together that season by Grau, which with some changes for the better remained with him for several years, was perhaps the most remarkable selection of singers that the world has ever heard.   It is amusing, when turning over my programs, to note that " The Mastersingers " was given with a cast comprising one Russian, two Germans, two Poles, three Americans, four Frenchmen, and five Italians. This German opera, conducted by an Italian, was sung in Italian before an English-speaking audience. It was not long, however, before " The Mastersingers " fell into line in German with the other Wagnerian operas we performed. It sometimes happens that with such a polyglot cast, in which every singer knows the music but has the words in his native tongue only, the audience will be treated to Italian, French, and German in alternation, from the lips of representatives of as many as six nationalities.

Among the prima donnas of that time the beautiful Americans, Lillian Nordica and Emma Eames, reigned supreme. Madame Nordica was married to a Hungarian singer, who considered himself engaged to the prima donna before she had left for America the previous year. It is said he was kept aware of her movements in America by her maid, who before long informed him that attentions were being paid to her by another. He thereupon set sail for New York, and on his arrival made his way to Nordica's hotel. Upon being announced and received by the beautiful artist, he, so the story goes, drew a pistol from his pocket and threatened to shoot her then and there unless she married him immediately. Influenced both by awe and admiration of so doughty a lover, the fair Lillian went with him to a clergyman near by who married them, the clergyman's wife being the witness. She later averred that the soprano was in such a torrent of tears that she could not answer the questions put by the clergyman during the wedding ceremony; while the bridegroom, with flashing eyes and mustache on end, commanded the minister, "Go on! Prima donnas always behave this way when they are getting married."

Although Lillian Nordica learned her rôles with difficulty, she had the determination which carried her to such artistic heights that she will never be forgotten in musical annals. Her grit, reënforced by her beauty and her lovely voice, enabled her to do an amount of work which is truly astonishing. She was a worthy model for younger artists, any one of whom would do well to walk in her way.

French and Italian held sway as formerly, and under Mr. Grau English was seldom used during his régime. He was not particularly musical, and did not believe that anything but light opera or oratorio, in which he was not interested, could be sung in English. He also confessed to me that, if he had his way, he would never have any advanced Wagnerian music at all in his repertory. "Still," as he said, "the public seem to like it — I don't know why; but if they want it, it is my business to give it to them."

I had made arrangements with a concert manager to provide for me as many engagements as possible outside of my operatic work, and soon after my initial performance in New York, inaugurated a series of concerts in America that probably has few equals in the history of the profession. If the work of a busy singer is hard, it certainly is agreeable, and the successful artist has nothing whatever to complain of either in appreciation or in material gain, be the work ever so arduous.

As a matter of record, however, it may be of interest to the student to know that I appeared during the season of 1896–97 in America, before returning to Europe, eighty-three times; thirty-four of them in seven operas, two of the rôles being new in my repertory.

In concerts I sang forty-nine times in seventeen cities, introducing at several of these for the first time in America, not only Brahms's " Magelone," but the same composer's latest work, the " Four Serious Songs," which I had given in London the previous season almost immediately after Brahms had issued them.

It was doubtless through my association with Anton Seidl, as conductor at the Metropolitan opera, that I was engaged by the Philharmonic Society, which he also directed. Seidl was always friendly to me, seemed to take special interest in my work, and suggested that on the occasion of my first appearance at these concerts I should perform with Madame Clementine de Vere the duet from the second act of " The Flying Dutchman." At my second Philharmonic appearance, later in the season, I decided upon selecting two groups of Schubert's songs. Seidl later showed me his orchestral accompaniments to certain of the ballads of Loewe, and asked me to sing some of these at one of his Sunday night concerts at the Metropolitan Opera House. He was a great enthusiast, and I am proud to have come into as close touch with Richard Wagner himself as I did, through the artistic friendship of and much work with his two faithful disciples, Anton Seidl and Hans Richter. They handed on the brightly burning torch lit at the shrine of the great master whose works and methods they understood better than any one else — even than Cosima Wagner herself, who never ceased to inject her own ideas into the representation of her great husband's operas, which took place under her direction after his death, until Bayreuth became nothing less than a hotbed of jealousy, dissension and musical politics.

I have been informed by a well-known soprano that toward the end of her engagement at the Bavarian shrine, things became so disagreeable that she, like Lilli Lehmann, Madame Materna, and various other shining lights before her, was constrained never to appear there again, as the honor was by no means commensurate with the mental and spiritual discomfort, not to speak of the artistic belittlement to which well-known singers were subjected. In the case referred to the artiste was obliged to take orders from Cosima's daughter's maid, who attempted to instruct the experienced singer in the manner of wearing her garments and walking upon the stage, with the result that the soprano complained to the fountainhead, informing Madame Wagner in no uncertain terms that, while she was proud to obey her, she could not delegate this power to her daughters, much less to the servants of her daughters.

Singing under Seidl and Richter, no one was subjected to any supercilious treatment. These great men knew exactly what was to be done with the music, and every one associated with them knew that they knew, and accepted their readings and interpretations as authoritative beyond question.

It was during the last days of 1896 that the brothers de Reszke made their first appearance as Siegfried and The Wanderer respectively. The occasion was made trebly interesting by the appearance of Madame Melba as Brünnhilde. It was also Madame Melba's first appearance in German opera, and I well remember wishing her luck when, having finished my part as Hunding in the second act, I found her upon the stage with Jean de Reszke, who was assisting her to the rocky couch beneath the great tree, where presently the audience was to see her surrounded by the flames which Wotan called forth at the conclusion of " The Valkyrie," and in the sleep from which Siegfried was presently to awaken her. I took my place in a box to witness the remainder of the performance. Melba was extremely nervous, not only because she was singing in a language to which she was unaccustomed, but in a part which was entirely unsuited to her, and which, though she knew it perfectly, she was ill-advised to have assumed at all.

In this act Melba, accustomed to the older repertory, was apparently forgetful of the Wagnerian tradition to remain well within the scene, and Jean de Reszke, in the heavy fur coat of Siegfried, was kept busy patrolling the forward part of the stage to keep the white-clad Melba from rushing into the footlights, over which she had so many times sung to delighted audiences. Unfortunately for the celebrated and gifted prima donna the task she had here set herself was too much for her vocal powers and she sang but little in the subsequent performances of the season.

As the act progressed my mind was carried forcibly back to a scene that had greatly impresed me in boyhood. I had been to a fire at night in which an enormous barn and stable connected with a stock farm were completely destroyed. Many cattle which had been driven into adjacent fields were so attracted by the flames that a considerable force of men was kept busy preventing the animals from rushing headlong to death. Near where I stood in the night a white calf in great excitement was

trying to make its way toward the fire, but the field between the young animal and the conflagration was in this
instance patrolled by the mother cow, whose maternal
instinct was superior to the call of the light.

Illustrative of the vagaries of artists, I recall a Sunday
night concert at the Metropolitan Opera House, when
Calvé was on the bill with Plançon, myself, and others.
Opera singers are often not accustomed to concerts. Bare
boards without scenery; musicians on the stage instead of
in the orchestra pit; waiting through a disjointed collection of instrumental and vocal numbers until one has
to appear on the platform without that make-up which
is such a disguise and inside of which one feels so much
at home — such things as these often tend to make the
opera singer extremely nervous. Upon the occasion I
refer to, Madame Mantelli was calm, as indeed altos
usually are; the tenor Cremonini was moderately excited,
but Plançon was weeping violently, mopping from his
cheeks and beard the tears that continued to flow until the
moment for him to walk upon the platform; when, having given vent to his emotions in song, he quieted down
for the rest of the evening. I myself was somewhat upset by these manifestations of the idiosyncrasies of vocalists, especially when Madame Calvé demanded that the
orchestral accompaniment to her piece be transposed into
a key that was uncomfortable to the players as well as
for her voice. Later she had such a quarrel with Alvarez, the tenor, that as they performed in " Carmen "
together I was much relieved to find that Alvarez had
not planted his dagger between her shoulder blades as he
seemed to do, almost pinning her with his knife against
the door of the bull ring. But the curtain went up at

the end of the performance upon Calvé, smiling and beautiful as usual, while she and the tenor in all his glory took the rapturous curtain call.

That spring I visited Chicago several times, not only with the opera but for concert engagements. It happened that at this time Henry Irving and Ellen Terry were acting in the windy city. I found myself staying in the same hotel and on the same floor with Miss Terry, whom I had known in London for a number of years. Hearing me singing, she sent word by her attendant to ask if I would not do her the pleasure of rehearsing in her sitting-room. She wished to hear the music of which she was so fond, but of which naturally enough she could get but little, as she was constantly working and unable to attend concerts.

I was glad to do as the celebrated actress requested, and, though she remained much of the time in another room, she could hear everything that went on through the open door while I rendered several selections from my forthcoming concert. Presently Miss Terry entered the room and sat down quietly to listen. At the conclusion of the songs, she said: " I like some of those things very much, but what were those wonderful songs you sang half an hour ago? I could catch words from the Bible, and they sounded like the grandest sermon I ever heard in my life." I took from the piano the " Four Serious Songs " by Brahms, which she looked at and handled with a reverence that shed new light upon the character of this brilliant creature, whom I had already seen and admired in most of her repertory. I had frequently met her in private, but here she was at eleven o'clock in the morning, fresh and alert as always, clad in a comfortable dressing gown and slippers, looking like the mother of all the characters in which I had seen her upon the stage.

Earnestly she requested me to preach her that sermon over again. " Now," she said, " I am your congregation and will sit under you to listen to the truth, for I am persuaded that music is a part of the voice of the Almighty."

Though Brahms was not essentially dramatic in his style and never composed an opera, yet he gave out in this swan song something of the poignancy of the emotions which he felt, but which he so often elected to conceal from the world.

Never have I sung more feelingly to the largest of audiences than I did that morning to my audience of one. Carried away by the situation as I stood behind the back of a chair, I found myself actually using such gestures as an earnest clergyman might use, as he expounded to his congregation the Word of the Lord. As I finished, the tears that coursed down Miss Terry's cheeks were the most graceful tribute I had ever received, and yet the tribute was not to me, for I was merely the mouthpiece, the interpreter, of noble music wedded to words of power.

CHAPTER XXIII

FORTUNE GOOD AND ILL

Take all that comes, the hard goes with the soft;
All are from God and His decrees fulfill
— *From the Arabic.*

IN the classic auditorium of the Academy of Music in Philadelphia, assisted by my friends, the gentlemen of my beloved Orpheus Club, I gave early in the season one of my own concerts. No more loyal body of men ever supported an artist in his native city, after what they were pleased to call my triumph abroad, than this body of enthusiasts, who made me feel that the old saying, " A prophet is not without honor, save in his own country," was completely disproved. No one could have been more highly complimented than I was when they made me an honorary member of their society, and I almost came to believe that the world was assuming a fresh outlook on things, by which musical people would forego all symptoms of jealousy.

Perhaps the reason is to be found in the attitude of such societies of amateurs as the Orpheus Club, which in their intimate associations are on the plane of the dilettante, even though some of their members may be professionals, and do not allow any spirit of envy to enter the realm of art. The spirit of the amateur, the true lover of music, reigns supreme. I can truthfully say that when I myself was an amateur, I looked forward through each recurrent week to the Monday night rehearsal of this club with a delightful anticipation of the work which nothing else has ever given me.   True comradeship is incited by song, a oneness of heart and of purpose seldom aroused by other occupations.   I hope such bodies may spring up everywhere throughout the United States, each to become a nucleus around which a more extended musical life may grow.   Orchestras may well be founded in the same way from small beginnings, and thus may native talent, both vocal and instrumental, be cultivated to the great advantage of every community.

Early in January, 1897, I gave at the Carnegie Lyceum, the cozy little auditorium in the basement of Carnegie Hall, the first of my New York concerts, assisted by Miss Marguerite Hall and Mr. Gregorowitsch, the Russian violinist.   Upon that occasion, besides examples from the older classics, and the " Four Serious Songs " by Brahms, I gave a group consisting of six songs by living American composers: Dudley Buck, Henry Hadley, Reginald de Koven, Arthur Foote, H. H. Wetzler, and George W. Chadwick.   Ever since that time I have endeavored to keep before the American public the work of its own gifted men.   I was and am still well aware of the all but universal tendency to consider the work of any foreigner superior to that of our own people, but I have never held with that view, insisting that much foreign music is quite as bad as any that could possibly be produced in America.   Though naturally enough the best is always sought for, yet many are the mistakes which have been made in the concert room and at the Metropolitan Opera House in bringing forward compositions by foreigners, while well considered and carefully prepared material by our own native musicians has been deliberately put aside, or when performed has met with scant courtesy at the hands of press and public.

This attitude on the part of Americans is one that has puzzled me considerably. In the intimate social circles which supported imported art there were few with the courage to proclaim America and Americanism as Walt Whitman proclaimed it two generations ago, and the grand substratum of Europeanism remained. Most American men of leisure wanted to take their holiday in Europe, and American women knew that when they died they would go to Paris.

I gave that season three concerts of my own in New York, still assisted as in London by other artists. The brilliantly gifted Madame Corinne Moore Lawson, Miss Lillian Blauvelt, and the Kneisel Quartette added a distinction to my programs which otherwise might have been lacking. I was rapidly finding sufficient artistic poise for recitals alone, and before long I was able to dispense with any assistance but that of my own accompanist.

At first, not finding any one able to place himself entirely at my disposal, I was constrained to accept the services of pianists who, however talented, were unaccustomed to me and my ways. Let me say here, for the benefit of my successors, that it is obvious that the artist should not be obliged to fatigue himself with rehearsals just before the concert of which he is to bear the brunt. It will be found in the long run far better to undertake the expense of a permanent accompanist than to run the risk of a bad one or the nervousness of singing for the first time with any one, no matter how good.

Once, when I had been careful to send my music ahead to the pianist who had been selected for me and whose ability was vouched for by one whom I considered competent to judge, I found the clever young instrumentalist in such a state of alarm at the prospect of playing for me that, for all his ability, my concert was nearly ruined; certain pieces he was unable to cope with at all, and in their places others had to be substituted at the last moment.

Sometime before starting from London for New York, I had been asked by a friend to hunt up a brilliant musician named Blank, whose address was not given me. Upon reaching New York I inquired for him without avail. Later in the season, after returning from an operatic performance to the St. Botolph Club in Boston where I was staying, I sat at supper with two men who were quietly conversing as I read my letters. One of these was from my friend who, having learned Mr. Blank's address, sent it on to me. As I read the words, "Henry Blank can be found at such and such a place," I became aware that my two friends were speaking of Henry Blank. Hearing them I asked, "Whose name was that?" They replied, "Henry Blank, an excellent pianist. You should have him as your accompanist." I asked his address, one of them told it to me, and they were as surprised as I when I showed them my letter which I held in my hand. Whether this be a mere coincidence or a stroke of fate I am unable to tell. The result was that Blank was saved from suicide, contemplated because of lack of work, by the telegram I sent him that night. In a few days he became my accompanist and remained such for some time. The fact that he left me because his name appeared on the program was nothing against his artistic ability, but only proves my contention that artists should be treated differently from other people. Blank, it seems, did not wish to be known as an accompanist; he considered himself a solo pianist, and he would have been a fine one had his peculiarities not interfered. One of these peculiarities was to insist that his name should be omitted from any program in which he merely figured as an accompanist. Of this I was not aware and, of course, gave him credit upon the program at which he first appeared. I found him to be deeply offended, and was requested in no uncertain terms to leave his name off in the future.

It so happened that sometime later I was requested by the promoters of a concert in a city where I was to appear to permit the inclusion of certain piano pieces played by a local artist who had had considerable success in Europe; this I was, of course, glad to do. Unluckily it happened that Blank was known by those interested in this concert and they, finding his name omitted from the program which I had sent to the printer, inserted it without my knowledge. The result was that my eccentric friend was with difficulty persuaded to play for me at all that evening. Though he did so, he kept his word in the future and never played for me again, though I had some six weeks of concerts still to perform, which he had carefully prepared with me in advance. For the rest of my American season I had to get along with any one I could pick up, greatly to my disadvantage.

From that time Blank went down, and though we remained friends, yet he had difficulty in making a livelihood, and I, with others of his acquaintance, was called upon from time to time to see him through. At last it seemed to us that he could go no further, and he finally disappeared from our ken. We all recognized his talents, but were unable to make them work.

Some years afterward in London, Blank's card was handed in at my apartment, and what was my surprise to find, instead of the down-at-the-heels, shabby man whom I had last seen in New York, a beautifully dressed, clear-skinned, bright-eyed, healthy Englishman, none other than my old friend, who, as he took his leave after a pleasant conversation, told me that he had come to his senses and gone back to his home and family. Before leaving he casually remarked: " By the way, you were always very good to me, and saw me through some pretty hard times in my life. Let me see, I think the amount would add up to about so much, would it not? I never forget my friends "; and he proceeded to write a check for the amount of his indebtedness, which was at once honored. The talented Mr. Blank then disappeared out of my ken as suddenly as he had come into it.

The artist's life, like the policeman's, is not always a happy one. During my first American season it was necessary for me to go to a certain city to sing at a concert, where I was pursued almost on to the stage by an officer of the court bearing a legal warrant to collect out of my fee, if he could, certain moneys to satisfy a debt contracted some time before by the person who booked me for this concert. I have always thought it an outrage that the law should permit the public performances of an artist to be interfered with in this way, even though the money should be rightly due from the artist, who by the interference with his performance would naturally be rendered incapable of earning the wherewithal to satisfy his debt. The biblical narrative tells how the severe creditor threw his debtor into prison till he should pay to the uttermost farthing, but surely we have grown beyond this antiquated code!

Fortunately, in my case nothing untoward happened. By calling upon all the resources of the actor, I managed so to scare the officer of the law with my pretended rage that he begged for mercy and tried to find the door to get away from the madman, who he thought would do him bodily injury. Those who saw the scene begged me to calm myself, reminding me that I had to sing in a few minutes, and were surprised to see me come smiling out of my anger the instant the door was closed behind the minion of the law.

Upon another occasion, at one of my concerts in a city that shall remain nameless, great was the apparent concern of the local manager who stated that, though the concert had been successful, for it was given before a large audience, he was unable to pay me for my services because of an action taken by his creditors. But he reëngaged me to come again with another artist, when, as he said, he would be able to give me a check for both appearances. On the second occasion, however, the manager of the assisting artist, learning what had previously taken place, put a representative into the box office on behalf of his client, with the result that when he had his money and other creditors obtained theirs, I came for the second time empty away.

Such experiences have been infrequent, I am glad to say; but a number of years afterward, upon visiting the same city to appear in an orchestral concert, I was waited upon by the president of the society, its conductor, and its treasurer, to whom as we sat in my room I narrated what had happened at my earlier appearances. We all had a good laugh over it and I was assured that nothing of the kind could happen now, as a splendid audience would be in attendance. On proceeding to the rehearsal I found to my disappointment that the orchestra was a scratch affair, the occasion not being one of any importance, so that the ultimate performance was poor and resulted in my getting a check for one-sixth of the amount of my contract, the balance of which I have never been able to collect to this day. Needless to say I shook the dust of that town from my shoes for ever. Let it be clearly understood that such occurrences as those I have related are very rare; I do not wish to besmirch the reputation of the music givers of America, to whom I am so greatly indebted.

CHAPTER XXIV

CYCLES OF SONG

For doth not Song to the whole world belong?
Is it not given wherever tears may fall;
Wherever hearts can melt, or blushes glow,
Or mirth or sadness mingle as they flow —
A heritage for all?

— Author unknown.

ALTOGETHER I had a busy, valuable, and interesting season in my native country and returned to London rather pleased with myself over having made such a good beginning. There was a certain amount of *kudos* gained from the fact that I, an American, had been asked to go with the foreigners to the United States. Few of my countrywomen had returned from Europe to sing upon the operatic stage, and no American men, so that I may be said to have been the first.

Soon after reaching England I gave another of my own recitals, bringing forward what was, in its entirety, as new to the London public as it was to New York, "The Beautiful Magelone," by Brahms, and telling in a few words between the numbers the story by Ludwig Tieck, a quaint little mediæval tale upon which lovely lyrics are strung as pearls upon a thread.

All the great song cycles are founded upon poems of romance. Beethoven's early attempt, "To the Distant Beloved," is one of them; a breathing out of emotion, of longing to be again by the side of the dear one, and has no great depth of sentiment. In Schubert's "Songs of

204

the Mill " and " The Winter Journey," we find veritable gems of song. Schumann, in setting Heine's " Dichterliebe " (Poet's Love), had at hand something of a tragedy, for the lady jilts her lover and marries a rich man. In his still more beautiful cycle called " Frauenliebe und Leben " (Woman's Love and Life), domestic happiness is revealed.

All of these, however, except Woman's Love and Life, are songs for a man, though women frequently undertake them, perhaps not realizing the artistic error into which they fall. Yet it is said in England that one of the most beautiful musical experiences ever known was that of hearing Jenny Lind render the " Songs of the Mill." I asked Otto Goldschmidt why his wife had sung songs intended for a man; but he seemed to find that there was nothing incongruous in it, in view of the fact that she had sung them so exquisitely.

I happen to have in my possession a letter from Professor Max Müller, the son of the Wilhelm Müller who wrote the poems. Max Müller I knew rather well; he was fond of music, and attended my first production of the " Müller Lieder " at St. James's Hall. In thanking me for what he seemed to feel was a new light which I had shed upon these, he told me in his note that many years before Jenny Lind had sung them for him, thinking he would like to hear his father's poem rendered by her. It is known that her voice went off considerably in her middle life, and I imagine it was partly because of this that the philologist expressed himself as being so deeply disappointed by the great cantatrice's rendition.

My work during the London season of 1897 was almost entirely confined to the opera; though, besides my own concerts, a few other appearances preceded the open-

ing of the opera season. One of these was with Mottl
in the third act of Wagner's " Parsifal," in which I
again had the great artistic joy of singing the noble
phrases allotted to the anguish-ridden Amfortas. The
two months following were so filled with operatic performances and their necessary rehearsals that little work
could be done outside Covent Garden. There I had
twenty-five appearances in seven master works within two
months. My own efforts were entirely devoted to the
operas of Wagner, with the single exception of Kienzl's
" Evangelimann," in which I played the part of the
scoundrelly brother Johannes to the saintly Mathias of
Van Dyck and the Magdalena of Madame Schumann-
Heink.

It may be interesting to students to know that when in
America during the previous few months I had studied
this rôle while on tour by means of the recorded music
upon the pianola. Not having an accompanist always at
hand, I would take the perforated rolls specially prepared for me, place them upon an instrument in my
apartment, and turn on the music. The accompaniment
was thus played mechanically and could be turned back
whenever I made a mistake and wished to begin over,
while I, the book before me, committed the lines to
memory, and either closed my eyes or turned away as I
desired to repeat my part without looking at the notes.

The other characters performed that season were Telramund, Beckmesser, Kurwenal, Alberich, Wotan, and
Wolfram. All these were, of course, by this time sung
in German with the exception of " Tannhäuser," which,
owing to the presence of French artists at Covent Garden
that year, was sung in the French text prepared by Wagner himself for the first Parisian production. I origi-

nally studied the opera in Italian; then in German; while on the occasion of the performances of the fiftieth anniversary of the work it was given in English; and now it was in French! Journet was the Landgrave, Van Dyck Tannhäuser, and Madame Eames Elizabeth. The conductor was Mancinelli, to whom it was all one in what language anything was sung; his language was the language of music.

At this time I had an interesting evening with Henry Irving. No one had been a harder worker than he, nor in his day had played more parts. He said, " Ah, my boy! " in his peculiar manner, " I see what you are doing at the opera — something different every time you play, eh? It reminds me of myself once; nowadays I have long runs. Yes, yes, so much for success; but the time was when I had to play a different thing every night, too; more of them than you do now, many more, only all that I did was in our own language; you have to sing sometimes in Italian, sometimes in French, sometimes in German, besides singing in English. Then, there's the music! How the devil do you know what is coming next? How do you keep one opera separate from the other in your mind? I can't make head or tail out of it. Ah, but it is a great life; yes, yes, my boy, a great life! Hard work, though — what? — hard work."

" Well, Sir Henry," said I, " hard work doesn't seem to trouble you at all."

" No," said he, " I like it; the more of it the better for me. As long as a man is interested he's happy, if he is happy he is content, and if he is content he is all right. Work as hard as you like, it will not hurt you, if you're happy and content. So, my boy, even with all those languages and all that music, if you like it, you're all right! But what puzzles me is, how you know when to come in! I don't know much about music," he added, " but I like a tune, and I don't find any tune in that damned German music!"

The company at Covent Garden that year was indeed of the best, including all the great people, and under Anton Seidl I had the joy of singing Wotan in " The Valkyrie " with Van Dyck, the talented American, Susan Strong, Schumann-Heink, and the superb Marie Brema.

My inches are not great, though my voice was adequate for that and many subsequent occasions as the Master of the Gods; but to simulate a height much greater than my own was a rather difficult thing to do, particularly when I was contrasted with persons taller than myself. It is interesting for an amateur and student to know how an artist supplies natural deficiencies. In my case, there being no secret about it, I confess to availing myself of every aid that costuming and make-up can afford. On my feet were buskins with heavy soles, including insoles and high heels, which together gave me an extra three inches. The cloak that hung from my shoulders reached nearly to the ground in perpendicular lines to add to the effect of height, there was long blond hair and beard, a helmet crowned my head with two great eagle wings rising from its sides, and I carried a long spear. As I am sturdy of build, the effect was remarkable from the front. I was constantly surprising myself in my make-up, as the god Wotan one night and the dwarf Alberich the next; now the stalwart Telramund and then the querulous Beckmesser. But these things are " all one," as the Clown says in " Twelfth Night " :

> " But that's all one, our play is done,
> And we'll strive to please you every day."

DAVID BISPHAM

as Wotan in Wagner's "Valkyrie."
From a Photograph by Arnold Genthe, New York

Before leaving for America I had an invitation to sing at the Birmingham festival in the autumn of 1897, and while in New York had been engaged to appear at the festival at Worcester, Massachusetts, which began only two weeks earlier than that at Birmingham. It will readily be seen that it was necessary for me to bestir myself if I were to sing at both of these gatherings. That feat, however, was accomplished after a holiday taken to recuperate from the fatigues of the London season, by returning to America in September, just long enough to take part in four of the Worcester concerts. What was most vividly impressed upon my mind there was the performance of Horatio Parker's beautiful oratorio " Hora Novissima," Madame Gadski, Gertrude May Stein, Evan Williams, and myself being the quartette fortunate enough to render this distinguished composition.

In this connection I am glad to say that upon my return to England I not only carried word of the success of Parker's work to the directors of the Birmingham festival, but took with me as well a copy of the music, which I placed in the hands of Richter, by whom it was at once appreciated. He showed it to others, with the result that not long afterward this work was performed in Worcester Cathedral at the Festival of the Three Choirs, and because of its English reception our distinguished American musician received an honorary degree from Cambridge University.

It is unnecessary to give the programs of the two functions at which I sang in such close proximity; suffice it to say that our oldest American festival did not in the least suffer, all things being considered, by comparison with the splendid performances of the much older institution at Birmingham. There is in America, however, a lack of ceremoniousness, almost amounting to informality, in contrast to similar occasions abroad.   I recall two cases of assumption on the part of great prima donnas who took part in such entertainments in the United States which could hardly have happened in England.   One of these queens of song entered the artists' room in the festival hall, stared around superciliously, and inquired, "Who are all these people?"   She was told that they were the other principals, members of the committee, and others having official relations with the function. Haughtily declining an introduction to any of them, she demanded a dressing room of her own.   One was hastily extemporized in a corner of the auditorium near the stage, from which my lady emerged in her royal raiment, as frigid as an icicle, leaving her audience fairly frost-bitten.   Even more famous was the other diva who found the hall at the dress rehearsal crowded with auditors. She demanded to know who they were, and what they were doing at a rehearsal.   It was explained that the houses for the regular performances had been sold out, and the public demand was so great that these townsfolk had been admitted for a small sum to hear as much as they could under the circumstances.   "If they have paid you," the songstress rejoined, "you will have to pay me." When the music began, she sang under her voice so that she could not be heard by the orchestra.   It was explained that she must sing louder.   "Send these people away, then!" she ordered.   The management had to do as she wished rather than submit to an extortion, and the audience, departing, carried word of such arrant cupidity throughout the city, to which neither lady ever returned.

Quite otherwise was a certain artist treated at one of the English festivals, where no such nonsense is put up with. The festival opened at the customary hour or eleven o'clock in the morning. One of the principal soloists had not arrived, and did not arrive, for over an hour. Another artist sang her part, for she had forgotten that she had to appear, and was sound asleep.

When she arrived at the hall she was ushered into the committee room, where the heads of the festival threatened to terminate her engagement then and there. On her knees, before the outraged committee, she was so far forgiven as to be permitted to finish her engagement, but that door for further advancement remained forever closed to her.

At Birmingham, besides " Elijah," " The Messiah," and many other choral and miscellaneous works, there was given Purcell's " King Arthur," which in its quaint old style was extremely effective, reproducing in 1897 the work first heard in 1691. This contains the remarkable Frost Scene, which I have since so often performed in my concerts. Love comes to the frozen North and bids the " Genius of Cold awake, and winter from his furry mantle shake." Then is seen to arise the majestic figure of the Frost King, icicles depending from his hair and beard. As he shakes himself free from the snow, he addresses Love in shivering accents; but to utter Dryden's extraordinary lines effectively is a task which might puzzle any vocalist, for the voice must shake, literally shake and chatter, with the cold. The piece cannot be sung, in the ordinary acceptation of the word *song;* it has to be rendered, but rendered effectively; and I may say, without boasting, I have known half the women in the audience to draw their cloaks about them before I had finished my declamation of this two-century-old novelty.

Richter prepared this antiquated music with great care,

amusing us by his quaint pronunciation of English. When he first came to London, his accent and general manner caused many stories to be told about him. On one occasion he had been invited with his wife, whom he adored, to go for an extended visit to a country house not far from London. Richter had to come up to town every few days, and at the railway station bought a return ticket for himself, and a single ticket for his wife. To the amusement of the bystanders he was heard to ask in a loud voice, " Giff me two tickets, vone for me to come back, and vone for my vife,— not to come back! "

During their residence in England Mrs. Richter became ill and was afflicted with attacks of fainting,— what the Germans call *schwindeln,*— and had to lie down. When some one solicitously inquired of the great conductor after the health of his wife, Doctor Richter replied: " My vife, she is very bad; venn she does not lie she schwindles."

It was rather a rush to sing upon Friday evening in Worcester, Massachusetts, and catch the steamer on Saturday morning in New York in order to present myself a week later at Birmingham, England, where I had faithfully promised the committee to be for the final full rehearsals. Richter was satisfied before I left for America that I knew the work that I was to perform; but I was not prepared for a heavy fog off the Irish coast, which did not allow my vessel to land in Liverpool until Sunday. I sent a telegram from Queenstown and, much ashamed of myself, arrived at Birmingham on Sunday morning during a rehearsal. All went well, however, and I was forgiven, as I had to contend against *force majeure.*

A few days after the conclusion of the Birmingham

festival, I was invited to appear before Queen Victoria at her Scotch country seat of Balmoral Castle. Great statesmen and brave warriors had quailed before that little old lady, who knew everything that went on within her realm; and I have rarely been afflicted with such an attack of nerves as that from which I suffered that evening before a company of ladies and gentlemen, many of whom I knew. All of them probably understood what was going on under my evening coat and in the neighborhood of my knees.

The castle, by the way, is not a castle but merely a good-sized country house, much less ostentatious than those occupied by many of the English nobility and gentry. I was put up at a neighboring inn and brought during the evening to the royal residence, where I was made comfortable until, dinner over, the Queen, having reached the drawing-room, would be ready to receive me.

I was informed by one of the gentlemen-in-waiting how to make my entrance into the royal presence. On stepping into the room I was to bow once, take two steps forward, and bow again; two more steps forward, bow again, and I would then be at my place beside the piano. My accompanist, having done likewise, was to take his seat, and the music was to begin immediately. The little rehearsal having been gone through satisfactorily, I tremblingly entered the august presence, did as I was told, and proceeded to sing, the program having been arranged beforehand by correspondence with one of the ladies of Queen Victoria's immediate circle.

The Monarch was seated at a little table in the middle of a rather large room, the windows of which were hung with tartan plaid. She had on enormous spectacles and with the aid of a magnifying glass she consulted the program, which had been written in large letters and placed upon the table beside her. It happened that as I was singing Schubert's " Who is Sylvia," the Queen lifted the glass to read my program, just as I sang the words:

> " Love doth to her eyes repair
> To help him of his blindness."

When I came to this passage, she quickly dropped the magnifying glass and put down the program, as much as to say, " I need nothing to help me of my blindness! " I afterward learned that she was sensitive about her rapidly failing eyesight. Upon finishing the first half of my short selection of songs, the Queen's principal lady-in-waiting came forward and took me to her Majesty, who spoke with me some minutes kindly, asking about myself, my English ancestry, and my American life and artistic desires. When the concert was over she expressed her gratification at the performance, and I departed from the presence to be entertained at supper by some of the gentlemen of the household. A few days later I received as a memento of the occasion a beautiful scarfpin from Queen Victoria, with an appreciative note thanking me for the pleasure the music had given her Majesty.

CHAPTER XXV

BEETHOVEN IN DRAMA

This is our master, famous, calm, and dead,
Borne on our shoulders.— *Robert Browning.*

AFTER all my experience I seldom felt that I was really acting in opera, and always longed to take part in straight drama; though opera was my business and my pleasure as well, I nearly always felt myself in an anomalous position. To sing was one thing, to act quite a different matter; but both to sing and act seemed to me somewhat artificial. I have found operatic acting so limited by the music that it imposes a restraint upon the performer and often obliges him to make gestures which carry no conviction. But some gestures have to be made; the singer cannot stand motionless as in a concert. Opera acting is *sui generis* and would be entirely out of place and grotesque in drama. Yet fortunately such parts as generally fell to my lot on the lyric stage were so strong in character that they are not open to these objections.

Some years before, when living in Florence and studying for concert work, I was shown by a friend an old photograph, which at first I took to be a copy of Beethoven's portrait. This was not the case, however, for the picture was the representation of a well-known Viennese actor in the part of Beethoven in a little play by Hugo Müller called " Adelaïde." I was greatly interested and realized that I, too, could look like Beethoven. I made

215

up my mind to act the part, though I did not know where the play could be found. Several years later I mentioned the matter to a friend in London, who said he knew of the play and had seen it in Germany. As he was starting for Berlin that very day he promised to make inquiries of an actor of his acquaintance and try to obtain it for me. A few weeks after, I was delighted to find that he had brought me a little pamphlet yellow with age which he had seen by chance upon a second-hand book stall in the street and bought for a few pence. With my German master I immediately set to work translating it, though there seemed then to be no opportunity of performing the piece. This opportunity came, however, as all things come to him who waits.

Soon after I reached America in October, 1897, my friend Morris Bagby, at whose now famous Musical Mornings I had already sung twice, asked me if I had anything new to vary the character of these entertainments, particularly of that with which the ballroom in the new Waldorf-Astoria Hotel was to be opened on December 6. I told Mr. Bagby of my musical find in the Beethoven play. Very enthusiastic, he immediately made arrangements to produce it and to have Anton Seidl with his orchestra render a short program of the master's music before the play began. In the cast were Mrs. Wolcot and Mrs. Whiffen, two of the most distinguished elder actresses of the American stage, and the beautiful Julie Opp, later Mrs. William Faversham, who was admirable in the title rôle. The services of these three ladies were loaned me through the courtesy of my friend Daniel Frohman, from the famous company of the old Lyceum Theater, which then stood in Fourth Avenue near Twenty-fourth Street. I had the further assistance of Miss Nita Carritte and of MacKenzie Gordon, the sweet-voiced Scotch tenor, who played the other male part and sang Beethoven's exquisite lyric, "Adelaïde."

The piano on the stage, which represented as nearly as possible the interior of the room in which Beethoven died, was the master's own concert grand, which had been kindly loaned me for this occasion by Morris Steinert of New Haven, out of his famous collection of old instruments.

As I sat in my dressing room before the play, I had beside me on the table a bust of Beethoven, from which I was making up. The touches here and there, added to the assumed expression on my own countenance, made the resemblance between my face and that of the bust quite remarkable. A friend, entering the room at my back, saw my face in the glass and that of the bust over my shoulder, and in amazement exclaimed, " If you were whitened or the bust colored no one could distinguish between the two heads." Thus encouraged I went on with my part. At the conclusion of the play, Seidl came on the stage, his eyes all red, and said to me in a broken voice, " You are ze only man vich haff effer made me to veep."

The occasion was memorable to me in more ways than one, and led to many subsequent performances of the piece that season in New York, Philadelphia, Boston, Chicago, and also in London during the following summer. There were changes of cast, which included the names of Yvonne de Tréville and Kitty Cheatham as Clara and Hilda Spong as Adelaïde; and I had on several of these occasions either Mr. Damrosch to conduct the Beethoven program for my play, or the Dannreuther Quartette to play the master's chamber music, or Ma-

dame Gadski to sing. The performances without exception gave pleasure and made an indelible impression on
the minds of our audiences, but for some reason the Press
has with almost one accord objected to the presentation
of Beethoven on the stage, several critics even going so
far as to hold that I was trespassing upon sacred ground
in impersonating him.

Events had brought about a cessation of opera under
Mr. Grau, but my second American season began, nevertheless, at the Metropolitan Opera House, where I assisted Madame Marcella Sembrich at her first appearance
in concert in America, when that celebrated and gifted
lady sang in superb fashion. On several subsequent occasions that season was I honored by Madame Sembrich's
request to participate with her in her concerts in New
York and elsewhere. It will be recalled that we had
both been pupils of the old Italian master, Francesco
Lamperti. Sembrich had the advantage over almost any
singer I ever knew in being so musical as to have practically mastered both violin and piano before taking up the
study of the voice. Being so fine a musician it is no wonder that she was able to accomplish what she did in her
later years. Added to these accomplishments was a
great histrionic talent, which made her one of the outstanding ornaments of her profession.

The season upon which I embarked in this way turned
out to be one of the busiest of my whole career: it gave
me 112 appearances in 28 American cities, in most of
which I had not sung before, embraced every kind of
vocal work, including opera, oratorio, my own individual
song recitals, miscellaneous concerts, and musical festivals, such as those of Indianapolis, of Ann Arbor, and
the famous Cincinnati festival, with which my season

closed. During these appearances I sang in ten different oratorios or works of a similar nature. For the sake of the student I will mention their names: Handel's " Messiah," Mendelssohn's " Elijah," Beethoven's " Missa Solemnis," Schumann's " Paradise and the Peri," Berlioz's " Damnation of Faust," Gounod's " Redemption," Benoist's " Lucifer," Massenet's " Eve," Grieg's " Olaf Trygvasson," and Stehle's " Frithiof's Return," besides selections from " Parsifal " and other Wagnerian music dramas.

However interesting such concerts and festivals as these may seem to the singer, however valuable they are to his artistic standing, it is nevertheless a fact that grand opera exercises the greatest influence upon the mind, not only of the participant, but upon that of the public as well. The average music lover thinks more of an opera singer than he does of an oratorio singer, nor is the reason far to seek — the glamour of the stage holds undisputed sway, and a story told in choral form is far less impressive than a story told in costume, with action, and upon a stage furnished with appropriate scenery.

While singing at the Metropolitan Opera House, during the previous season, we were given to understand that most of the money made in New York was lost during the opera company's visit to Chicago. Whatever may have been the reason for the temporary abandonment of opera, the fact remains that Maurice Grau did not have an opera company in New York during the season of 1897–98. During the previous year, Walter Damrosch had conducted a season of grand opera in Philadelphia, and, the field being left open in 1897–98, in conjunction with Charles Ellis, manager of the Boston Symphony Orchestra, he inaugurated in the Quaker City that winter a season of opera, which was continued in New York, Boston, and Chicago and which yielded the new firm of impresarios a handsome return. Even Chicago, which the previous year was loath to patronize opera, now turned out its beauty and fashion and mightily encouraged the young impresarios who had dared to tread the path which such a master as Maurice Grau had followed almost to his ruin. The motto of Damrosch and Ellis might well have been " Nothing venture, nothing win." As a matter of fact they did venture, and they did win.

An admirable company had been gathered together, headed by Mesdames Melba and Nordica, and also the talented young singer Madame Gadski. Among the tenors were Salignac the Frenchman, and Kraus the German; among the barytones and basses were Campanari, an Italian, Emil Fischer, and myself; and a considerable repertory of opera was given, standard works of the French and Italian schools, but more particularly of Wagnerian music-drama, of which the public of those days never had enough.

Any opera season is likely to have its surprises, and the surprise of that year was the success of " The Flying Dutchman." The character was not new to me, yet was one in which I had never before felt myself entirely at home. Doubtless the reason for its popularity that season was that Damrosch took up the work with enthusiasm, whereas my previous performances in London had been conducted in a perfunctory manner by those who did not really care for the music, characterized by Madame Eames at the time as a " back number." Then, too, we had the great advantage of the assistance of Madame Gadski, who perfectly suited the part of Elsa.

I have often wondered whether the public can realize what the work of a busy artist obliges him to do. The opera season in Philadelphia was so arranged that about two weeks elapsed before I had to appear again with Mr. Damrosch's organization; my manager booked a number of concerts which I proceeded to fulfill meanwhile. After singing with the Boston Symphony Orchestra in Philadelphia, I appeared the following evening in Washington as Telramund in "Lohengrin" with our opera company. Proceeding immediately to Brooklyn, I sang again with the Boston Symphony Orchestra at the old Academy of Music on the afternoon of December 17. That evening Ysaye, the Belgian violinist, and I appeared with Anton Seidl and his orchestra, this being the last time I ever had the opportunity of singing with that great conductor. I sang once more with the Boston Symphony under Emil Paur the following evening before taking a train for Milwaukee, where I appeared in " The Messiah " on December 20. Repeating that oratorio in Chicago on December 21, I was off for St. Louis for the same work and sang there December 22, thence back to Chicago again for " The Messiah " the evening after. Jumping to Nashville, Tennessee, I took part there on Christmas Day in a recital of songs, returning to New York for " The Messiah " with the Oratorio Society at Carnegie Hall on December 29 and 30, and sang in Philadelphia on December 31 in " The Flying Dutchman " under Mr. Damrosch's conducting.

Seated comfortably at breakfast, audiences of a previous evening read the accounts of the music they have heard, but we artists are not enjoying the repose which most people think we take to a much greater extent than

themselves. Far from it! A busy vocalist has probably taken a train after the evening performance, traveled all night, been obliged to get up in the early morning, make a hasty toilet, get a hurried breakfast at the
hotel, and attend a rehearsal by ten o'clock for a performance that afternoon or evening. After which, even
if a night in bed is possible, comes a call at five or six
o'clock in order to catch a train at seven for a journey all
day to appear in another city. This is not in the least
uncommon; yet I have often been taunted with the laxity
of my life; with the late hours in which it is supposed that
I indulge myself, and with the comfortable sleep that I
am believed to be enjoying in the lap of luxury until near
noon. Nay, nay, admiring public; such is not the case!
The singers who you think are getting fat from laziness
are in all probability getting fat because they have not
time enough to take the exercise they would like, or, during the time they might be exercising, are too tired to indulge in it, but have to go to bed half dead.

The last opera to be performed in Philadelphia at the
close of a repertory which included the whole of the
Wagnerian " Niebelungen Ring," was Damrosch's " The
Scarlet Letter," in which Gadski and Kraus were admirable as Hester and Arthur respectively and in which
I reveled in the disagreeable but interesting character
part of Chillingworth, a part that I regret not having
had any further opportunity to perform, as this interesting work has never, to my knowledge, been revived.

Mr. Damrosch tells an amusing story of a supper
party given in his honor by those who participated in
" The Scarlet Letter " after the occasion of a previous
presentation. It is to be supposed that the artists were
foreigners and did not in reality understand the mean-

ing of the words they were singing in English, or they would not, with considerable ceremony and many complimentary speeches, have presented Mr. Damrosch with a large scarlet letter A which they placed upon his breast.

CHAPTER XXVI

MY NATIVE TONGUE

The more I sang in foreign tongues the more I loved my own.— After De Belloy.

I HAVE ever inveighed against the custom, so happily on the wane, which for so long obliged us English-speaking artists to sing in England and in the United States in the languages, French, Italian, or German of our musical *confrères,* who are too indolent, to say the least, to learn English. In Italy the audiences desire to hear operas sung in their own beautiful accents. Germany and France have long ago broken away from singing operas in Italian. The Germans love their rich but rough tongue, while the French treat their exquisite language with the highest respect and the government maintains theatres and opera houses, where French only is spoken or sung and where it must be enunciated to perfection. In England and America, as has often been pointed out, operatic and orchestral music has, for many decades, been imported. It took a long time for the English to understand that their own people were able to write music as well as the inhabitants of any other country. Once let us learn the art and encourage the practice of it, and America will surely realize that the same idea should prevail here.

Though I have studied Italian, French, and German and have sung in them for years, I cannot be said to be proficient in those languages, and it has always seemed a pity that we should be obliged to sing in tongues which we can only partly understand, to English and American audiences who do not understand us at all. There is nothing bad in English, as a medium for song, except bad English.

It was early in 1898 that the Liza Lehmann song cycle, " In a Persian Garden," the words selected from the Rubáiyát of Omar Khayyám, was performed in New York for the first time after its English *première*, from the music which I had brought from London, by a quartette consisting of Mrs. Seabury Ford, soprano, Marguerite Hall, alto, MacKenzie Gordon, tenor, and myself, bass, under the direction of Victor Harris, who presided at the piano. The entrancing strains of this exquisite composition were frequently rendered by us during that and subsequent seasons and were taken up by many other quartettes throughout the country, and it soon became widely known, individual numbers even being sung in churches.

The season following it was revived by me at one of my concerts in London, but, whatever the reason, it never became as popular in its native land as in the United States, notwithstanding its beautiful and thoroughly intelligible English.

At the conclusion of this season I gave a concert at Mendelssohn Hall, when I was surprised in a way that I had not thought to be by an American audience. Hitherto, though singing frequently in English, I had yielded to the tastes of the public and performed in other languages. But on this occasion my recital consisted entirely of, and was called, " Gems of Song in English," with the result that I had a larger and more enthusiastic audience than I had ever had before. I received an eye-opener as to the gradually changing tastes of the public.

So great was the success of this concert that I repeated its program upon various occasions elsewhere, and continue the practice of singing in English to this day, unless there is some special reason for doing otherwise, as in the rendering of the cycles of songs by Schumann, Schubert, or Brahms in the original German, rather than in an indifferent translation. Yet at that time, when singing Brahms's "Four Serious Songs," I remember being taken to task by some one who wanted to know why I did not sing them "in the original German." My reply was that I considered the words of the Scripture to be sufficiently original for English-speaking people, and that we did not need a German translation for what was our daily bread, or ought to be.

Of course, I was rapidly making acquaintance with American musicians. Among these was the talented young composer, Henry Hadley, to whom I am indebted for many engagements and many of whose earlier songs I helped to bring out. I sang the clever reconstruction made by Henry Holden Huss from the memoranda Beethoven had made for a setting of "The Erl King," and also Huss's musical setting for "The Seven Ages of Man," which I first gave in 1898 in America, later in London, and which I continue to sing to the present time.

After the opera I had a busy and interesting season of concert engagements at various music centers, including the festival in Indianapolis under Van der Stucken, and at Ann Arbor, Michigan, under Professor Albert A. Stanley of the University of Michigan, who has been one of the great forces in music in America for the past twenty-five years. Nearly all the principals at the festival were Americans, with the exception of a man whom I had never thought to be associated with, it had been so long since I, as a youth, had seen him in his prime upon the operatic stage. I refer to the Italian barytone, Signor Giuseppe Del Puente; he sang that year in Verdi's "Manzoni" Requiem Mass. Though his voice was diminishing in volume, his art was still supreme. Del Puente had been living and teaching in Philadelphia, where I had met him shortly before. I remember him running to compliment me in the old-fashioned, spacious, portrait-hung greenroom of the Academy of Music, as I came off the stage after singing in some opera. "Ah," he said, "you move your tongue in just the right way; I can see everything he do."

This was a curious sidelight upon his vocal methods. I had always admired Del Puente's luscious tones, never thinking of how he made them. He seems to have thought that the tongue should stand up at the end while I had been taught it should lie flat in the mouth. If my tongue was unduly prominent it was from accident rather than design; according to Del Puente's method I should have intentionally let the audience see it at work. Each vocal teacher has his own ideas and becomes set in his ways, perhaps thinking that similar methods will bring forth equally good results with his pupils. Of this I am not at all persuaded. Any means to a vocal end should be concealed as far as possible from the public. It is, however, difficult in singing either to practice what we preach, or to preach what we practice. The proof of the vocal pudding, however, is in the hearing; what is really good to hear has been properly produced, and *vice versa.* What is not agreeable is either not naturally good, or, whatever the care spent upon it, has been injured in the making. More likely than not too many cooks have helped to spoil the broth.

The most important festival of 1898 was that of Cincinnati, where for the first time I sang under Theodore Thomas, whom I had admired from boyhood. Though he did not know me, it so happened that I had the lion's share and opened with Berlioz's " Damnation of Faust." The following afternoon and evening were miscellaneous concerts with symphonic music by Mozart, Beethoven, Franck, Brahms, Weber, and Dvořák, vocal numbers from Handel, Weber, Schubert, Wagner, and Liszt, and choral work by Bach and Grieg. The fourth concert was devoted entirely to Beethoven, Symphony No. 5 and the " Missa Solemnis." The fifth concert entirely to Schumann: the Fourth Symphony and his choral work, " Paradise and the Peri." The sixth concert consisted of symphonic and vocal music of modern composers, Brahms, Marschner, Rimsky Korsakoff, Dvořák, Smetana, Berlioz, Ponchielli, Saint-Saëns, Boito, and Hugo Kaun, the American. The final concert was entirely Wagnerian, with copious selections from " The Flying Dutchman " and " Parsifal."

This thirteenth biennial festival afforded as fine a feast of sound as any one could wish to hear, carried out under one of the world's ablest conductors, who had under his baton a superb orchestra of his own choosing and a chorus which had behind it many years of work and a great reputation, which it nobly supported at his command. Again were the principals all Americans, with the exception of the Scottish soprano Miss Mac-

Intyre and the tenor Ben Davies, with whom I had been so frequently associated in opera in England. With that festival ended my second American season, which in the total amounted to 108 appearances.

CHAPTER XXVII

ENTER DANNY DEEVER

If a man were permitted to make all the ballads, he need not care who should make the laws of a nation.— Andrew Fletcher.

TOWARD the end of 1897 Walter Damrosch had been devoting his attention to the composition of a few songs and among others produced admirable settings of Rudyard Kipling's " Mandalay " and " Danny Deever." When I first sang the latter at the Academy of Music in Philadelphia, December 11, at a concert of the Orpheus Club, I had no idea that it would soon become famous throughout the United States. The ballad had already been set to music several times, though the compositions authorized by Mr. Kipling in England were not known in artistic circles, but were sung only by Tommy Atkins at large. In America Richard Harding Davis, who by the way was a kinsman of mine on his mother's side, conceived a good straightforward tune which was sung by the students at Princeton, and I first made its acquaintance through the splendid bass voice of my friend Booth Tarkington, who trolled it out with fine effect. It was not long, however, until all rival compositions gave way before the virility of Mr. Damrosch's conception of the piece.

When Kipling visited New York in 1899 I met him at an evening reception given in his honor at the house of the editor-poet, Richard Watson Gilder. Though it was not a musical party, toward the close of the evening

I was requested to sing " Danny Deever," by that time famous everywhere. At the conclusion of the song Kipling rose, hastily said good-by to his hostess, and left the room, to the surprise of every one present, who wished to congratulate him on the power of his text. After recovering from the attack of pneumonia brought on that very night through leaving the hot drawing-room for the snowstorm outside, he returned to England.

The next spring I had a visit from a gentleman who called ceremoniously and politely informed me that his friend Kipling, who was in the country, sent me his apologies and regrets for what I might have thought rudeness in leaving the room so suddenly after my singing of his " Danny Deever " in New York the winter before; but Mr. Kipling would like me to know that he had been so powerfully affected by my rendering of the ballad that he could not trust himself to speak and had to say good night as quickly as possible. Here was indeed the *amende honorable.*

The public performer is rarely left to take his leisure peacefully; where it is known he can sing, it is thought by the public that he ought to sing; and, if he does not want to sing, that he should be made to sing. When I was requested to sing " Danny Deever " once at a concert on shipboard I had difficulty in getting out of appearing, but with the legitimate excuse of a cold I was at last allowed to remain out of the bill.

As I sat in the barber's chair on the morning of the concert, the voluble tonsorial artist spoke of the entertainment as he shaved me and hoped I would reconsider my decision not to sing. He would not be satisfied without an explanation of my refusal, as he had heard me before. I told him of my heavy season in America and that I needed rest on the sea. " I can understand that," he replied sympathetically. " It is just the same with me, sir. I never look at a razor when I am ashore."

There was a notable company aboard and a superb concert resulted, some of the celebrities being Melba, Nordica, Jean de Reszke, Plançon, Sarah Bernhardt, and Coquelin. While I did not sing, I disposed of a large number of tickets; and, having had several programs autographed by the principal artists, I sold these at auction during the intermission in the concert, securing $800 for the benefit of the Sailors' Home. Upon reaching the smoking room after the concert I was accosted by a passenger who complimented me upon my efforts, saying, as he drew his business card from his pocket, " I am a New York auctioneer. Whenever your voice gives out just let me know and I'll give you a job for ten thousand dollars a year to sell our stuff."

It is not always that incidents are amusing, and public performers are often looked down upon. Early in the year 1898, when the Ellis-Damrosch Company was playing at the Metropolitan Opera House, which also contains apartments, one of which I was then occupying, I had a sharp attack of my old enemy, lumbago. We on the stage are like soldiers and must do our duty regardless of personal inconvenience. The audience has nothing to do with our maladies, physical or mental, but unfortunately, one of these attacks came upon me in the midst of a busy time. I had to sing at several performances at the Metropolitan Opera House, to give one of my own concerts at Mendelssohn Hall, to take part in " The Messiah " in another city — and I could scarcely get out of bed! I sent a telegram the day before to the oratorio committee telling them of my plight and that I had at my own expense engaged an admirable artist to take my place in the oratorio.

As I was preparing to take my painful ease, I received an urgent message from Mr. Damrosch, who knew that I was ill, asking me, if it were possible, to dress, wrap up warmly, come down in the elevator, and step inside of the opera house, it being only a few yards from my door to that of the theatre. When I arrived I hobbled, supported by a friend and nearly bent double, to the stage, where a chair awaited me, and an overcoat and rug protected me from the draught.

As I sat there humming through my part, I noticed two strangers standing near the wings. When my work was done one of these introduced himself as one of the committee of the oratorio society who had come to see if I was able to keep my engagement. I rose from my chair with difficulty and explained the plight in which I found myself. He agreed with me and with the friend who had come with him, that I could not be expected to travel, go through a difficult performance, and return the following day in time for " The Flying Dutchman " in New York. They bade me good-by, saying that they would explain the matter to their committee. My visitors, however, upon reaching their home reported that they found me busily rehearsing upon the stage and seemingly in perfect health, and the committee refused to permit my substitute to sing in my place.

I thus found myself a victim of the caprice of my friends. I was severely censured in the newspapers and for some time was made to feel the disapproval of the public, who doubtless thought that here was merely another example of the idiosyncrasy of a spoiled artist.

During a visit to the Pacific Coast I attended the

Chinese Theatre in San Francisco and once was taken behind the stage after the performance to see where the actors lived in cellars even two and three stories below the ground.   Here these men smoke their pipes, say their prayers, burn their joss sticks, and study their enormously lengthy parts.   They act every night in plays which it sometimes takes weeks to finish, and fine actors many of them are, among the best I have ever seen.   Asking when these artists took their exercise, I was informed that they went out only at night.   When I voiced my surprise, I was told that they dare not go abroad in the daytime, for they would be insulted by the populace, mal-treated, beaten, stoned, and driven back to the burrows of their theatre, where the audience thought they be-longed and nowhere else.

Thus we have up to the present day a continuance of the hostile attitude toward our craft inherited from the older times, when the actor had no rights, could not be married or buried by the clergy; but remained a vagabond, alive or dead, and was legally so termed.   A strolling player, because forbidden to settle down any-where, was obliged to keep going, no matter what his talents, no matter how much he contributed to the joy of his audiences or, in later years, to the education of the public.

I believe, disagreeable as many aspects of life upon the stage are supposed to be, that the personnel of the dramatic and operatic profession to-day is far superior in morale and in morality to what it ever was before. For generations in England a stage career was consid-ered beneath the dignity of a gentleman, and the great Lord Chesterfield was evidently trying to save his son from such a fate, when he said, " If you wish to hear music, by all means pay a fiddler to fiddle for you, but by no means fiddle yourself." I cannot insist too strongly that the stage is no more dangerous an occupation than any other, and the sooner the public gets over such an idea the better it will be for stage and public. In the freer life of these days, young men and women of good family and excellent education are quite properly seeking the dramatic or musical field of endeavor as a means of livelihood and as an outlet to natural impulses which are not to be denied. Every one likes to make a speech, to hold forth in a recitation, to act, to sing, to give vent to artistic emotions, and those sufficiently gifted may thus be led to take up music and the drama as their work in life.

Notwithstanding this it is my invariable custom to counsel my pupils or those who seek my advice not to give up any other pursuit by which they make their living in order to follow music as a profession, unless they possess the necessary gift in an unusual degree, and not to take to the stage even then unless after the most careful consideration, serious preparation, and intensive training of all the faculties needed in their occupation, they find their fitness beyond doubt, the call for their services undeniable, and their prospects more than ordinarily good.

Almost immediately upon my arrival in London I gave at St. James's Hall one of my own concerts, opening with songs by Schubert, and closing with a group by Schumann which had been written to words by the English poets, Burns, Moore, Byron, and Shakespeare, which, of course, I sang in the original. Among other interesting features then brought forward I introduced a group of songs by Americans, Harry Rowe Shelley, Clayton Johns, and Walter Damrosch. This was the introduction into England of Mr. Damrosch's song, the newly popular "Danny Deever," but, owing to the strict copyright on this poem, I was unable to print the words in my book of words. Kipling's prohibition of the use of his ballad, even in the printed copy of music as it appeared in England, left it another "Song without words."

That summer I rested for a while in a little old-fashioned place which was many centuries old and which I had rented from an ancient Gloucestershire family on whose estate had stood Fair Rosamund's Bower. My cottage, so called, a substantial structure of beautifully carved stone, might have been the bower of the Fair Rosamund herself and the place where the King visited her. At any rate it is said there were ghosts in the house, and sure it is that from the cellarage a subterranean passage extended for two or three miles to another and more considerable ancient dwelling. While I enjoyed this rural pleasaunce, I could not keep long away from the metropolis, and soon I repeated, at a theatre I took for the purpose, my Beethoven performances, supported again by Miss Julie Opp, the program being enriched by a first part of Beethoven's music in which I was assisted by Miss Fanny Davies, Johannes Wolf, Hollman, and others; and last, but not least, by Madame Blanche Marchesi, daughter of the famous Parisian vocal teacher.

Of course my association with persons of distinction in the artistic world was of great interest to me, but after all, the most enjoyable evenings of my recollection were those so often spent in the hospitable home of William Shakespeare, the great singing teacher and my very good friend. His *soirées* were exemplars of what musical evenings should be. He had among his intimates some of the finest artists of the day, and though he never imposed upon them in return for the many favors he and his good wife had rendered them, they were only too willing to be associated with anything he might suggest in the way of entertainment of his friends, as held in that modest drawing-room at No. 14, Mansfield Street. To this house many noted people resorted, glad to partake of the generous cheer always to be found at the hands of their jolly host of the great name and remarkable likeness to the poet-dramatist.

How often have I not heard in such intimate surroundings the greatest artists of Europe playing or singing in those rooms, where, be it said, they always arrived early and never left until correspondingly early in the wee sma' hours of the following morning!

On one of these occasions some of the noblest chamber music had been played in the most inspiring manner by Joachim and his quartette. At the close of the concert, as the guests were listening to the dying strains so perfectly rendered in surroundings the most sympathetic, the grandfather's clock at the head of the stairs struck twelve. Even this was in tune with the circumstances, and not only in tune but in rhythm, for as the four last majestic bars were played in three-four time the clock joined its voice to those of the instruments and in perfect unison and harmony brought to an end one of the most remarkable musical séances imaginable.

CHAPTER XXVIII

WHERE ANGELS FEAR

Nothing so difficult as a beginning,
. . . unless perhaps the end.— *Byron.*

THE musical man in the street on New York's Great White Way and he who attends the opera, and the musical woman in the street, she who attends the concert, probably give little thought to the preparation of the entertainments they so enjoy. Even performers themselves fail to realize what must be done before a concert can be given; and a concert is the easiest kind of entertainment to provide.

A small percentage only of those who set forth upon a public career ever get far. If by reason of strength and talent and a combination of favorable circumstances, a few out of the great number who try are able to continue on a long and honorable career, their strength is often but labor and sorrow.

I must admit that the labor is pleasurable and that, as God tempers the wind to the shorn lamb, so does He assuage with the joys of success the bitterness of the struggle made to attain it.

The few that win out attain their positions by hard work alone, bringing into subjection material already more than ordinarily good, for only too often the most musical are not blessed with voices of paramount beauty, and those who have fine voices are often not gifted with musical temperaments. Lack of studiousness is a common thing, and all who teach should make plain to their pupils the enormous amount that must be learned, from which, after all, only a small part may be retained as one's habitual working material. The voice must be fine, the ear must be good, the mind must be sound, the body must be healthy, the spirit must be indomitable, and fair musicianship is an absolute necessity. But while all these things may coincide in the persons of a few, opportunity may not offer itself or, if it does, may not be seized. One's clients must be convinced before an engagement can be arranged even for a single concert. How much more difficult is it to appeal for a year's work to the organists of churches and their music committees, or to the conductors of oratorio societies and their boards of directors for high-class engagements! Should the young man or woman possess such qualities in fair proportion and in such favorable combination as to attract the manager of artistic opera, then how far from probable is it that these talented individuals have given any thought to languages or to the art of acting?

To be reasonably at home in the concert room or on the oratorio platform is one thing, but to create an impression upon the operatic stage is quite another. A reputation made before the concert-loving public may easily be lost in a night by one who has been unwisely attracted by the glare of the footlights, the glimmer of the golden horseshoe, the far-resounding fame of the tenors and prima donnas. Few realize that these artists, after every imaginable obstacle has been overcome, find themselves in a position of such eminence that they are in momentary fear of dethronement by new rivals and compelled to curry favor with press and public, day and night, in season and out of season, in order to maintain their hard-won position.

Even though there are more schools of music and opportunities are more numerous, musical competition is consequently much keener. In spite of this, the American student does not yet realize the importance of early and careful preparation for a career so arduous as the one I have been sketching. Those who engage musical talent do so with their eyes, and particularly their ears, wide open, and after long and careful thought secure the services of those only who, in their opinion, will attract and continue to please their audiences.

We often hear of vocalists as being wedded to their art; but in such musical, as in human, unions there is many a mistake made. Years, that should have been those of preparation, have been wasted. Then after an elopement with the Muse, comes the bitter sense of error. Then the Muse, unsatisfied, breaks away to leave her whilom partner sadly musing upon the caprice of Art, never realizing that the so-called artist is the capricious one. Art is the ever fixed pole, immutable and undying. It is we miserable pygmies, philanderers with her majestic form, who are to blame. Then let all take heed, nor contract an alliance with one of the immortals unadvisably.

During my career as a singer I have marked the growth of interest in musical art in colleges, both for men and for women, and in universities throughout the country, where music is now a recognized part of the curriculum for anybody to study it who will if he has the requisite ability. Apart from annual festivals at many institutions of learning there are musical functions at frequent intervals throughout the whole of the collegiate year. At many of these I have been privileged to assist.

Upon returning to New York in the autumn of 1898,

I found a number of such engagements which had, of course, been secured by my manager months in advance. I opened at Vassar College, following with Oberlin and Wells, and sang also at Bryn Mawr and at my own beloved Haverford. To all these I have often been asked to return, thus assisting in keeping the flame alight, not only at those named but at many other places where music is being appreciated throughout the United States. My college programs were always constructed with a view not only to the art of music but for its educational influence, and included selections from the works of German and Italian masters of olden times; selections from operas nowadays infrequently heard; examples of the French school and of English lyric grace at its best, and the folk songs of all nations, not overlooking modern tendencies nor American composers and their work.

After a dozen such appearances, I joined the Maurice Grau Opera Company which opened in November, 1898, in Chicago with a splendid roster of artists at the Auditorium Theatre, one of the most remarkable opera houses in the world and, considering its vast size, one possessed of acoustic properties of an extraordinary character. It was there that Ernest Van Dyck, the Belgian tenor, made his first appearance in America as Tannhäuser, supported by Madame Eames as Elizabeth, Miss Olga Pevny as Venus, myself as Wolfram, and Plançon as the Landgrave, with Schalk as conductor.

Little did I think, when years before I saw Van Dyck lose his wig in the second act of " Parsifal " at Bayreuth, that I should take supper with that bald-headed gentleman that very night, and that time held in store for me many an operatic thrill at closer quarters, after a lapse of years. But it had so happened, in the enchant-

ment scene in the lovely garden of Klingsor's castle, while
Kundry, in the person of Madame Materna, was exercising her blandishments upon the youthful and unsophis-
ticated Parsifal, that Van Dyck, starting from the maternal embrace of the enchantress, stepped a few inches
further back than was necessary and a lock of the fair
hair of his wig caught in the branches of the magic wood
which had enclosed the couple with its alluring charm.
At that moment a change of scene took place; the tangled
leaves and tendrils of the verdant coppice began to arise,
and in the presence of the spellbound audience gently
lifted the covering from the shining poll of Parsifal.
With the spring of a cat the guileless one leaped into
the air and tore down the rapidly rising wig, which fell
upon the stage at his feet. Before he could adjust the
peruke upon his head Kundry had ceased singing and
Parsifal's reply was forthcoming.

Through my opera glasses I could see the great beads
of sweat start out upon Van Dyck's head, neck, and bare
arms, as in an agony of rage and of frenzied embar-
rassment, he put the wig on his head — wrong side before! As his back was to the audience, his baldness was
all the more apparent. When he turned to face the
footlights, the audience was not only amazed but amused
to see the smooth face of the man covered with what
seemed to be a long full beard. Everybody burst into a
ripple of mirth as unfortunate as it was uncontrollable.
As Parsifal went on with the scene, he reclined again by
the side of Kundry who, with admirable presence of mind,
stroked Van Dyck's forehead, parting the hair from his
face on either side in order that he might give expression
to his vocal raptures. A few moments later in the scene

Materna had a considerable passage to sing alone, when Van Dyck took advantage of this and left the stage in order to put his wig on properly; but, in his haste, he tore it off his head before he got out of sight of the audience, and this time there was not merely a ripple but a loud roar of laughter. It would have spoiled the scene for any singers other than two such consummate artists as Van Dyck and Materna.

On the evening of November 7, 1898, at the Auditorium in Chicago, the American public first saw the name of Ernestine Schumann-Heink, which has come to mean so much in the musical annals of the United States. As Ortrud in " Lohengrin," she made an immediate success which was at once recognized by her impresario and the public. I am proud to have been associated, in a cast including Andreas Dippel and Madame Eames, with one who since that night has become one of the greatest figures of contemporary musical annals.

A few nights before, upon emerging warm from work into a cold wind from Lake Michigan, I had caught a cold which was beginning to lay me low. As a matter of fact, I did not sing again for about a month, for upon the urgent advice of my doctor I immediately took train for Philadelphia, where I could be near my own people in case of an unfavorable turn in my malady, which proved to be a sharp attack of influenza.

I had never before been near death, but now I was told by my physician that I must look the possible consequences in the face. As I lay there I thought of Browning's " Prospice," the words of which I had sung so often to Stanford's music, and repeated the powerful lines: " Fear death? To feel the fog in my throat! . . . Yet the strong man must go! . . . I was ever a fighter, so one fight more, the best and the last."

I lay quietly, seeking strength to continue the silent struggle, alone then as I had been in all the struggles of my artistic life. Fortunately I pulled through, with nobody any the wiser. For I do not believe in emulating the example of those of my *confrères* who advertise their disabilities, when their abilities alone ought to be permitted to speak. I could never endure managerial apologies for an artist, from the days I first heard them before the curtain at the opera when I was a young fellow, as some one stepped out to ask public indulgence for Madame So-and-so, who was suffering from a severe sore throat, but who presently appeared singing as well as she ever did.

My code is that if an artist makes an engagement it is his duty to try to fill it, whether he is well or ill. It often happens that though one may not be feeling in the best of voice, the effort to pull oneself together is the very thing that overcomes one's difficulties, perhaps to learn that he never sang better before; though as a matter of fact he was far from doing so, but was acting as becomes a man, and trying to do his best to satisfy his public.

The repertory of operas performed that year was large, including "The Flying Dutchman," "Lohengrin," "Tannhäuser," "Tristan und Isolde," and the four sections of "The Ring." Besides the artists of whom I have already spoken there were Madame Nordica, Jean and Edouard de Reszke, and Miss Meisslinger. Early in 1899, Mesdames Calvé and Sembrich, Mr. Salignac, the superb-voiced Anton Van Rooy, and Madame Lilli Lehmann came to add the distinction of their presence to a company already as notable as any brought to New York in years.

My own season comprised about a hundred appearances divided almost equally between opera and concert. In regard to the latter I always stipulated that I was to be allowed to accept as many engagements as could be conveniently arranged in connection with my appearances in opera. By contract I was guaranteed fifty operatic performances, including Sunday night concerts. The other concerts Grau arranged for me himself. If for these he obtained more money than the pro rata amount, the opera company was to benefit by the excess. This was satisfactory to me inasmuch as all my expenses, except hotel bills, during the fulfillment of such engagements were defrayed, even to the salary of my accompanist. As Mr. Grau explained, Plançon had been such a money-maker by the acceptance of outside engagements that he had cost the company nothing. Mr. Plançon's contract provided that every journey he took should be paid for by the company, with every wig, costume, and property that he had used in years. He was a handsome figure of a man, and to dress him handsomely in accordance with his handsome voice was the only handsome thing for a manager to do, and handsomely he did it.

Maurice Grau reveled in difficulties and delighted in fitting together engagements for his artists in concert and opera. He was a great card player, expert at chess, and an inveterate operator on the Stock Exchange, and viewed the profession of an impresario in the light of a complicated and highly interesting game in which, when his partners did not upset his calculations, he was usually successful.

I remember that I came into Mr. Grau's private office one day and found him in the midst of a discussion of the most intricate nature, arising out of the illness of several of his principals and the need for filling their places in compliance with their contracts, taking into further account the probable effect upon the public of the changes in the casts. At the same time he was hearing a complicated report from the managers of the company; discussing the terms of his written agreement with an artist without referring to the document, except to prove the artist wrong; speaking as many as three foreign languages in rotation with men of as many nationalities about him; calling up his broker in Wall Street to give him orders to buy and sell, and evidently calculating the possible gains and losses mentally as he spoke. He had indeed a photographic mind, the absorptive and retentive power of which I have never seen equaled.

It takes a clear head to run two monster companies in two of the greatest opera houses in the world with the ocean rolling between them; but this Mr. Grau did, in addition to many other theatrical and musical ventures, making for himself a name that will go down in history as that of one of the ablest impresarios of his day.

CHAPTER XXIX

HAPS AND MISHAPS

— Grasps the skirts of happy chance,
And breasts the blows of circumstance.
— *Tennyson.*

UPON my recovery from influenza this is the sort of work I had to do. The opera had finished its season in Chicago and elsewhere and had come to New York, where on December 9, 1898, I sang at the Metropolitan with Van Dyck and Nordica. The 11th I sang in the Sunday night opera concert in solos and in the duet from " The Flying Dutchman " with Madame Gadski. On the 13th I gave with Arthur Whiting the whole cycle of Schubert's " Müller Lieder " in Boston, repeating that program two days later in New York in the afternoon, and the same evening appearing with Madame Nordica at the house of the elder J. Pierpont Morgan. The following evening I declaimed Alberich at the opera, with Van Rooy as the Wanderer, making six performances in eight days.

Then, fortunately, I had a little rest, just a breathing space, like the whale, only he comes up to spout but seldom, while the artist has to remain up, if he can, and spout continually.

When it was decided that I should give the " Müller Lieder " in Boston I felt a distinct sense of alarm. I had looked up to Boston from my youth, and now that I visited its classic precincts, though I found the Bostonese

much the same as other people, yet there still clung about
them and their city and everything pertaining to it, from
its hallowed Common to its crooked streets, from its
Handel and Haydn Society to its Symphony Orchestra,
something indefinitely alarming which a mere Philadelphian could not consider without trepidation.

That curious assumption of right, that distinction of
superiority that hangs about Boston, is undeniably felt as
we approach the Hub from any quarter. We sense it,
as we would Rome, with a feeling of something everlast-
ing, as being the mundane spot where Deity deigns to
touch the earth and make it brighter. As we approach
we remember that we have heard of the sounds which
turned out to be its people reciting Browning, and as we
approach still nearer we recognize an odor — can it be
that of sanctity?

Upon stepping across the threshold of our American
Mecca even the negro porter who carries our bags at
the railway station has something superior about him; it
must be that he knows more than the porters of other
cities. The bell boys and the bootblacks at the hotels —
have they not access daily to the Boston papers? They
must know all about us who make music, from these.
I feel a vague alarm that critics — Boston critics — shall
be at my concerts!

Will any one recognize me in Boston? Ah, yes, I
am recognized; the manicure has heard me sing in New
York! Oh, joy, the waiter at the table remembers me
from Europe! I am called upon by one or two friends.
Though I have been there many a time, I have wondered
at my temerity in tempting fate, and wondered, too,
whether such visits were not made in a sort of bravado,
not in the endeavor to conquer Boston, but just to show

the rest of the United States that I am not afraid of it.
Though it did not need my attention, I was not to be induced to pass by on the other side. I have felt that it
might be well to receive from Boston that little corrective
of which my system was in need, after a good deal of
feeding up in other parts of the country — the feeding
up that makes one feel so good and yet is so bad for
one; the success that is so beneficial and yet so harmful;
the sweet little morsels rolled under the tongue which
are said to be so deleterious.

But to continue. Four days' rest; and on December
21st I gave a song recital at Hartford, Connecticut. As
I distinctly remember, my eccentric accompanist, Mr.
Blank, refused to carry my music on the stage, and at the
end of the concert threw it on the floor behind the door
instead of placing it on the table at hand — capricious as
a soldier mutinying over a matter of daily routine. The
next evening I gave a concert at the Brooklyn Institute,
the program consisting of sixteen songs, different in
every instance from those sung in Hartford. The following night, December 23, I sang my old part of Telramund with Madame Eames and Dippel. December 25
I sang " The Messiah " in Boston, repeating it there the
next day. December 30 in the afternoon I took part in
" The Messiah " in New York; that same evening singing
in " Tristan and Isolde " at the opera. The following
afternoon, December 31, we repeated " Lohengrin," and
in the evening I sang " The Messiah " at Carnegie Hall,
making nine heavy performances in eleven days.

The year 1899 opened almost as strenuously. January 4 I sang in " Siegfried " in Philadelphia, on January
5 a whole recital program in Orange, New Jersey,
January 7 an entire program again of a different nature

in Troy, New York; January 8 at the opera house in the Sunday night concert, January 9 "Lohengrin" in the same auditorium, January 10 the same opera in the Brooklyn Academy of Music, and January 12 Alberich in "The Rheingold" on the occasion of the first performance of the entire Trilogy given in New York under Mr. Grau's direction: — seven performances in nine days.

A summary of the work which I have just sketched shows that besides six appearances in opera I sang "The Messiah" four times and the whole or part of ten concerts. I also rendered Brahms's "Four Serious Songs" several times, Beethoven's cycle, and three performances of Schubert's "Müller Lieder"; besides other vocal selections. Indeed, those days were crowded full; as the Bible says, "pressed down, shaken together, and running over" with interest, excitement, hard study, and constant work, and this for a man who had just arisen from a sick bed! The whole season went on like that, numbering almost a hundred appearances before I went across the ocean again.

Such casts as we then had may be well looked back upon with pride. Nordica would be the Elsa in "Lohengrin" one night, Emma Eames the next. Jean de Reszke or Van Dyck as Lohengrin, Edouard de Reszke the King, Madame Schumann-Heink the Ortrud, Van Rooy the Wotan and the Wanderer in "The Ring," with Van Dyck in his superb impersonation of Loge; Lilli Lehmann as Sieglinde or Brünnhilde; Jean de Reszke as Siegfried, with his brother Edouard as Hagen, with Nordica and Schumann-Heink in the cast. Great nights!

There were, however, times when mishaps took place. At the close of the first act of "Siegfried," in the scene of the forging of the sword, the young hero proves the temper of his blade by bringing it down upon the anvil, cleaving it in twain. But more than once the anvil split apart while the sword was still poised high in mid-air for the blow, leaving the actor looking silly at having nothing to do except to wish that he could hide the enchanted weapon and his own confusion as well. The Germans with one accord blamed the American management, though the fault lay wholly with the German subdirector, who had pulled the string that parts the anvil at the wrong moment.

Often, too, when the curtain fell, it left the anvil, split as it was, outside, for awkward removal by the stage hands, ruining the climax of the act. Here again the blame was attached to the English-speaking persons who paid the German stage manager his salary not to leave the anvil outside. That worthy ever insisted upon placing the unfortunate object so near the curtain that the usual draught from the auditorium was bound to sway it back too far. It was a law of nature and not an American plan for Teutonic confusion; but no German, in or out of the cast, would have it so.

In the gyrations of the Rhine daughters, suspended in air to simulate the appearance of swimming in the river, their attempt to escape from the embraces of Alberich looks easy. But often the complicated machinery by which they are held and moved got out of order at the critical moment. Once the Rhine maiden, Flosshilde, was left in mid-air at the end of the act, almost necessitating the call of the fire department to release her; and the other time Woglinde lost the brace that held her shoulders and was hung upside down by one foot, screaming until the house was in alarm.

Accidents are bound to happen on the best regulated

stages. I remember that at an afternoon performance of "The Valkyrie," desiring to save myself in the extreme pressure of the season, I remained in bed during the morning in my apartment above the Metropolitan Opera House and had no luncheon, but asked to have it supplied me after the first act, in which I was impersonating the character of Hunding. It was ordered from the restaurant, then in the Fortieth Street corner of the opera house building, and it was to be brought in at the Fortieth Street stage door to my dressing room on the Thirty-ninth Street side. The scene represents the interior of Hunding's hut, built around a great tree which rises through its roof. Madame Eames, always the best of Sieglindes, was seated at the table beneath the tree on the right hand of Hunding, her lord and master, on whose left sat Siegmund. Our meal was scanty and consisted mostly of arid drinks from empty cups made of the curved horns of cattle. While grimly listening to the story of Siegmund, I became aware of a commotion at my left just off the stage, where through the wings I saw my waiter from the neighboring restaurant standing, his white apron showing against the dark background and the tray with my frugal meal poised on one hand above his head. At that moment I had to sing and, though the waiter did not recognize me in my disguise, he knew me by my voice, and so made a dash for the table at which he saw me sitting. He was caught by the coat-tail just as he was about to make his first appearance upon any stage. I was so upset with mirth that I could scarcely continue my part.

Nothing was finer in the series of operas that year than Van Dyck's impersonation of Loge, the fire god in "The Rheingold," and such an embodiment of the Spirit of

Flame surely was never seen before. Would that my own frequent rendering of the Frost Scene from " King Arthur " could in any way have matched it! Yet I once so impressed an American poetess as the Genius of Cold that she attempted to dramatize the Glacial Epoch in Kansas!

Hard as all this music is to learn there are certain parts of it which are most baffling in their complexity. Even Beckmesser is scarcely less puzzling than Alberich, and in that part perhaps the most difficult scene of all is the quarrel with Mime at the mouth of the dragon's cave in the second act of " Siegfried." I have often performed this, but each time approached it with fear and trembling. At the rise of the curtain, Alberich is found lying outside the cavern in the dusk of the early morn, keeping watch over the ring and the sleeping dragon, its guardian. There is something primal about the part of Alberich, who is, after all, the *deus ex machina* of the whole Niebelungen story. But the supreme moment is when Mime appears and the quarrel between the two brothers ensues. That scene takes about one minute and a half to enact. After ten days spent in learning it I thought I had it fast, patted myself on the back, and slept in peace until rehearsal the next day. When I awoke in the morning I could not remember a word of it! These things settle eventually into the mind; but let me assure the student that the trick of learning parts, even comparatively easy ones, is an accomplishment to be acquired early in the game, or valuable time will be lost and a greater effort made necessary than should be required. We Americans have to work harder than most Europeans to learn operatic rôles, partly through lack of early training in the essentials of the calling, partly because we have so little preliminary education in foreign languages.

For myself I can only say that, while it was a drudgery, it was one that I was glad to undergo. At last Alberich and all my other characters got well into my emotional nature and I was able to make them effective accordingly. Artists differ greatly in their ability to memorize words and music. Some learn with ease and forget equally rapidly; others learn slowly and have retentive memories; some learn slowly and forget quickly, and others learn quickly and never forget. Luckily for me I read music well, though I play it badly, and I do not need aid from the piano after a certain stage in learning any rôle. I have seen Madame Schumann-Heink reacquiring a part she had not sung for years from the score in her lap while we were traveling. Madame Melba's extraordinary memory has enabled her to sing a rôle without an error which she had sung but once, and that six years before. But memory is only one of many requirements. One singer who was in our company for years was the quickest study and most reliable artist I ever knew, yet he remained a nonentity, his very name unremembered, through lack of the mysterious gift of personality.

In Washington one spring, Madame Sembrich, usually the most trustworthy of vocalists, was compelled by sudden illness to excuse herself from singing. The management was notified of it early in the morning, and Madame Nordica was begged to assume the part, after several seasons spent in Wagnerian rôles. But Violetta is so different from Brünnhilde or Isolde that the *diva*, good-natured and obliging as she was, was almost prostrated with nervousness at the thought of stepping into Sembrich's shoes, often as she had sung the rôle in years gone by. And not only Sembrich's part and shoes had to be considered, but Sembrich's costume, for Nordica had brought nothing of the sort with her, never expecting, of course, to be called upon in this way.

Many were the consultations in the old Shoreham Hotel between Sembrich downstairs and Nordica several floors up. Messengers were kept going between the manager and the prima donnas, both of them popular, but knowing the risk of disappointing a public. To relearn an old part is not a light task, but it is no less difficult to change an operatic bill and still conform to the singers' contracts. Those who sang a night or two before may flatly decline to appear again until the time and in the rôle set down in the understanding. There is the orchestra; there is the conductor; there is the chorus; everybody but the one person needed, who will not budge a hair's breadth to oblige the distraught impresario.

Nordica was willing, but was she able? If willing and able, could she get into Sembrich's clothes? Their maids were called in. Nordica's accompanist began teaching her the music afresh, playing and humming over page after page, because it would never do to rehearse all day in full voice the piece to be done that night. Doctor Stengel, Madame Sembrich's husband, haunted Nordica's door, anxiously inquiring how the part was progressing.

Twelve o'clock came, two o'clock came, messengers came and went to and fro, hurrying and scurrying hither and thither with notes to this or that member of the company, who might be able to oblige in the embarrassing moment. But no! Unless the opera were changed Nordica would have to sing; and Nordica had not said yes. All the time, however, she was doing her best, fitting her-

self into her old part while Sembrich's clothes were being
fitted on her as she stood by the piano. As Nordica,
becoming more familiar with her rôle, began to act it,
moving to and fro in the room, she accidentally bumped
into the tall workbasket as it stood by the open window,
knocked it over and out on the balcony, sending its contents through the latticework to be blown by the stiff
breeze all over the street several stories below.

Returning from the theatre after seeing whether I
should be required in case of a change of opera, I found
in front of the hotel silk and velvet, linings and brocades,
skeins of varied colors and spools of thread, scissors and
thimbles, scattered over the sidewalk in process of collection by maids, bell boys, Doctor Stengel, street urchins
and newsboys, negro porters and cabmen, all called into
the chase as the wind merrily blew the treasures up and
down. At last all were corralled, the costumes fitted,
and Nordica assured Mr. Grau that she knew the part.
It was sung accordingly and the day was saved; and if the
day was saved the night was a triumph for one of the
most beautiful and obliging prima donnas that America
ever produced.

Madame Lilli Lehmann joined the company that season, and then New York heard after a lapse of several
years one of the greatest artists that ever adorned the
European stage. I had seen her many times in Germany,
admiring her immensely from the audience; now I had
the pleasure of appearing with her when she sang Fricka,
Sieglinde, and the Brünnhildes, Ortrud, and Isolde.
Artists have their individual ways. Accustomed as they
are to their work, some are never at ease unless being
prompted from the little round box down in front of the
footlights; and, though the public should not hear his

voice, it is comforting to a person like me to find such an ever present help in time of trouble. But Lilli Lehmann would have none of it. I have seen her walk to the prompter's box and request that she be not prompted in anything at any time, and with a stern look on her handsome face declare that she knew her part and that any interference only embarrassed rather than helped her in rendering it.

This superb woman lived with her sister Marie in an apartment in the Metropolitan Opera House building, where several of us also had lodgings, including the barytone Maurel. Calling one afternoon upon Lilli Lehmann I found her domestically darning the barytone's stockings and greatly enjoying the home-like service. He was not arrayed for conquest as was his wont, and she was not expecting visitors. The apron that adorned her queenly form and the gray hair that crowned her regal head came to me as something of a shock, in spite of my knowledge that artists beneath their disguises are nothing but mortals.

That winter Maurel's apartment was set on fire. My rooms were a few floors above his and up the stairway and elevator shaft were wafted great clouds of pungent smoke from the transom of his sitting-room. He had gone out while his servant was preparing a posset to fortify his master against the evening performance. The concoction was on the hob to simmer. The man forgot the mixture when he left the room, and returned to find the door broken in by the fire department. The mess had boiled over, set the rug on fire, climbed the mantelpiece, and generally created a tempest in a teapot, one result being that Maurel was sued for damages by the lady from whom he had rented the room while she was off on a concert tour. One may well say, " Behold how great a matter a little fire kindleth."

Among my programs I find one bearing the following in regard to the performance of " The Rheingold" of January 27, 1899: " Special notice.— Miss Marie Brema is suffering from a slight cold and begs the kind indulgence of the public."   Miss Brema's cold became so bad that she could not sing and Madame Lilli Lehmann took the part of Fricka to study at four o'clock in the afternoon and sang it that night for the first time. She told me this herself. On this occasion the great artist needed not only the prompter, but all the prompting she could get, and every help was given her to get her through the evening as comfortably as possible. One or another of the assistant conductors stood ready to give the word at the least sign of trouble, to whichever side of the stage she moved. Her sister Marie was rendering a similar service, and to her Madame Lehmann chiefly looked. The sister told me later that Lilli had sung in " The Ring" so often and in so many parts that she was already somewhat familiar with the rôle; but let me say that there is not one artist in a thousand, perhaps not another in the world, physically, nervously, mentally, and musically able to perform such a feat or, if able to perform it, willing to do so to help another artist and assist the management in its duty to the public.

Goldsmith says in " She Stoops to Conquer," " Women and music should never be dated," but though she has now passed the threescore years and ten allotted to mortals, there is certainly no artist in the history of the modern lyric stage who has performed so great a number of parts or performed them with such uniform distinction as Madame Lilli Lehmann.

CHAPTER XXX

THE UNFLYING DUTCHMAN

As idle as a painted ship
Upon a painted ocean.
— *Coleridge.*

I HAVE spoken of the square dealing of Maurice Grau in certain matters, though in others he was almost parsimonious. On our tour that year, Grau, desiring to save as much as possible in the transportation of scenery, communicated with the managers of the theatres we were to visit, asking what scenery of theirs could be used, to save us the expense of bringing our own.

If I mistake not, it was in Baltimore, when I was performing in " Lohengrin," that an incident occurred of which the German stage manager had a perfect right to complain. The curtain rose on the first act and everything went on musically to perfection. We, the participants, were facing the audience, with the chorus on the elevated parts of the stage behind us. At the approach of the Knight of the Swan the chorus moves aside as Telramund goes up stage and hurls defiance at Lohengrin when he is magically drawn in on his boat by the swan, along the river Scheldt near Antwerp. But, turning, what greeted my eyes, those of my associates and of the astonished audience, was the river Thames at Henley crowded with house boats for the famous regatta! This was the river scene asked for from the New York office, and it was idle for poor Paul Schumann to try to wash his hands of the affair among the painted boats upon that painted river.

After an adjourned farewell of opera at the Metropolitan, the company as a whole — chorus and ballet, but not orchestra — set sail for London, where we immediately opened under the conductorship, as far as the German operas were concerned, of Felix Mottl and Doctor Muck, both of whom were later to come to America. The former was greatly disappointed because he did not meet with the success in New York he considered justly his; and though the latter became conductor of the Boston Symphony Orchestra, it will be remembered that during the war he was obliged to retire as an alien enemy.

On May 23, 1899, Madame Gadski and I were billed to present "The Flying Dutchman" at Covent Garden, where in rapid succession I had also been singing in "Tristan and Isolde," "Tannhäuser," "The Mastersingers," and as Wotan in "The Valkyrie." I had rendered "The Dutchman" before in London, and knew the vessel of that antiquated skipper on the Covent Garden dry docks to be at least as old as himself. I asked for a rehearsal with my craft before I ventured on board of her to sail the operatic sea. That the stage at that time was extremely busy, I had to admit. Rehearsals were going on in every available room in the opera house — in the foyer, in the old greenroom, in front of the curtain, in the orchestra, and behind the curtain on the stage; in short, upstairs and downstairs and in my lady's dressing room. There was no time to get the old tub out and polish her up; but my prophetic soul knew something was about to happen. As I entered the darkened stage I saw that

sheer hulk lurking in the offing and my mind was filled
with a ghostly apprehension.

We had at the time a bustling little mustachioed German stage manager, always in his evening clothes, with
white kid gloves and an opera hat, and wearing several
decorations on his coat lapel. I came from my dressing
room when I heard the overture begin, and to my horror
found that the Herr stage director had ordered the ship,
for this occasion, at least, to be lighted up; indeed there
was, as the Italians say, an *illuminatione al giorno*. He
had two large lanterns set on the high poop deck of the
Spanish galleon, with a dozen or more tallow dips in
each, all of which had just been lighted by an obedient
English stage hand, who of course knew nothing of Wagner's directions for the opera prescribing that the ship,
dark, ghostly, and with blood-red sails, shall be seen approaching. I had barely, Boreas-like, blown out the impossible candles, when I was compelled to climb aboard,
take station, and sail across the uncharted deep of Covent
Garden stage, filled with an ancient and fish-like smell,
and full of cracks, as well, between worn boards that had
probably been trodden by Garrick, Kean, and the Kembles.

This night the sea was lashed into a fury by the gale,
though it was merely the light playing upon the dust ac-
cumulated upon that floor cloth, as several sturdy men
behind the wings on each side shook it into the simili-
tude of billows, while street urchins from the purlieus
of Covent Garden, Drury Lane, and the land of Charles
Lamb and Dickens hunched up their backs and walked
hither and thither beneath the painted ocean which rolled
these billows without in any wise affecting the phantom
ship. She proceeded on her even keel of a half dozen

iron wheels, propelled from beneath by three or four stalwart stage hands. At a given moment the vessel should reach the rocky shore, and Vanderdecken step off; all of which usually happens most unseamanlike but successfully, and the great scene should begin with the words, " Die Frisst ist um "— the term is past.

My ship had been guided by her invisible pilots on to the stage, and after a graceful turn should have entered the harbor. Fate that night was against me, and guided one of those submarine wheels into a broad crack in the stage at the bottom of the operatic sea. There, about eight feet from shore, my vessel stuck.

The night was dark and the wind howled dismally, as the storm subsided. The orchestral prelude ended; but I could not disembark. I felt the men beneath me trying to lift the ship out of its predicament. I hoped against hope that my term was indeed past, but nothing happened; I was condemned to remain aboard that fated ship. Doctor Muck, who was conducting, looked up and gave the sign for me to advance and sing. I stolidly met his gaze, but did not move. Becoming impatient he made a sign or two more, and then laid down his baton, bowed over it, put his head in his hands and shook with laughter. I knew what he was thinking: " That *verdammte* Covent Garden stage management again! " But what would he have said had I not put out those tallow dips!

By this time the orchestra men began to stand up and peer over the footlights, and the audience was evidently in a hushed excitement. Suddenly the masts of the ship began violently to shake, as the stern arose a full foot in the air and bumped back again with a crash. Some one in the audience tittered, and there was a sound of

" Sh-sh-hush ! " in protest; was not Wagner being performed, and was it not by just so much a sacred occasion? Suddenly I heard a series of grunts from the
bowels of my craft as it again rose and fell back without
moving an inch forward. Then came the voice of one
of the stage hands from the vasty deep. " Why don't
you shove 'er along, Bill? " he said, so that the whole audience could hear; whereupon Bill replied still louder,
" 'Ow can I, when the blasted thing is stuck fast in the
stige? " With this all bounds of gravity were overcome
and the audience burst into a roar of laughter, such as
might have greeted the wittiest sally of any comedian in
" The Gaiety Girl," then running at a neighboring
theatre.

I, holding my own, not only with a forced composure,
but with a firm grasp upon the shrouds for fear I should
be tilted overboard, had been tempted to jump ashore;
that, however, would have been dangerous in the dark.
It would not do to climb down and swim to the land;
that would have been ridiculous. Suddenly a light began to break; from one corner of my weather eye I observed the head stage carpenter, who, when his attention
was called to the mishap, had hurried around behind and
from somewhere brought a plank ten feet long, which
in his shirt sleeves he bore, both hands lifted high above
a head crowned with a derby hat. Wading out into the
middle of the ocean, almost up to his neck in its water,
this worthy placed one end of the plank upon my vessel
and the other upon the rocks, and very politely turned
to me, touched his hat, and said, in a loud voice, " Now
you can get off, sir," and took his departure.

With such a prelude was I obliged to proceed, accompanied not only by the orchestra but by the gradually

subsiding merriment of an audience that must long have remembered what is unforgettable to me.

That was not all. In the last act the Dutchman is supposed to sail away, imagining that Senta has been untrue to him. Such, however, was not to be the case. The Dutchman remained perforce, because his ship got stuck in another crack and would not budge more than an inch. Senta is supposed to throw herself into the water, and by her sacrifice save Vanderdecken's immortal soul; but Madame Gadski was barely able to squeeze herself between the shore and the ship, and as she gradually settled out of sight in the waves a tin cupful of water, by way of splash, was thrown upon the stage by one of the urchins concealed behind the scenery by the bedecorated stage manager, who had also instructed one of the sailors to throw a modern life preserver, conveniently at hand in expectation of the catastrophe, into the sea in the vain attempt to save Madame Gadski's life.

In anticipation of accident or the inability of the two principal artists to reach the ascending trap in the back of the stage in order to take part in the beautiful transformation scene with which, if Wagner's directions are followed, the opera is brought to a conclusion, the management provides two persons made up and costumed like Senta and Vanderdecken. But on this unlucky night, I, from my post of vantage on the deck of the recalcitrant vessel, saw arise from the bosom of the deep, clasped in each other's embrace, not our counterfeit presentments, but two little children twelve or thirteen years old, looking not in the least like either of us!

During Queen Victoria's Diamond Jubilee Year, 1899, the sixtieth year of her reign, I had the honor of being invited again to sing in a State Concert at Buckingham

Palace, under the conductorship of Sir Walter Parratt. I sang with Madame Emma Nevada, the American prima donna, long absent from the stage, but now induced to come forth and sing the celebrated Bell Song from "Lakme," which she did charmingly. Madame Brema was superb that night in "Plus grand dans son Obscurité" from Gounod's "La Reine de Saba." De Lucia the tenor also sang and, besides other numbers, I rendered one of the duets from "Don Giovanni" with Madame Albani.

This occasion was attended by a most gorgeous array of dignitaries — no other words describe it. All the diplomatic corps from every country in the world were present, every one in full regalia. The Prince of Wales held court in the place of his august mother; but amongst all the royalty, the Indian princes, the great nobles, and fair, coroneted ladies present, the one figure that stands out in my mind is that of Lord Kitchener, who, head and shoulders above almost any one in the room, was one of the most striking personalities in that incomparable assemblage.

I was in demand among royalty that year and was gratified, not to say flattered, to receive another note from Sir Walter Parratt reminding me of my singing before the Queen in Scotland, and adding that it was her Majesty's gracious pleasure to command me to sing again for her, this time at Osborne House in the Isle of Wight. There I had the pleasure of appearing again with Madame Marie Brema. Before returning to London, we were presented by the Duke of Connaught with mementos of the occasion and the thanks of his royal mother, who had already graciously complimented us upon our performance, which took place in the presence

of Arthur Balfour and many distinguished statesmen or
Great Britain and of Europe.

Lilli Lehmann was a member of the London company
that season and again I sang with her frequently, while
among the splendid array of women, one appearing in
England for the first time was our American, Louise
Homer, who has since risen to such heights.   The ranks
of the men were also materially strengthened by the engagement of the barytones, Maurice Renaud from Paris
and Scheidemantel from Dresden, with whom I appeared
in my old rôle of Beckmesser to his noble Hans Sachs.
But of all the Sachses with whom I ever did sing, Edouard
de Reszke was the best, more completely in nobility of
voice and of personal appearance realizing the part, to
which he brought a greater degree of *bonhomie* than
any other of the numerous artists, even Van Rooy, with
whom I have sung in " The Mastersingers."

All barytones owe a great deal to Victor Maurel,
who was again with us that year in London and who had
been in America so many times.   I frequently heard him
as Don Giovanni.   I admired him enormously as Rigoletto and as Amonasro and in many of his other rôles,
including his later masterpieces, Iago and Falstaff, and
it is safe to say that for over a generation no barytone
in Europe was his equal either as a singer or an actor.

The cast with which I enjoyed appearing more than
any other was that which became so famous on both sides
of the Atlantic.   Indeed the public seemed to want us,
and Mr. Grau, always with his ear to the ground with
respect to what the public desired, put on Jean and Edouard de Reszke, Madame Nordica, Madame Schumann-
Heink, and myself upon many occasions.   It so happened
that it was this ensemble which, by royal command, sang

at Windsor Castle on the evening of May 24, 1899, on the occasion of Queen Victoria's eightieth birthday, when her Majesty heard " Lohengrin " for the first time.

We were ushered about eleven o'clock into what is known as the Waterloo Chamber, hung with portraits of the great generals who overcame Napoleon. There, upon the temporary stage, always ready to be put together, we performed, under Mancinelli, the first and third acts of the well-known opera. The Queen was literally surrounded by royalty and every one of her immediate family was there. Half the crowned heads of Europe were present, and it was a splendid sight to see the most celebrated monarchs of the modern world under such circumstances.

The opera over, the Queen, always considerate, desired the artists to appear with her guests in the Green Drawing-Room, requesting us not to change our costumes as the hour was so late. Mesdames Nordica and Schumann-Heink, Mr. Muhlmann, and the brothers de Reszke came in their mediæval robes, Jean de Reszke in his silver armor, Edouard in the costume of the King, and looking every inch a king.

The first and third acts of " Lohengrin," it will be recalled, take place in the same stage setting, which was one reason why this opera and these portions of it had been chosen. I, as Telramund, am slain in the second act, to appear in the third only as a dead body borne in upon a bier. Having ample time to do so, I changed into my evening suit, leaving my make-up on, since only my face is shown above the pall. It happened that the bearers were two tall Germans and two short Italians, these latter being on the side toward the audience. As a result the bier slanted so that I had to hang on to it with one hand to keep from being rolled off on the stage in my swallow-tail, clutching the pall firmly with the other lest it slip off and disclose my incarnate anachronism, both dead hands busy.

The great Queen, a little woman eighty years of age, was, after all, the Personage of that distinguished assembly, and no one who has ever seen her under circumstances of state but realized that she was the mistress of all she surveyed.

Her Majesty spoke kind words to us, and we in turn felicitated her upon her birthday, of which she was to have so few returns. Many of those present that evening have suffered defeat, banishment, ruin, death; but the royal family of England still retains the respect of the world.

As we passed from the drawing-room the Prince of Wales led us into the famous Holbein Room, and there, surrounded by the portraits painted by that old master, the Prince took from a large table the gifts placed there by his royal mother's direction, and with many pleasant words handed them to his son, now King George V, who presented them to each of us. I do not know what the others received, but when I had a chance to open the green leather case embossed with the royal arms I found inside a gold cigarette case and match box, mementos of an evening that will never pass from my memory.

I had cheerful reflections, upon this momentary association with resplendent royalty, of the little red-headed Quaker lad who had become the singing representative at that moment of a family that had left England generations before eschewing music and protesting against the pomp and vanity of the world.

CHAPTER XXXI

A BAFFLED IDEAL

Who shoots at the midday sun, though he be sure he shall never hit the mark, yet as sure he is he shall shoot higher than he who aims at a bush.— *Sir Philip Sidney.*

AFTER having been in the presence of the greatest monarch of modern times I now found myself the guest of one of the richest and most notable men in the world, the great ironmaster, Andrew Carnegie, at Skibo Castle in Scotland, golfing, fishing, and shooting deer with him, and moreover with a chance to discuss a matter near my heart: the foundation of what I called the Classic Theatre. It was to do for the drama in the United States all that the Metropolitan Opera Company does for music. Now that I was here, filled with my fine project, it seemed a happy conjunction of the time, the place, and the man.

Often as I had sung in public in Scotia, this was my first visit to the private house of any Scot. Though the new castle was built soon afterward, this admirable example of a Highland country home still stands out vividly in memory. Warm was the hospitality of the Master of Skibo! As I dressed for dinner the first evening, I heard resounding through the house the strains of an approaching bagpipe while the guests were assembling in the drawing room, and presently, playing down the hall, a magnificent piper in full Highland costume came to the door. Thence he led the way, Mr. Carnegie just behind, to the dining room, walking around the table

until the master's chair was reached, and continuing to
stand there and play until the guests were seated. He
betook himself then to his own place, playing himself
out in Scotland's wholly original and inspiriting manner. We heard him no more until the following morning, when he awoke the household by skreeling for half
an hour beneath our windows, marching up and down the
terrace, which overlooked a glorious lawn, and arousing
us in fine spirits for the day.

The day before my visit came to an end, Mr. Carnegie and I were fishing on a distant loch, which gave
me a further opportunity for discussing the Classic Theatre with him. He was unquestionably interested, but
weighed the pros and cons — particularly the latter —
with care. He did not think the country ready for such
an enterprise; I did not agree with him. I believe the
time came long ago when people of cultured tastes and
no great means would interest themselves in a theatre
where plays are performed which they are willing to
hear, and to have their children hear, acquainting them
as they grow up with the masterpieces of the drama,
whether of our own day or of other countries and other
times, and with the greatest examples of all — Shakespeare and the old English comedies.

Mr. Carnegie himself was one of thousands who will
not squander time and money and insult their intelligences
by attending such plays as are often provided, to the ex-
clusion of the masterpieces found enjoyable by the peoples
of other countries, especially of France, where the Comédie Française serves as a model for all institutions
such as Granville Barker, William Archer, and others
interested in developing the theatre would call into
being.

Many anecdotes were current of the men who now direct the dramatic destinies of America, men uninterested in theatrical progress, unable to recognize good drama when offered them, ignorant of the past of the theatre or the literature of the stage, and without holdings in any of the finer arts. To one of these came a youthful artist with sketches for the scenery and costumes of a forthcoming production. "Who'll carry them out?" asked Mr. Manager. The young man in a spirit of pleasantry suggested the name of Michael Angelo; with the unexpected reply, "I'll have none of those damned Irishmen about the place!"

A good play of which Major André was the hero was brought out by a firm of Broadway managers. The public was not attracted by the story of a British spy in Revolutionary times, and the play was a failure. Said one partner to the other, "Why didn't you tell me Major André was a spy?" Said the other partner to the one, "How did I know he was a spy!"

Mrs. Sarah Lemoyne and Otis Skinner put on the stage as a play Robert Browning's dramatic poem, "In a Balcony." Such a work produced by two such capable actors attracted the most favorable attention of those interested in the best, wherever the piece was given. News of its success was brought to one of the gentry who then commanded Broadway, and he was asked why he did not do something of the same sort. "Who is this fellow Browning?" he asked; and he was told that Browning was a poet. "Well," said the manager, "tell him to come around Monday and show me some of his stuff."

As Mr. Carnegie and I fished and talked of these things, a gentle wind blew our boat up the lake, far from the little inn where we had left the brake and the horses.

Mr. Carnegie listened with interest to my idea of an exhaustive dramatic library in connection with the Classic Theatre, a library which should contain everything pertaining to the history of the drama: rare manuscripts and early editions of the plays of noted authors acclaimed in other countries, with books of costume, of biography, of anecdotes, and of criticism. This interested the Laird of Skibo more than anything else.

By that time our boat had drifted some three miles up the lake, and nearly to the farther end of it. The ironmaster, eying his watch and the declining sun, exclaimed, "Good gracious, we can't row all the way back! How are we going to make the men know we wish to return?" A brilliant idea struck mine host, and he said, "I have often heard you sing against a full orchestra in the Wagnerian operas; your voice must be very strong to carry through all that noise"; and, with a twinkle in his eye, he quietly challenged me to make myself heard the length of that three-mile lake. The breeze had died down, but what little remained was going toward the inn. I lifted my voice, half singing my call. Those afar off in the inn heard the voice; and out came tumbling three or four men, two of them the servants. We could see them looking this side and that, not thinking of the little speck of a boat so far away on the bosom of the water. Standing up I waved my coatless arms and called again, bidding them bring the brake to the end of the lake and pick us up. Whether I used the correct method of deep breathing, I know not, but my ample lungs were expanded, my diaphragm in good working order, and my nasal resonance in the finest sort of condition that afternoon, and my words, wafted on the wings of the wind, brought the desired result. I

have sung out of doors many a time, but I doubt if another opera singer has ever done what I did then.

Later in New York the subject of the Classic Theatre
was broached again and, at Mr. Carnegie's request,
though without committing himself, I asked my friend,
the distinguished architect, Stanford White, to make me
a sketch plan of such a building as I proposed. His
attitude reminded me of the story of two Highland poachers, who were fishing on a lake where they had no business to be, when a tremendous storm came up, a Scotch
mist came down, and the waves rose so high their little
boat was threatened with immediate swamping. One
pulled with all his might, though he could not see which
way they were heading, while the other knelt among the
fish in the bottom, praying the Lord to deliver him and
promising, if saved that time, he would never use bad
language again, never drink again, never poach again,
when — " Hold on! " cried the other, " hold on, Sandy,
dinna get yerself into any mair obligations; the boat's
ashore! "

I indicated to Mr. Carnegie the place where I should
like the theatre to stand; at the southern end of Central
Park, between Sixth and Seventh avenues, facing south
and crowning the top of the high, rocky hill which rises
above the lake far beneath and to the east of it. " Ah! "
said Andrew, as we drove past, " the Lord must have
thought of this as the place for your theatre when He
made the world." He then took me to see his new house
in Fifth Avenue; it was nearly completed and he took
me, not to the pinnacle of the temple, but to the flat part
of his roof and there, without tempting me in the least,
showed me certain of his possessions, the New York
building lots in the immediate vicinity, with the remark,

"How strange it is how money makes money! Some years ago when I bought this property around here, my friends thought I was crazy. Nobody at all lived up here then, and they thought nobody ever would; but I tell you — and mark my words — within fifty years there will not be a private dwelling house on the whole of Manhattan Island.

"I paid," continued Mr. Carnegie, "So-and-so much for this land and it seemed a high price then; but property has so risen in value that with what I have sold already, including that lot over there which Mr. Belmont signed for yesterday, I have regained, not only the original cost of the land, but enough more to build this house and to buy the whole of the Skibo estate "— which I had been told was over a hundred square miles in extent —" and enough more to build the new castle I am contemplating; and yet I have left this lot and that and that," pointing as he said the words to several lots still vacant near by.

I felt no pang of envy of that rich man, for a kindlier soul never existed, nor one readier to do good according to his lights. My own few wants I have been able to supply ever since I left my $10 a week job in the wool trade and entered into the less tangible pursuit of song, and I have often wondered what I should do with money if I had a large amount of it. I think I should found the Classic Theatre.

Mr. Carnegie then lived at No. 1, West Fifty-first Street, and asked me to lunch and bring the sketch Stanford White had made. During the meal our host spoke of his fondness for acting and of his early youth as a telegraph boy in Pittsburgh, when he and his companions would postpone delivering telegrams received toward the

close of the day and addressed to the theatre, until the
box office opened.   Andrew and the other boys, poor then
but rich now, when they took the messages over would
ask if they might not have seats in the gallery to see the
play.   In this way the young enthusiast saw many a shining dramatic light.   It was truly enjoyable to hear him
tell of the encounters he and the other lads would have
spouting Shakespeare and shouting, " Lay on, Macduff ! "
beating each other about the back yard of the telegraph
office with swords made of laths and bucklers from the
heads of empty barrels.

Such an encounter was in progress when young Andrew
saw the fight from the back second-story window.   At
his side stood a bucket of water, and near it a tangled
mass of the tape used for stock quotations.   Soaking a
double handful of this in the dirty water, just as a youthful tragedian below felled his opponent with a doughty
blow of his broadsword while the vanquished one lay
crying for mercy, Andrew let fly the dripping tape straight
into the open mouth of a boy who is now another of the
world's richest men.

Jumping up from the table with a hearty laugh Mr.
Carnegie said, " Come now, come!   I am all eagerness
to see the plans."   With excitement I laid the precious
drawing upon a little table in a bow window of the library.
Many a time since have I seen that spot, and thought of
what ensued.

Soon after this I was asked to speak at the Art Theatre Society, but postponed for several days making any
notes of what I intended to say, and the night before the
meeting went to bed feeling concerned about the address
expected of me.   I had just dozed off, when suddenly I
found myself wide awake.   Springing out of bed I rap-

idly wrote down what had come into my mind on the instant, and when called upon at the dinner read the following:

THE EPISTLE OF DAVID

A manuscript has lately been brought to light, dating from the first century A. C., and bearing closely upon the well-known Gospel according to Andrew.   The narrative has every internal evidence of being genuine, and is a colloquy which took place about the first year of the reign of Theodorus the Strenuous, between Andrew, surnamed Crœsus, and David, the Singer of the Church at Philadelphia.   To David are we indebted for its preservation. It reads thus:

I, David, had traveled much and had seen the theatres at Athens and at Rome, and had approved the judgment of Paris, and with a deep thought in my mind I journeyed to the Land of Scotia and abode certain days in the hill country in the castle of Andrew the Rich, surnamed Crœsus.

Now Andrew the Rich is of small stature but of great heart, whose head ruleth and his hand is stayed.   And Andrew treated kindly his visitor, David the Singer; and unto him at a propitious moment David made known his desires, saying:

O, Andrew, thou hast flocks and herds and lands and palaces. Are not thy riches famed even unto the ends of the earth? Naught is impossible unto thee.

Come now, therefore, be it known unto thee that the New World crieth out for a worthy home for the drama.   Do thou, therefore, build us a theatre, even a Temple unto Thespis like unto naught the world hath seen before.   Let not the unbelieving daunt thee.

Build thee not, O, Andrew the Rich, a place alone for the presentment of the grace of dancers, but for the elevation of the mind of man, and if so it seemeth good in thy sight, secure it well and grapple it unto thy heart with bonds of steel.

Do thou call its name The Institution of the Classic Theatre, wherein the greatest works of men may be performed in the

vulgar tongue understanded of all the world; that men may flock
thither and partake of the benefits of thy largess.

And Andrew pondered these things and then he spake: O,
David, in pleasant converse there is much delight, and in thy
mind there is a mighty thought. Tell me now, I pray thee, how
great a price hast thou deemed should be paid for such a work?

And I answered and said: O, Andrew, do thou apportion
and set apart for this work ten millions of sestertii, and do thou
take counsel of such and such men, skilled in letters, poets, and
wise men of affairs; and do thou form affiliations with institutions of learning, both for men and women, in the land of thine
adoption; and do thou bind together such of those whose business drama is, and take thou advice even as to the foundation of
a true profession whereof the men and maidens of our land, of
good education and birth, may be proud.

And Andrew answered and said: Verily, how noble a deed
would this be, could there be but found the actors, who could
present worthily the plays thou namest. And then I showed
unto him the names of these, and spake of the great ones skilled
in acting, who would be bespoken to perform even upon the stage
of the theatre which he had builded, and of the rising generation
who would follow in the paths his wisdom had shown.

But Andrew questioned and looked on all sides, as is his wont,
and he said: If thou sayest that there be men who can present
worthily these plays, then to whom can they play them? For
verily I perceive an audience will be lacking, nor do I believe it
is in the heart of the people to interest themselves at all in this
matter.

Have I not builded an hall and founded it in my own name?
And did I not place therein Walter the Musician? And, verily,
he piped, but the people danced not unto his piping! Nor came
they to hear his music in sufficient numbers, and my venture rewarded me not. Truly, in order that I should not lose, I builded
me studios upon the building. Howbeit, continue! Thine enthusiasm almost persuadeth me.

Then I enlarged and unfolded to him all that was in my
thought; and he strode to and fro within the room, and his
hands worked beneath the raiment behind him. And he spake
in a low voice, as if unto himself saying:

Of the making of books there is no end, and they shall not go houseless. Verily am I sent to prepare a place for them. I will build me libraries that my name shall live among men on the earth for ever!

And after a time we crossed over and came to the other side of the sea, and met again in the New World. And there I spake to him further on the matter, saying: O, Andrew, be thou informed that no fame like unto the fame of having builded such a temple of art can belong to any man, and the glory of thy name shall be undying.

Thereupon Andrew said: O, for thine enthusiasm! Had I thine enthusiasm I should own the world! Do thou bring me a plan of the temple I should build. And he fixed a day to see the same.

And I departed and took counsel of a great architect, who made me certain drawings, and I went and sat at meat with Andrew in his own house, wotting not that one of his kinsmen there was also a builder of edifices. And after we had broken bread, Andrew called for the parchment and marveled at the dignity and beauty of the art of the great architect who had conceived them. Then, turning toward his kinsman, he said unto me:

If thou wilt have this young man to build me the theatre, lo, I will have my purse bearer pay unto thee ten million sestertii. Whereat his wife and those who stood by rejoiced greatly; but I departed with mingled feelings in my heart and sought out the architect, and told him what had befallen.

He smote upon his thigh saying: By all the gods, let it be so. I care not who the builder be, so long as thy servant may oversee the work. Thy thought is so mighty that it must be put into form, no matter who doeth it. Go thou then and say unto Andrew as I have told thee, and bid his kinsman come straightway and consult with me.

Then went I in haste and wrote unto Andrew what the architect had said. But the next day there came no word from him whose surname is Crœsus, and a great fear fell upon me.

The second day came a letter from Andrew bidding me remember well that of the making of books there was no end, and that the housing of them was as the breath of his life. He had considered my plan well, determining that the man who builded the theatre would be a benefactor of mankind, but he said:

Though in pleasant converse there is much delight, yet many words may be had without money and for small price. Utopia is no more, neither is the time ripe for the realization of thy dream. Therefore I pray thee, have me excused.

So I returned to my abode, desolate, and pondered over these things in my heart.

CHAPTER XXXII

ACROSS SEAS AND CONTINENTS

There is no feeling, perhaps, except the extremes of fear and grief, that does not find relief in music — that does not make a man sing or play better.— George Eliot.

EARLY in 1900 I began my experiment of reciting to music with Tennyson's " Enoch Arden," to which Richard Strauss had fitted the music. Ernst Possart, the German actor, had been giving the piece *in extenso* with the composer at the piano, and George Riddle had rendered it in America with a few cuts in the text; but I deliberately omitted enough of the unaccompanied lines to bring the performance within an hour when I tried it out at a few private hearings, and ended my program with some of Strauss's songs.

The most satisfactory of these musical recitations has been Longfellow's " King Robert of Sicily," with the noble music of Rossetter G. Cole. The poem is a clear-cut, plain-sailing, straightaway story, with incident enough to hold the attention, characterization enough to avoid monotony, opportunity enough to display every inflection of the speaking voice, and the final advantage of being familiar to every one in the audience, with effects greatly enhanced by organ tones in the accompaniment.

The manuscript of Arthur Bergh's fine musical setting of Poe's " Raven " had just been submitted to me when I received a telephone message from a professor at the New York College asking me to read the poem at the approaching centenary celebration of its author's birthday, with the intention of compelling the inclusion of Edgar Allan Poe's name with those of other American worthies in the Hall of Fame, a colonnade running around the assembly hall of the college. I replied that I was at the moment looking over Mr. Bergh's music, and promised to render it. My reading, with the composer at the piano, took place at the end of a program in which eminent men spoke in praise of Poe, and I like to think that my contribution aided in changing the hearts of the nominating committee, which soon after added the poet's name to those of the other Immortals.

In giving this I act out the character of the distraught and grief-stricken soul, tormented by the hallucination of the raven's entering his room to reiterate the cheerless refrain of " Nevermore." I think this the one artistic interpretation, enabling me to enact the part of a man driven mad by memories of a lost love; and deem this to be the only possible rendering of the piece, to which the accompaniment is entirely suitable. Mr. Bergh has also adorned " The Pied Piper of Hamelin," Robert Browning's narrative written for a child, with music as exquisite and fantastically fitting as that to " The Raven " is full of tragedy.

I also use the accompaniment written by Max Schillings for Wildenbruch's gruesome ballad, " The Witch's Song," which demands a full orchestra for its best effect. I have performed it in this way a number of times, of which the most notable was with the Chicago Orchestra under the conductorship of Frederick Stock, for which several interesting rehearsals were held. After the second of the week's pair of performances I was honored with a request from the orchestra committee to repeat the work at a special concert the week following. This rare distinction had been previously conferred upon but two artists, Ysaye the violinist and D'Albert the pianist, leaving me the first vocalist to receive it.

I freely confess that my fondness for reciting to music is primarily due to my love of the histrionic art. In default of other dramatic chances, I am thus able to combine my love for music with my ambition to act. But let me warn those who intend to devote themselves to melodrama that it is very difficult to do acceptably. The music so covers the tones of the speaking voice that both power and clearness of utterance beyond the average are demanded, yet the vocal tone must have distinct reserve, never trespassing upon the region of song. In spite of the fact that the female voice is essentially less effective in speech than in song, this difficult task is much more frequently attempted by women than by men. I think this desire to perform the impossible results from the greater artistic enthusiasm of our sisters, who allow themselves to be carried away by impulse where men think twice before embarking upon so unusual and so technical a venture.

Often as I have indulged myself in this form of art, and thoroughly as my efforts have been enjoyed by my hearers, the leading music critics of America seem to feel that the words and music stand in each other's way; that the text cannot be understood for the music, or the music for the text. As this seems to me like the ancient complaint of the man who could not see the forest for the trees, I have gone on in my own fashion, partly because I enjoy reciting to music so much myself, and partly because I have repeated proofs that my audiences enjoy it too. Certainly the happy wedding of music to dramatic art cannot result in illegitimacy.

In February, 1900, I was invited to sing at the executive mansion in Albany, New York, while Theodore Roosevelt was governor of the State. I had met this eminent American more than once and knew members of his family, and was specially asked that evening by Mrs. Roosevelt to sing for her guests from the best in my repertory, which included classic songs and old English lyrics to end with, but was as particularly requested not to sing my war horse, " Danny Deever," my hostess thinking it so gruesome a piece of realism that she preferred not to be harrowed by it again. Surely this was a compliment as great as that paid me afterward at the White House by President Roosevelt himself.

In the spring of 1900 Walter Damrosch organized a tour during which Madame Gadski and I rendered Wagnerian selections separately and together to Mr. Damrosch's admirable piano accompaniment. After a few concerts in the Eastern States, he opened his season on the Pacific Coast at the Simpson Auditorium in Los Angeles, on March 2. I had first to fill some engagements in Chicago, the last of which was with the Apollo Club on the evening of February 26. I took the midnight train for Los Angeles, where my associates had preceded me, due to arrive the morning of our opening. Awakening next day I found the train so stuck in a snowdrift on the prairie that several hours were lost in getting through. The following day was like midsummer, and a succession of hot boxes held us up. The third day a bridge, nearly washed away by an Arizona cloudburst, delayed me more. My anxiety was great lest I miss my concert. A Los Angeles newspaper that met the train published our program, which I ran over and, after getting into evening clothes, I stepped from the express into a cab and arrived

after a journey of some 2500 miles at the door of the
concert room on the minute of 8:15, the manager greeting me with the flattering statement that my reputation
for promptness and reliability was so great that he knew
I would have found some way to reach the concert even
if our train had broken down.

Thus began the first of many successful tours on the
Pacific Coast, all of interest but not different from concertizing elsewhere, always excepting the climate, the
scenery, and a sense of freedom not found elsewhere.
The idea of the Classic Theatre was still uppermost
in my mind, in spite of my disappointment at the hands
of Mr. Carnegie, and I suggested the foundation of such
an institution to Mrs. Phoebe Hearst. She was interested then, and had it still in mind when I called upon
her in New York afterward, going so far as to say that
she would be glad to coöperate with others in providing
the money necessary for the enterprise. She asked me
why I did not appeal to her son, William Randolph
Hearst, saying that she believed he might take it up. I
did not feel that I knew Mr. Hearst well enough to
approach him, but I cannot help thinking that his mother
may have done so, for it was not long before the Greek
Theatre at Berkeley was built by him.

This beautiful structure, modeled after the Athenian
amphitheatres, is an outstanding feature in the artistic
life of the Pacific Coast. Without fear of interruption
from the elements, large audiences may gather in the
open air within its ample confines to hear fine music, see
great plays and marvelous pageants, by day or at night,
and many such celebrities as Sarah Bernhardt and Margaret Anglin have begun there a tradition of artistic
loveliness which will doubtless prove lasting.

Our journey took us as far as Portland, Oregon, whence we returned by way of Winnipeg, St. Paul, and Minneapolis, meeting on the way a little Italian concert party headed by Madame Sophia Scalchi, then nearing the close of her career, but remembered by me from my youth; the majesty of her art in rôles of the old Italian repertory, particularly her Orfeo in Gluck's masterpiece, is never to be forgotten. Madame Scalchi boarded a train at a place in Dakota, and I wondered at so eminent an artist's visiting so small a town. But in a country like ours, its builders have gone from the larger centres in the East, where they were formerly acquainted with good music and are in their new surroundings in constant need of it to lighten their lives. It was not long before I myself was besought to travel to all sorts of places, where the women and their clubs demanded the influence of music. Many little towns of twenty years ago are large cities now, and I look back with pride in having helped to bring the comfort of song to many thousands of thirsty souls.

Returning to New York I revived my Beethoven play "Adelaïde," the title rôle played charmingly by Hilda Spong, with Mr. Damrosch presiding over the orchestra.

Immediately after this I left for Detroit, where I performed "Elijah," and after much work of great variety under other distinguished auspices, I took part, for the second time, in the Cincinnati Festival of 1900 under Theodore Thomas, at whose concerts in Chicago I had sung earlier in the season. At the conclusion of the festival I appeared in Rochester, New York, in joint recital with the celebrated Kneisel String Quartette. An enthusiastic audience protracted the concert, though

both Kneisel and myself had to catch night trains to keep
our respective engagements the next evening. They
went to Chicago, and I to Columbus, Ohio, to sing with
the Arion Club. Though I rendered three groups of
songs with encores for the first and second groups, at
Rochester, it was impossible to give an encore to my third
appearance. I barely caught the train as it was; while
Kneisel and his associates, ending the program with the
Quartette by Grieg, were also obliged to cut short their
acknowledgments of the pleasure of the audience. As
a result we were severely criticized in the next morning's
papers. That we had played and sung well was not the
point; we were taken to task because we had not played
and sung more.

When I returned to London that year I was asked to
appear in opera in Spain, and subsequently was obliged
to decline an invitation from the Royal Opera of Berlin.
Indeed I have never sung professionally on the Continent, being so constantly occupied in England and
America. London was kind enough to keep me busy,
and my intercourse with persons of distinction in the
musical world was as interesting as ever, including among
others frequent association with Kubelik, whom I first
met at the house of his patroness, Lady Palmer, who
gave the black-haired wizard of the violin a Stradivarius
said to be worth 2000 guineas. Sir Walter Palmer, her
husband — they are both gone now — was of Quaker
stock, a kindly man whose wife was a miniature Ellen
Terry with a flair for celebrities and a piano seldom in
tune.

Before leaving England in October, 1900, I again took
part in the Birmingham Festival under the conductorship
of Richter; singing in Bach's " Passion Music," Brahms's

" Requiem," Dvořák's " The Spectre's Bride," and other works. Edward Elgar's " Dream of Gerontius " was then first produced, and another English composer lifted to the pinnacle of fame.

During its performance I sat behind the wife and daughter of Edward Lloyd, the tenor to whom had been assigned the title rôle. Nearing the end of his career as he was, and not in his usually good voice, I knew him to be very nervous over the task before him. The soloists sat in chairs on either side of the conductor as is customary, rising to sing and seating themselves when finished. In " The Dream of Gerontius " the tenor seems to be for ever rising and sitting down again. I could hear Madame Lloyd speaking to her daughter quietly, nervous for her husband so ill at ease himself. At last Mrs. Lloyd could contain herself no longer, and her stage whisper must have been audible to many besides me, as she said, " Mary, if your father gets up again I shall scream! "

At this festival was performed, though not for the first time, the beautiful music to Longfellow's " Song of Hiawatha," by the gifted English negro composer, S. Coleridge-Taylor, a musical genius of whom more than passing mention should be made.

English audiences do not share the American aversion to persons of African descent in connection with serious music. Coleridge-Taylor was much in demand to conduct his own choral work, and was invariably cheered to the echo by chorus and audience alike. He was a pleasant and highly educated man, and reminded one in his personal appearance strongly of Beethoven. Early in Sir Hubert Parry's directorship of the Royal College of Music, I was invited to hear a quintette composed by Coleridge-

Taylor, then a highly esteemed student there. It was rendered for the benefit of no less a personage than Doctor Joseph Joachim, with whom and Villiers Stanford I went to listen to this fine composition, afterward performed by Joachim and his associates in Berlin. When " Hiawatha " was performed at Birmingham in 1900, Doctor Richter conducted it at the composer's request; it need not be said that such distinguished musicians would not have recognized Coleridge-Taylor thus had he not possessed more than ordinary musical ability.

He had consulted me, before coming to America, about his chances of success in conducting his own work, which he hoped to have performed by our choral bodies; and I regretfully informed him that the feeling in the United States against people of his race, owing to their former enslavement, was such that the only engagements he could obtain would be with negro choral societies; and this indeed was unfortunately the case.

One day in London I received a visit from a gentleman who brought me such songs by Coleridge-Taylor as were suitable for my voice, asking me to sing them as often as I could in order to introduce to the public the young genius whose supporter he had been, explaining that he was taking to other musicians vocal and instrumental compositions suitable to their talents written by his protégé. He said that with this final step his association with Coleridge-Taylor ended, though it had lasted from the composer's infancy, and told me the following story.

He was a bachelor of large means living near London, with only one desire — to discover and educate musically gifted English youth. More than twenty years before he learned of the remarkable talent of a negro child, whose mother was a servant in a lodging house. He went to see her there, and heard her dusky four-year-old child play almost incredibly well, standing before an inferior upright piano. Inquiring into the child's history, he learned from his white mother that the father was a full-blooded negro from Sierra Leone, Africa, sent to London to be trained as a medical assistant to the missionaries when he went back to his native land. His father had left England never to return, and the child's benefactor entered into an agreement with the mother by which her son was to be thoroughly educated, special attention being, of course, paid to music. The young composer's benefactor, far from regretting his action, professed sincere admiration for Coleridge-Taylor both as man and musician.

It is said that, at a dinner party given Coleridge-Taylor by some of his own people in New York, the host, while carving a fine turkey, jocularly asked the composer if he would have some of what is called our " national bird," to which he replied as he passed his plate, " Thanks awfully; but do you really mean it is an eagle? "

CHAPTER XXXIII

GOING TO AND FRO

God is its author, and not man; He laid
The keynote of all harmonies He planned,
All perfect combinations; and He made
Us so that we could hear and understand.
    —*J. J. Brainard.*

EMULATING the example of Satan was I during the busy autumn of 1900, "going to and fro in the earth, and . . . walking up and down in it." My second visit to the Pacific Coast was with the company from the Metropolitan Opera House of New York; one of high distinction, as ever, with the names of Mesdames Melba, Nordica, Eames, Gadski, Schumann-Heink, and Olitzka, with Edouard de Reszke, Van Dyck, and many other prime favorites with the public. I sang frequently, and in the parts with which my name was associated.

At Christmas and other times I sang in oratorio, and brought out in concert such new works as Liza Lehmann's setting of " In Memoriam " and Arthur Somervell's " Maud," Tennyson's fine poems fitted to beautiful though somewhat somber music. American composers were also urged upon the public attention, for I sang the songs of Howard Brockway, Herman Wetzler, and John Alden Carpenter, who has come to be one of the best of our native writers. Singing with me were Miss Lillian Blauvelt, the soprano, Mrs. Morris Black, known in the opera houses of Europe as Madame Cahier, and the late Evan Williams, a Welsh tenor with a voice of gold. Several times I appeared at miscellaneous entertainments with Monsieur Coquelin and Madame Sarah Bernhardt, whose impersonation of Hamlet that season afforded me the most interesting evening I ever spent in a theatre.

Early in 1901 I sang at the Philharmonic Society's concerts in New York, under the conductorship of Emil Paur, Richard Strauss's noble songs, " Hymnus " and " Pilgers Morgenlied," settings of poems by Schiller and Goethe respectively. Though I know of no other singer who has thus paired these compositions, I recommend them to the attention of all barytones.

In opera that season we had Madame Milka Ternina, a Croatian whose majestic appearance, splendid voice, and great histrionic power placed her high in public esteem. Walter Damrosch first brought her to America, but some mysterious nervous trouble kept her from appearing after she had been announced. Upon her recovery she rendered Wagner's heroines superbly, her Isolde being one of the best I have ever seen. There was never an artist more serious, but once when I was singing with her in " Tristan und Isolde," as I came forward on the deck of the ship in the first act to tell her my master would have speech with her, to my amused amazement the stately Ternina calmly winked her right eye at me, not once but several times. She forgot her lines as she did so, but had the presence of mind to remain silent till she had collected herself, coming in at a convenient place in the music soon after. While she was silent she crossed the stage, contrary to the directions, and forced me to accommodate myself to the new situation, sorrowfully realizing why she had taken so unusual a course. For her cheek thus turned from the audience, after her winking had become constant, began to twitch in a most painful manner. No operations on the nerves of her face gave permanent relief, and in her forced retirement the stage lost a brilliant ornament.

Jean de Reszke was stricken by influenza early in the year, and sang only a few times after his recovery. Andreas Dippel, from whose tongue opera seemed to slip, was his substitute, and has been known to dress in the cab between his hotel and the opera house on a call following de Reszke's sudden illness; but neither he of the hundred rôles nor any others of the company could, alone or together, fill the vacancy Jean de Reszke left. Dippel was not heroic enough in figure to fill the eye, Van Dyck's mode of singing left too much to be desired by the ear, Burgstaller had too small a repertory, Kraus was so vast that his Siegfried in armor looked like a huge armadillo, even Tamagno the Italian and Alvarez the Spaniard, admirable artists both, could by no means vie with de Reszke in the extent of their repertories. Taking him for all in all he was the finest artist of his generation, a tower of strength to our company, and a vocal and physical adornment to the stage he elevated by his presence.

I sang with de Reszke for the last time at the farewell performance of the season at the Metropolitan on the evening of April 29, 1901, when Monsieur Coquelin and Madame Bernhardt also bade a temporary good-by to America. The remarkable program comprised the first scene of the third act of Gounod's "Romeo and Juliet," with Salignac and Suzanne Adams as the lovers, Miss Bauermeister as Gertrude, and Plançon as the Friar; the second act of "Tristan und Isolde," with the brothers de Reszke and Mesdames Nordica and Schumann-Heink; the Mad Scene from "Lucia," sung by Madame Melba in wonderful contrast to the preceding; Gozlan's comedy in one act, "La Pluie et le Beau Temps," exquisitely rendered by Coquelin and Madame Bernhardt; the evening concluding with the third act of "The Valkyrie," in which I as Wotan supported Madame Nordica's Brünnhilde, as so often before.

When Madame Bernhardt was playing in Louisville, Kentucky, the home of our own Mary Anderson, the fashionable attendance on her opening night was so great that she could not get a carriage to take her to her theatre. *Faute de mieux* she hired an old-fashioned coach in rags and tatters, drawn by a rawboned nag, and driven by a good-for-nothing, white-woolled darky in an ancient suit and forlorn top hat. Something about the combination struck the fancy of the divine Sarah, who ordered the ramshackle vehicle to return for her. When the play was over Sambo drew up at the stage door, only to be ordered away by a policeman, who would not believe the ragged driver's assertion that Madame Bernhardt had used his vehicle. Ordered away the second time by the officer, the aged negro descended from the box, opened the door of the barouche with a flourish, and said: "Look here, boss, if you don't believe I done brung Miss Sarah to this here theatre, just you smell my hack."

During the spring of 1901 I was singing in Chicago at one of the series of popular four o'clock concerts, the orchestra being under Theodore Spiering. As I was to appear in Philadelphia the next evening, it was essential that I should catch the limited express after the concert. In my contract it was stipulated that the program was to be arranged so that I could finish in time to get my train. I had a cab at the stage door of the Studebaker

Theatre, in which were my impedimenta, and I had nothing further to do but to deliver the last group and go. After singing I jumped in, urged the driver to hasten — and the horse fell down! What to do? Get the horse up on four legs again. We did it with the help of several passers-by. I reached the station, the porter running beside me with my things, to find the train already moving; but I luckily scrambled aboard before the doors of the vestibule were closed. Audiences are never aware of the nervous anxiety incidents so slight cause the artist.

I went to London for the season of 1901 at Covent Garden, entering immediately upon rehearsals of Villiers Stanford's new opera in four acts founded upon Shakespeare's "Much Ado About Nothing," the admirable libretto in English made by Julian Sturgis. This really fine work was rehearsed and played with great enthusiasm by those of us who sang and had been written with equal gusto; as Stanford told me in his delightful Irish way, "It ran right out of the end of my pen." But the London Press would have none of it, though they had heralded it in glowing terms, and were so disappointed in the outcome that they said they had made "much ado about nothing." To my mind this judgment was entirely unwarranted. The work is beautiful and will well repay study by those interested in opera in English. Marie Brema was enchanting as Beatrice, I was Benedick, the English tenor John Coates was Claudio, Robert Blass made an amusing Dogberry, Suzanne Adams was lovely as Hero, Plançon superb as the Friar, and the part of Leonato was assigned to the gifted American basso, Putnam Griswold, who ere long joined the great majority, to the infinite regret of his friends and of the public.

Many and notable were the occasions upon which I sang

that season in London, the most distinguished being at a
memorial concert to Queen Victoria under the patronage
of Queen Alexandra. My own song recital the next day
was equally important to me, as I then introduced to the
London public among classics of the best sort the American negro melodies arranged by Henry Burleigh, " I
Don't Want to Stay Here No Longer," " The Blackbird
and the Crow," and " Joshua Fit de Battle of Jericho,"
which I consider to be as legitimate examples of folk
songs as those of Germany, England, and Ireland with
which they were grouped. London for the first time
had a taste of the real as distinguished from the spurious
article sung by the Christie Minstrels or the politely artificial negro songs of my friend Alfred Gatty.

The next evening I sang for the first time the difficult
but fascinating part of Iago in Verdi's " Otello," with
Tamagno in the title rôle, under the conductorship of
Mancinelli. The advice given me years before by
Planchette had never been forgotten, for I had studied
with great care the barytone rôles in the operas of Verdi.
Unfortunately for me the barytone parts in Italian operas
are preëmpted by Italians, and Iago, created by Victor
Maurel, was also very finely sung by Antonio Scotti,
whose indisposition enabled me to assume the rôle on the
few occasions when I have rendered it.

At the end of the great jealousy scene, while the
populace without is acclaiming Otello as " The Venetian
Lion," he falls in a faint. Iago, triumphing over him,
sings, " Ecco il Leone!" and, as performed by Maurel,
sets his foot upon the chest of the prostrate Moor. I
adopted it as an effective, and to Tamagno an inoffensive,
bit of stage business; but when I sang it later in New York
with Alvarez, unconscious as he was supposed to be lying

there close to the footlights, he calmly raised his hand
and shoved my foot away from his manly bosom. It
almost upset my balance and completely upset the gravity
of those who saw him do it.   I concluded that it would be
as well, in the absence of rehearsals, to find out in future
whether the procedure adopted is held objectionable or
not.

While recrossing the ocean in October I met a musical
enthusiast who knew me by sight and who was eager to
learn of the plans of the opera company, which had already begun a season of French and Italian works in
Canada. Telling him I was to join the company at
Louisville, Kentucky, he asked me what opera we were
going to sing. I replied that it was " Lohengrin," with
Mesdames Eames and Schumann-Heink, Dippel in the
title rôle, and Mr. Damrosch conducting. He said, " I
will go to hear you." I asked if he lived in Louisville,
and he replied: "Oh, no; but I have a few days to
spare and I'm a fan on music; so I'll just go out there to
hear that opera, and then I will have something no one
can ever take away from me." Would there were more
people like him!

To southern cities we went, with Mesdames Sembrich,
Gadski, Melba, Louise Homer, and Emma Calvé.

Among the newcomers in our cast was the German
character tenor, Albert Reiss, who could properly boast
of being one of the most useful artists who ever appeared on the stage, in New York at any rate, and one
of the finest character actors in operatic annals. Van
Dyck covered himself with glory; Journet, the basso, became immediately a favorite; Salignac under the genial
influence of our great audiences gave his best; the barytones Scotti and Campanari were at the top notch of their

fame, and the sprightly Fritzi Scheff and the genial
Edouard de Reszke contributed a vivacity and amount of
fun to the company which permeated the whole body of
artists.   We were all like children out of school.

As far as I know every one returned to New York
well except myself; but in crossing the Rocky Mountains
in December I threw off my covers in the overheated
sleeper, and lay unconsciously with my back against the
window while the weather outside was 40° below zero.
In consequence I contracted a severe attack of lumbago.
Our first stop was Kansas City, and I can never forget my
servant's surprise on awakening me in the morning at
the hotel to see me crumple up and fall prostrate upon
the floor as I stepped out of bed.   The demon had laid
his hand upon the small of my back and I was as nothing
in his grasp.   My faithful Italian plunged me into the
hot bath already prepared, and by the application of
electricity to my back during the day I was enabled, by
evening, to move about the room.

I wondered how I was to get through my part of
Wolfram that night, but I made my way with the others
to the huge Convention Hall, where a crowded audience
had assembled.   When standing I could scarcely sit
down, while sitting I could scarcely arise, if I bent an inch
out of the perpendicular I was in great pain; but the performance had to be given as there was no one to take my
place.   My voice was in excellent condition, though I
suffered acutely with every inhalation.   I faced the ordeal
and went through the first act well enough, not being
obliged to do anything but stand during the concerted
numbers and solo that fell to my lot.

The second act I dreaded.   I had to appear as graceful as was physically possible, and after changing my

costume was almost incapacitated by pain. However, I
walked on with the rest in the scene of The Hall of Song,
which Madame Gadski had just greeted in the famous
solo, and it was to her that I had to pay my operatic addresses through the rest of the act. She, calm and
serene, accepted the homage I laid at her feet, little
aware that every move I made almost prostrated me
before her. I shall never forget when the quartette of
pages announced " Wolfram von Eschenbach, beginne,"
and I had to rise from my stool, my hand on my harp,
ready to open my address to the assemblage. I was
sitting as straight as possible, and managed to get my left
leg around behind my chair out of sight of the audience
and without disturbing my equilibrium. My right foot,
visible to the house, was projecting gracefully before me.
The moment arrived, the deed had to be done, and with
a mighty effort I stood erect. In so doing I emitted a
groan that must have been heard to the farthest seat in
the vast auditorium. I could not move forward and
had instructed the page in waiting to draw my chair
away. Several times during the solo it was so painful
to breathe that I doubted whether I could go on. When
the number was over at last, and the page replaced my
chair, I could not sink into it gradually as I should have
done ordinarily; at a certain point the nerves and muscles
of my legs and back gave way and I fell into the seat
with a thud, thankful, at least, that so much had been
done without a catastrophe. Things went better from
there on, but at the conclusion of the performance, which
took place upon a bitterly cold night, my costumes were
wringing wet with the perspiration my agony had started
from every pore of my body.

My lesson in the obligations of a public performer to

his audience was learned early. When a youth attending the variety performance to hear Max Heinrich sing
I saw an accident befall one of the acrobats in the trapeze
act. As one of the two gymnasts let go his hold on the
bar and swung into the hands of his partner, he was
caught properly, but their hands slipped on the return
swing, throwing him into the orchestra. I was shocked
at the accident, but felt relieved the next moment, when
the fallen man arose, scrambled back to the stage and repeated the act, this time successfully. I was pretty sure
that he was injured in some way, for he had landed on
his head and shoulders, and asked about him the next
day. Heinrich told me he was somewhat better, but had
been in delirium and convulsions all night long.

There was my lesson. A public performer is neither
more nor less than a soldier under fighting orders. He
engages himself to do something and, the engagement
made, he must carry it out, no matter how difficult or
dangerous it proves to be. As in Kansas City when
great discomfort told me to stay in bed and nurse my
ills, the thought of that acrobat, injured about his head
and spine but doing his work nevertheless, made a higher
appeal than my slighter troubles, however painful. If
he could do his duty, certainly I could do mine. Short
of actual incapacity, it is the singer's task to sing well
enough to overcome all lesser difficulties, to appear smiling before his public without a hint of his afflictions, and
to go through his performance with all the artistry of
which he is capable. His private ills are not the business
of the public, which had paid its good money and has the
right to expect value returned.

There are times, however, when an artist is absolutely
incapacitated and unable to contend against an acute

malady, as in the case of the American soprano, Miss Sarah Anderson, who but a fortnight later arrived at Carnegie Hall, New York, to sing with us in " The Messiah." She complained that, though perfectly well before dinner, she had been attacked as she left her house with a fit of sneezing so violent that it left her unable to perform. A specialist was called who pronounced it acute laryngitis, the sudden onslaught of which presently robbed Miss Anderson of the ability to utter a note. By chance, there was a teacher of singing in the artist's room who said that he had a pupil in the audience who knew the part, though she had never sung it in public, and would take the place of Miss Anderson, who had herself been engaged owing to the illness of Miss Esther Palliser. The newcomer sang most acceptably, having bridged a gap which is but seldom provided against. Indeed it is remarkable, and altogether to their credit, that concert singers so seldom disappoint their audiences.

CHAPTER XXXIV

COMPOSER AND CRITIC

Hope constancy in wind, or corn in chaff;
Believe a woman or an epitaph,
Or any other thing that's false, before
You trust in critics, who themselves are sore.
— *Byron.*

THOUGH Ignace Paderewski, musician and statesman, did not conduct, he assisted in preparing the first production of his opera " Manru " on February 14, 1902, at the Metropolitan, and was present at its American *première*. I sang the very arduous part of Urok in this extraordinary work, Bandrowski assuming the title rôle as he had abroad, Madame Sembrich the beautiful character of Ulana, supported by Madame Louise Homer, Miss Fritzi Scheff, and others. Altogether " Manru " was given nine times that season in New York and other cities. It was so full of musical color and action and the drawing power of the composer's name was so great that it not only made money but was seriously considered by Mr. Grau for revival the year following.

Paderewski had a musical idiom of his own, used freely throughout this work. Nevertheless he was accused of plagiarizing from Verdi, from Bizet, and from Wagner. He was greatly hurt by the charge, and at the banquet given him by the opera management and associated artists several New York critics actually twitted him face to face on the similarity of his work to that of his predecessors. He replied that he had wittingly appropriated no musical material that did not belong to him, and pointedly inquired if an architect is blamed for putting windows in a house because others before him have done the like.

A man highly placed once said to me as he looked over his newspaper, "Is it not amazing that Paderewski, a mere piano player, should become the Premier of Poland! Think of a man like that," he said scornfully, "being allowed to hold a position of such prominence." My acquaintance was greatly surprised when I told him that Paderewski was one of the finest linguists in Europe, one of the best informed men in the world, and a statesman whose political acumen was acknowledged by the principal figures of the Peace Conference.

It is extraordinary how generally musical reviewers attempt to impede, rather than assist, artists in their work, and to destroy rather than uphold well-established reputations. It is so easy to speak in dispraise of anything that, in order that the public may be better instructed regarding those who entertain them, I heartily recommend to all who criticize what Swinburne calls " the noble art of praising."

I sang that season six times in four oratorios, Liszt's " St. Elizabeth," Gounod's " Redemption," Verdi's " Requiem," and Rossini's " Stabat Mater "; in ten miscellaneous concerts, several of which put upon me the greater part of the work; in ten recitals of my own in which I did all the work, including two or three performances of Strauss's " Enoch Arden "; and in fourteen performances of opera, Wagner's " Rheingold," " Siegfried," and " Lohengrin," and Paderewski's " Manru "; making forty performances in all, including nine entire works and a list of sixty songs, and involving travel away from New York to eighteen cities between Florida and Canada.

Fortunately, such is the power of will over ill — for even my robust strength was severely taxed — that I was enabled, thanks to the powers that be, to emerge safely from the ordeal and sail for Europe in my usual good health, entering immediately upon another busy season on the other side of the Atlantic after having given 119 performances in my native land.

The season that followed in London differed in no particular respect from the many preceding it. I took my usual rôles at Covent Garden and added to my repertory the part of Rudolf in an opera called " Der Wald " (The Forest), a work already performed on the Continent. It was composed by the talented English-woman Ethel M. Smythe, and brought prominently to the fore the gifted Olive Fremstad, an American of Norse descent and German training, whom I had met a few years previously at the house of Madame Wagner at Bayreuth and with whom earlier in the London season of 1902 I sang in " Tristan und Isolde " and in " Lohengrin," her interpretation of Brangäne and Ortrud giving promise of the great things she was later to achieve as a Wagnerian singer.

As Miss Fremstad began to come into prominence, various stories were told of her. Some years previously she had been studying in Germany with Lilli Lehmann, who was then married to Paul Kalisch, the tenor, and it is said that the elder artist, becoming annoyed with Miss Fremstad, took a book of songs from the piano and flung it at her head, with the result that the fair Olive burst into tears and left the house enraged. As she went she passed by Mr. Kalisch, sitting at a table in great dejection with his face in his hands; looking up with tears in his eyes he said, " Olive, what is the matter? " To which Olive angrily replied, " I will never come here again; she has thrown a book at my head." The tenor to comfort her said, " Never mind, my dear, she does the same to me."

That season in London there appeared a woman who had already made a great success in Paris at the Opéra Comique and who was presently destined to become world famous, none other than Mary Garden, who sang the title rôle in Massenet's " Manon," giving London a taste of the thrill which later moved the whole artistic world.

During my residence in England I had many times been touched to the heart by the admiration of the public for American artists and by the sincere desire on the part of the British nation as a whole to make friends and to stay friends with its great offshoot across the water. I knew personally our ministers and ambassadors, Bayard, John Hay, and Choate, who was loved for his American wit and gallantry, for had he not said that if he could not be himself, he would prefer to be Mrs. Choate's second husband? There seems to be in the make-up of the Britons little place for jealousy. They are such good sportsmen that they admire talent wherever they see it and reward Americans as they would their own people with frank affection.

I possess in an old statuette of Benjamin Franklin, a curious exemplification of this earlier British feeling. Many of these figures of the celebrated colonial statesman and sage had been sold, when his attitude during his diplomatic negotiations with France caused him to be as heartily disliked as he had before been beloved, and the demand for his statuettes immediately fell off. In or-

der to dispose of the stock, the makers erased from the
pedestal his name, and substituted that of George Washington, whom they held in the highest esteem even though
he had just defeated them at the game of war.   My
Franklin figure bears the name of Washington.   With
the change the remainder of the stock sold like hot cakes!

One of my most interesting programs of the season in
1902 is that of the grand British and American Festival
Peace Concert in commemoration of the South African
war, at Crystal Palace, under the conductorship of Frederick Cowan.   The Handel Festival Choir and orchestra
of 3000 performers rendered various numbers, while the
soloists, alternately American and English, were headed
by the name of Madame Albani, who being a Canadian
was both American and English, followed by Ella Russell,
American; Clara Butt, British; Belle Cole, American;
Ben Davies, British; myself, American; and Charles
Santley, the grand old man of the vocal world, British,
thoroughly British.   How the audience did love him,
how they rose to him when he appeared, and how they
applauded him to the echo when he sang!

The program contained the portraits of King Edward
VII and Queen Alexandra and of President Theodore
Roosevelt.   May we Americans never fall out with our
noble and high-minded kinsmen across the water in the
little island from which so many of us have sprung, but
may we, on the contrary, assist the sons of that far-flung
race to maintain the peace of the world!

I am proud to say that my own countrymen were asking for my services more than ever, but I did not return
to America until I had filled an engagement once more at
the Sheffield Festival under the conductorship of Henry
Wood, now universally recognized by the English as one

of their real geniuses of the baton.   Though I gave three
of my own recitals at St. James's Hall in the summer of
1902, I sang little more after that time till 1906, when
I produced " The Vicar of Wakefield " in England.   It
was a regret for me to leave a country where for so long
I had been so well received.   At two of the three concerts to which I have alluded I repeated Strauss's melodrama " Enoch Arden," with my version of Tennyson's
poem and also introduced a number of Strauss's songs,
including the " Hymnus " and " Pilgers Morgenlied,"
these colorful rhapsodies contrasting strangely with, but
not at all to the disadvantage of, Handel's duet from
" Israel in Egypt," " The Lord is a Man of War," which
I rendered with the brilliant Ffrangçon Davies.

Ere long I began to make acquaintance with the songs
of Hugo Wolf, some of which I ventured to bring before
the public, which has at length accepted them and would
do well to look more carefully into their manifold
beauties, though many of them seem to be the result
of a mental abnormality.   To a greater extent this is
true of Claude Debussy, who was driven almost insane
by the overtones he alone could hear, but which led him
at last to write his master work, the opera " Pelléas and
Mélisande."

The composer Ernest Bloch has told me of his friendship with Richard Strauss and Debussy and of their manner of working.   The former, having finished an orchestral score, does not rest content till he has added still
more contrapuntal devices, piling complication upon complication; whereas Debussy was not satisfied until he had
taken out of his score as many notes as possible and
simplified it to the last degree.

While the vocal score of Debussy's " Pelléas and Méli-

sande " was in my possession for some years it remained
quite uncomprehended. When at last I heard the work
with Mary Garden as the heroine, I sat entranced. I
knew not whether I was awake or asleep, whether an old
Bayeux tapestry had come to life before my eyes, whether
I was witnessing music or listening to pictures, so magical
was the effect upon me of this Old-World tale told in
terms of tones tense, tender, tragic, translucent, tran-
scendental!

Quite otherwise was I affected by the music of another
modern. As the sounds proceeded I seemed to have a
vision. I thought I was in Verona, on top of the roof of
an ancient villa surmounted with Ghibelline battlements
of dark-red brick, beyond which tall, dark-green cypress
trees reared their heads and swayed in the wind of an
oncoming storm. It was night, with the moon, riding
high in a purple sky, sailing in and out of the clouds.
Presently, a cat emerged from the shadows and stood
waiting on the middle of the roof. His feline call was
matched by a wail of the wind. Another cat appeared,
and the two had a pitched battle, as the lightning flashed
and the thunder rolled in the distance. There followed
a calm; the moon shone forth in glory; while an exquisite melody arose from somewhere; but soon discord
began again, and in the midst of the fury of the storm
the cats fought to a finish. I awoke to the fact that I
was in a fashionable London drawing-room and that a
quartette of Max Reger's had just come to an end.

Some time ago I attended an orchestral concert at
which I heard a well-known soprano sing on the first half
of the program a pearly Mozart number which she, rendered exquisitely. Later in the evening, she gave an
ultra-modern composition which sounded to me like noth-

ing in the world so much as a madwoman singing a song
by a crazy man at an insane asylum concert.   During the
closing bars of the piece I again had one of my sudden
visions and was aware that a heavily laden motor truck
had run over a whole family of innocent children.

Though it is impossible to forecast the tendency of
modern music, which in the hands of futurists seems to
presage insanity, yet in my own practice as well as in my
preachments I strive to inculcate in others a knowledge
of, and love for, the classics of song.   These we must
know and learn to sing, for it is well-nigh impossible to
comprehend the most advanced vocal music of to-day.

CHAPTER XXXV

WOMAN AND SONG

Man has his will, but woman has her way.
— *Holmes.*

As in years before, I began the autumn season of 1902
with a concert tour. The end of November found me
in New York again, singing my familiar parts at the
Metropolitan, including occasionally the rôle of Iago, of
which I have never had enough. Several performances
of "The Niebelungen Ring" were given under Alfred
Hertz, in which Alberich was once more assigned to me.

The outstanding figures in the minds of that generation of Wagner lovers were the Erda and Waltraute of
Madame Schumann-Heink; the Brünnhilde of Madame
Nordica; the Sieglinde of Madame Gadski and Madame
Eames; the Wotan of Van Rooy; the Loge of Van Dyck;
the Mime of Reiss; and the Hagen of Edouard de
Reszke, though there were other famous men and women
in the company brought together by Grau, during what
proved to be his final season in New York and London.
After him came Conried and a deluge of talent unknown
to New York, while a dozen of us who were still prime
favorites with the public were not reëngaged. Thus
came to an end an aggregation of artists which had been
together so long as to be looked upon as having created
an epoch in operatic annals.

After all I cannot say that I was entirely neglected by
the little man who had been so successful in his manage-

ment of the Irving Place Theatre, for he did offer me an engagement as Amfortas in his American production of "Parsifal" which caused such discussion in musical circles.

Somewhat later it was also given in English under the direction of Henry W. Savage, by whom I was also asked to take the part of Amfortas during his season. To appear in that work alone would have necessitated my giving up a good many concerts. For this I asked him a goodly sum as we were crossing the ocean together. Later on he decided not to employ me, saying: "If I enter into a contract with you as the leading figure of my company, I will have to live up to it, and I am not sure yet whether I shall do 'Parsifal' or not. If I wanted to change my plans ten thousand dollars would be a big sum to cough up." The phrase was new to me; but he was a phlegmatic man.

As a successor to Maurice Grau various names were under consideration by the directors of the Metropolitan Opera House. Walter Damrosch tried for it, and I had the temerity to offer myself, but changed my mind after reflecting on the remark of one of the music critics who wondered what kind of insanity it could be that prompted a man to wish to become an operatic impresario.

I have before mentioned my love for the stage, and as I realized that my operatic activities might be coming to an end, I was considering the production of great dramas, which celebrated composers had embellished with music, as Beethoven did in "Egmont," and Bizet in "L'Arlesienne." I urged upon one of the theatrical managers to consider this and to give the "Antigone" of Sophocles with Mendelssohn's music, or Shakespeare's "Midsummer Night's Dream" as set by the same com-

poser. In this connection, by a bit of luck, Frank
Damrosch suggested that I should read the play at one
of his Symphony Concerts for Young People, and I was
thus enabled to act all the parts to my heart's content.
I was supported by a chorus of women's voices from the
Oratorio Society. Every note of the music of Mendelssohn was performed and I read my own version of the
play, which had been made with reverent care. This I
have since given many times, not only repeating it a few
months later in New York, but performing it with the
Philadelphia Orchestra in my native city, using then the
same desk at which, when a young fellow, I had heard
Charles Fechter read the entire play of "Hamlet."

In the spring of 1903 the New York Oratorio Society
gave the sacred cantata, "The Dream of Gerontius,"
by Edward Elgar, the first production of which I had
heard in England, and a year later I sang as Judas in
"The Apostles," by the same composer. These works
coming in rapid succession from Elgar's pen brought a
retiring man suddenly into prominence. In this country
his compositions, by reason of their great difficulty and
lofty, not to say abstruse, character, have never become
favorites, though his "Coronation Ode," written for the
accession of King Edward VII to the throne, is not only
of a more popular nature but contains music of great
strength and beauty. I brought to America for the composer, and presented to Walter Damrosch, who afterward produced it, Elgar's brilliant fantasy upon London
life called "Cockaigne." On the occasion of the performance of "The Apostles," the English alto Muriel
Foster was in an agony of dread and pain, because of the
approach of what might have resulted in lockjaw had it
not been taken in time. That evening she placed be-

tween her teeth, at the back of her mouth which she could open but with great difficulty, a wad of paper to keep her jaws from coming together. In this plight she bravely went through the performance, though the audience must have wondered at the strange enunciation which sometimes marred her otherwise distinct delivery of the text.

In contrast let me tell the following incident, of which I did not hear the last in the newspapers for many a day. I had gone to a New England town to give a song recital. Arriving several hours before the performance I rested myself with a nap before dinner. Upon arising to dress for the concert I found that my evening waistcoat had been accidentally left behind. It was vain to try to get into the waistcoat of my slender accompanist. At the last moment, I began telephoning about town to discover a man with a figure like mine, who would be willing to lend me the needed garment. The only one I could find in the time available was still six inches too small.

In my despair I called up the housekeeper of the hotel. She came, slit the waistcoat up the back, and pinned it to my inner garment under my arms. For a while all went well; but, as I sang, the expansion of my chest with every breath caused the misnamed safety pins to give way. As I sang "The Two Grenadiers," one pin loosed its hold; as I sang "The Evening Star" the other began to slip, and I was in dread lest the points should come in contact with my cuticle. It happened, as I feared, during my rendering of "Why do the Nations So Furiously Rage Together." I took an unusually deep breath to prepare for one of the runs, which caused the sharp point of one of the wretched pins to dig into my rib a savage jab and nearly spoiled the point of the piece, as the point of the pin remained imbedded in my flesh. Yet all the audience saw was the first convulsive twitch, which was impossible for me to control. When at last the story appeared in the papers I felt the force of the Shakespearean line, " He jests at scars that never felt a wound."

So thoroughly had the German element pervaded America that much admirable English music has been excluded, yet it has always been a surprise to me that Villiers Stanford's sparkling " Irish Symphony " is not a favorite in our concert rooms. Perhaps the reason may be thought unsound, but the fact is that not many of his compatriots are supporters of symphonic music in the United States and therefore may never have made the acquaintance of their gifted countryman's orchestral work which Damrosch has lately reintroduced.

Yet many amusing stories are told of the love of the Irish in Dublin for Italian opera, to which in years gone by they used to crowd when some company from London touring the British Isles would appear in the Irish capital. It was there, during an early performance of Gounod's " Faust," that the trap in the stage stuck fast just as Mephistopheles, in obedience to the older stage directions, endeavored to disappear into the lower regions. An uncomfortable stage wait ensued and the music stopped for a moment, when a boy in the gallery shouted out, " Hurrah, boys; hell's full! "

On another occasion a tenor was holding out a long-drawn high note, which he was, with admirable breath control, spinning out almost to the vanishing point. The audience was breathless with admiration when from the topmost gallery, a stage whisper could be heard all over the house, " Whisht, boys! 'tis the gas." There was instantly a commotion, laughter on the part of some, hisses from many because of the interruption, and cries of " Put him out ! " with one irate Hibernian demanding that the offender be thrown over the balcony. Another shouted out lustily, " Howld on, boys! Don't waisht him; kill a fiddler wid 'im."

It was in the latter part of the year 1903 that I began during my concerts to say a few words as I went along about my programs, giving my audiences some indication of the meaning of each song when desirable. I have kept up this custom, thus interesting and holding the attention of my auditors and often enlivening with some carefully chosen anecdote, what might be, to persons unaccustomed to many vocal pieces rendered by one voice, a tiresome succession of unintelligible songs.

A famous artist after attending one of my concerts, and hearing me recite " Enoch Arden," at the conclusion of a program of song, assured me that if I both spoke and sang the effort of declamation would ruin my singing voice. This is not necessarily the case, though I am aware that many singers remain silent all day before any public appearance. No rules can be laid down about this any more than about eating before performances. Many eat several hours prior to singing; I have tried this and it does not suit me. I eat my dinner and go upon the stage immediately. Most of my colleagues wonder at my habits, and to them it may be appropriate to remark that, in the words of the ancient saying, " One man's meat is another man's poison."

Here let me record my obligations to the many women in America who have helped me in carrying out my ambitions and to whom we may all be thankful for the growth of music throughout the country. It is indeed

interesting to me to look over any musical journal at
the present time and see the names of so many enthusiastic and artistic business women, with whose musical
beginnings I was associated and whom I have to thank
for so much in my career. There is not a page to which
I turn but I find the names of places in which I have
appeared and of individuals to whom I am indebted.

Were it not for the artistic aims and the business
probity of the hundreds of women's musical clubs everywhere in the United States, America could not have
reached to the high level of musical attainment which
characterizes it above all other new countries. To
women's musical clubs, then, I desire to acknowledge my
deep indebtedness, for without them my enthusiastic
vision as I stood in the prow of the vessel on returning
from Europe as a professional singer could never have
been fulfilled. I could not otherwise have carried my
message, such as it was, to more than a restricted area
of the great North American continent, over which I
have traveled many and many a time, until my trail
on the map looks like a veritable spider's web. I am
thankful that every one of these journeys was undertaken
with enthusiasm and fulfilled with loyalty, and can be
looked back upon, not only without regret, but as among
the great pleasures of my life. Of fatigues there have
been many; but what of that, when the joy of performance has been so great? There have been unpleasant-
nesses; but what of that, when it would have been far
less pleasant not to have been engaged in the work?
There have been a few disappointments, but again what
of that, when no work can be undertaken without disappointment?

I have been fortunate to be in love with my profession.

Happy indeed is the man who is enabled to do what he likes to do, has found an occupation he enjoys, and is successful in it! Many a time have I been reminded of Tennyson's line, "One clear call for me." Though in the poem that call is referable to the conclusion of mortal existence, I from the beginning have heard the one clear call that bade me take up a musical life and prosecute it to the end to the best of my ability.

CHAPTER XXXVI

THREE PRESIDENTS

The man who disparages music as being a luxury and a non-essential is doing the Nation an injury.— Woodrow Wilson.

THOUGH I visited the White House several times during Mr. Roosevelt's administration on private or public occasions, I sang there on January 6, 1904, at the first musicale given by President and Mrs. Roosevelt, when I was honored by being asked to give a program of American songs coupled with a group of ditties familiar to everybody. Accordingly I rendered Mendelssohn's "On Wings of Music," followed by my favorite Irish, Scotch, and English ballads, not forgetting North American Indian and Southern negro melodies.

But the principal group, used as a climax to the occasion, included the work of six living American composers, which I was glad to present before the many foreign representatives present in their official and diplomatic capacity. Again I was asked, as in Albany, by my hostess not to include the harrowing "Danny Deever"; but it was demanded by the guests. Its conclusion brought the President upstanding to his feet, and with hands outstretched he came forward, saying, "By Jove, Mr. Bispham, that was bully! With such a song as that you could lead a nation into battle!" Yet it was said of Mr. Roosevelt that he was unmusical and that he knew only two tunes, one of which was "Yankee Doodle," and the other — wasn't!

While " Teddy " was often loud of speech and hearty in his manner, full of fun and roaring with laughter in the family circle or among intimate friends, President Taft was quieter in his demeanor, a larger, slower-moving man, but one of great kindness and geniality, though I am not aware that he was particularly devoted to music. Once at a function in New York when asked to sing for him the ever popular " Danny Deever," I was all but prevented from doing so by the rush of people into the room, which was so filled in a moment that my accompanist was unable to get through the guards to the piano. As good fortune would have it a lady saw my predicament and volunteered to play from the music which I happened to carry in my hand.   Strange to say, she who was thus able to leap into the gap was the one who a few seasons before had without preparation stepped from the audience on to the stage of Carnegie Hall to sing the soprano part in " The Messiah," after two prima donnas had unexpectedly been incapacitated by illness.

On the contrary, President Woodrow Wilson is devoted to music and something of a singer himself, with a tenor voice of considerable power and sweetness. During his first term of office, while I was singing in Washington, he came to hear me and I called on him at the White House the next day, a meeting I sought in order to lay before him, as head of the nation, my wish to have vocal music taught in every school, college, or university in the land to every American from early youth to manhood, not in order that they should all become professional singers, Heaven forbid! but that, through properly equipped teachers and visiting artists, they might learn to sing simple folk tunes in our own language, in each upward grade studying music more diversified and better suited to their growing comprehensions. The makers of music would thus become known to our people and the works of the great masters would become as familiar household words to every one in our rapidly growing and amazingly diversified population.

As I pointed out to the President, nearly every one can by nature not only turn a tune, but sing better than most people — except their rivals — think they can, and it soon becomes obvious that opportunity and even a little cultivation brings out latent talent surprisingly. The President agreed with me. He was not expected to commit himself to placing my views before the educational chiefs of the country, nor did I ask him to; yet he was alive to the value of music in private and public life, speaking with pride of the vocal attainments of his daughter, Miss Margaret Wilson, who after study had taken her place in professional ranks, though, as he admitted, he had at first considered her to possess nothing more than what he termed " an inconsiderable little pipe."

I am proud of having known Messrs. Roosevelt, Taft, and Wilson and look back much further with interest at having met Grant and having seen Lincoln. The sons of both of these noted Presidents I have known, having been acquainted with General Fred Grant and with Colonel Robert Lincoln, both when the latter was the American minister to Great Britain and later in our native country.

Of him and his distinguished father there comes to mind a story told me by my father soon after the Civil War, which, so far as I am aware, has never before appeared in print. " Bob " Lincoln and his brother " Tad," who died in early youth, were taken to task by President Lincoln for a noisy quarrel which disturbed

him at his work.   Calling the boys before him, he sternly
demanded the cause of the trouble.   Tad in tears replied, " Bob's got my ball and I want it."   The President turned to his other son and said, " Bob, give Tad
his ball to keep him quiet."   Bob refused, defiantly saying, " I won't!   It's mine; and I want it to keep *me*
quiet!"

Though I did not sing in opera from early 1903 until
late in 1906, I was busily engaged on the concert platform and more enthusiastic than ever in giving my own
song recitals to such an extent all over the country that
I am surprised myself when I look back upon the amount
and variety of work I did in 1904.   Between January
11 and 26 I gave five programs in as many cities, each
differing from the others, yet all giving examples of the
older classics and English and American contemporaneous compositions, groups of songs by Beethoven, Schumann, Schubert, Loewe, Brahms, Jensen, Hugo Wolf,
and Richard Strauss, seventy-two songs in all, besides
the recitation of " Enoch Arden."

After this I went to Canada to sing " The Creation,"
and in working my way back through the Middle West,
still with differing programs, I remember that my accompanist asked me: " Why do you put yourself out
to give varied selections every night, when one program
would answer for all these places?"   Little did he know
me and my passion for work.   I have never let myself
settle down in a rut, nor have I cared how hard the work
is.   By so much as I am interested, by just so much I find
it easier; besides, it is not for my audiences alone that
I sing, it is for my own pleasure.   I enjoy explorations
into new musical fields and dislike taking my exercise
in beaten paths.   Surprises always pop up to lend a zest

to labor, as when I once arrived in my native city ready to sing, but had to send my audience away because there was no piano there and it was too late to get one. And not long before Fritzi Scheff and I went to Buffalo to appear together at the Teck Theatre, where I had to entertain the house alone until she arrived an hour late, her trunk having been lost in the hotel. I must not forget that the fair comedienne had just been married and her husband did not know American ways with trunks.

In 1904 Felix Weingartner, who was to become Mahler's successor as conductor of the Court Opera in Vienna, visited America, where he was being considered for the leadership of one of the principal orchestras. I sang at his concert in Carnegie Hall a number of his own songs, which he played for me with perfect sympathy and understanding.

After him came Richard Strauss. The tall, slender, quiet, business-like man so flustered me at first by his habitual coldness that, during his concert at Carnegie Hall on March 1, 1904, when he played his underlying music to " Enoch Arden " for me, though the piece had been in my repertory about four years and my ample rehearsals of it with him had been satisfactory, I suffered so from stage fright that I completely forgot my lines. I did not even know I had forgotten them; my memory became blank, though it is vivid enough .now as to what occurred. Strauss attempted to prompt me. At first I did not hear him at all, so lost was I to the world. He spoke a little louder. I was only a few feet away at the bend of the piano, and when I came to I found I could not understand a word he said, his English was so bad. His guttural whisper sounded worse than it looks on paper —" Unt vare vass Aynoch," which being interpreted signifies "And where was Enoch?"

By this time I was thoroughly aroused. My accompanist, seated at Strauss's left to turn the music, was too frightened to say a word while Strauss gibbered at me more unintelligibly than before over the pages of his beautiful music. The only time I have ever been so scared was when I was on the deck of "The Flying Dutchman" and unable to reach shore. But my seeming composure never forsook me; indeed, I rather suspect I gave the audience the impression that Strauss himself was at fault. It lasted only a few seconds, but it seemed an eternity. I suddenly recovered my presence of mind and the words of my text with it, and went on smoothly to the end. Moments like these have contributed to the whiteness of my naturally red hair.

Later I sang several times for and with Strauss at the piano, in Providence, Boston, and also in New York, where we appeared together at the Philharmonic Concert at Carnegie Hall on March 25, 1904, when it was indeed inspiring, now that we were better acquainted, to have his support in his beautiful "Hymn of Love," "Longing," and "Song of the Stonebreaker"— the latter one of the strongest, most savage, and altogether remarkable songs in all vocal literature.

Many stories were current about this remarkable man during his visit to New York. He led his orchestra in the auditorium at Wanamaker's store, where though many beautiful concerts have been given in that hall since, it was then such a departure from recognized custom that Strauss was upbraided by his friends for doing it. He replied that he had been well paid and did not care where he appeared, as he had come to America to make money. Though I cannot vouch for its truth, there was a report that he said he would stand on his head in the street if he was paid enough.

At the dinner given Strauss by the Lotos Club at its old home in Fifth Avenue near Forty-sixth Street, I sat next him while he wrote some bars of one of his own most difficult compositions for me in spite of the hum of talk and the blare of quasi-popular music about us. During a discussion about making musical sounds mean anything he said: " I can translate anything into sound. I can make you understand by music that I pick up my fork and spoon from this side of my plate and lay them down on the other side."

I attended the first performance anywhere of his " Domestic Symphony " in Carnegie Hall. Far from depicting domesticity, it seemed to me to represent a family row among all the gods of Olympus; while in the act of breaking up housekeeping in the midst of a primal hurricane that carried the roof off creation. Jove launched his thunderbolts, Vulcan smashed the furniture with his hammer, Mars let loose the dogs of war, Minerva and Venus were in hysterics, while the baby Cupid had a fit.

By singing in the principal cities of the United States my " Cycle of Great Song Cycles," I kept up, as 1904 ended, my reputation for a variety of interesting work, while in addition to a considerable number of miscellaneous appearances in other cities I still found time to prepare my own version of Byron's play " Manfred," which I produced with Schumann's music on December 4, 1904, with the New York Symphony Orchestra under the conductorship of Walter Damrosch.

It was a further attempt to fit myself for the dramatic stage, to which I ever felt strongly drawn. Schumann's music for "Manfred" had not been done in America since 1889, when Possart had given it, also under Mr. Damrosch. Previous to that, however, it had not been given since 1869, and then by Edwin Booth. For my performance Edwina Booth (Mrs. Grossman), the daughter of the great American actor, offered me the use of the copy from which her father had declaimed the lines. Upon examination I found this large and handsomely printed folio volume to be an English rendering with quotations from Byron of a freely expressed German condensation of the drama. I therefore discarded it in favor of my own version, which I found to fit very well with Possart's cues, which were still preserved in the orchestral score. Being assisted by several soloists and a fine chorus from the Oratorio Society, who rendered the vocal numbers allotted to the Spirit Voices, I keenly enjoyed the performance of a notable work which, except in part, I have never since brought forward, owing to the difficulty of its proper presentation.

At a concert in Cincinnati early in 1905, I had engaged to sing three songs by Van der Stucken, received only a few nights before; but as I had sung eight times in the ten previous days, traveling after each performance to another city, I had no chance to study the compositions. However, as they were to be played by the composer, I relied upon his help. After one engagement I was caught in a snowstorm and had to go by trolley car to wait at a small place until three o'clock in the morning. The train was late and I did not get to bed until four; hardly adequate preparation for the first of my song recitals in Chicago the next day. I got through with everything, though my Italian manservant fell ill. In one hotel I had neither sleep nor food, and when I got up the man in the adjoining room objected to my practicing. I reached Cincinnati just in time for the concert, owing to another late train, to find that Van der Stucken had cut his finger so badly he could not play the piano at all. My talented accompanist, Mr. Harold Smith, with no more chance than I to study these beautiful songs, was obliged with me to read them at sight before a crowded audience. If my effort was not a success, it was equally far from failure.

Later in the season I found myself in Texas, stranded at a railway junction on the prairie with the train several hours late. The night was cold and inside that little shack of a station was a stove almost red hot, around it as motley a crew of men, women, and children as one could well see — indeed I could scarcely see them for the tobacco smoke; but even through that an overwhelming evidence of their presence came to my nostrils. Cowboys, negroes, Indians, Chinese, European peasants, dogs, cats, and babies were too much for me, and rather than brave such terrors I faced the cool night air outside and went to bed at five o'clock in the morning when my express train came in. I reached Galveston and had several hours' rest before singing in the evening, when the pedals came off the piano in the middle of the performance and the rest of the concert was continued under difficulties. Such is the life of an artist.

CHAPTER XXXVII

SCULPTOR AND STAGE

Life is a stage, so play
The comic way;
Full soon the skies will bring
Some tragic thing.
— *After the Greek.*

Two men of the first importance in their respective arts were to make the world the poorer by their leaving it during these days, and both were my friends: the sculptor Augustus Saint Gaudens and the actor Joseph Jefferson. I saw them often at The Players, and though I have recollections of them personally and artistically that nothing will take from me, what impresses me most in my memories of them is an almost tragic coincidence, whereby their priceless possessions were destroyed by fire.

As I sat down to breakfast one morning at the club mentioned, Mr. Saint Gaudens quietly handed me a telegram from his wife which had just come to him, saying that his studio in the country had burned down in the night with all its precious contents. Understanding what such a loss meant to him, I expressed my sympathy, to which he replied without a show of feeling:

"My friend, I have learned to take things as they come in this life and I have no regrets for the destruction of what I myself have brought into being; almost everything of my own there was only a reproduction of what exists elsewhere. What I mind most is the loss

326

of the gleanings of a lifetime, the letters of celebrated personages the world over, gifts of drawings and sketches, bronzes, marbles, stained glass, none of which can ever be reproduced. But we have to take things as we find them. I am sorry that the workman my wife was good enough to allow to sleep in the barn should have chosen to light his pipe when the wind was blowing toward the studio. Won't you have some peaches?" With this he went on with his breakfast, quoting as he did so the old saying, " It's no use crying over spilt milk."

The loss of Mr. Jefferson's treasures did not occur during his lifetime, but the destruction is none the less lamentable. In my enthusiasm over the cause of the Art Theatre I had thought how fine it would be if in its foyer there were a collection of portrait busts and paintings of the shining lights of the American stage. When the New Theatre came into being I obtained promises of such mementos from several persons, among them the widow of Joseph Jefferson, who died in the spring of 1905. Not long after I obtained from the family a promise of a portrait bust made in Rome by the American sculptor, Hiram Powers. Time passed, the New Theatre was completed, and I spoke to William Jefferson about the gift promised by his mother, when with great regret he told me that, shortly before, the building in which his father's library and all the other relics of his artistic life had been temporarily stored was burned to the ground. What a loss to the history of the stage of the United States!

Mr. Jefferson was an ardent lover of the fine arts and had painted many canvases large and small, by which, though few admired them, he himself set great store. One of his intimate friends was President Grover Cleveland, whom Mr. Jefferson used frequently to visit at his country place on Buzzard's Bay, Massachusetts. Mr. Cleveland placed at the actor's disposal an ancient wind-mill on the estate as a studio, and there the good old player used to finish sketches made while visiting his host. To the windmill Mr. Cleveland would come and chat with Jefferson as he worked, and as the actor lovingly touched up some of his sketches one day, talking to his friend Grover the while, he said after a thoughtful silence, " Mr. President, though I have been an actor all my life I think that when I die I shall go down to fame as a painter." Dear, simple soul that he was, he little knew that the moment he had shuffled off this mortal coil, every landscape of his on the walls of The Players, of which he had been president since Edwin Booth's death, would be at once removed by the art committee.

I was very fond of Richard Mansfield, the actor, and found him to be the most courteous and considerate of men. I was ready to sing at his musicales, a fact which immediately put him in good humor, if he happened to be upset, and which invariably brought out in him his best qualities as an entertainer. He was an excellent pianist, possessed a beautiful singing voice, and his quaint-ness and originality in extemporization were remarkable. I have known Mansfield toward the close of one of his extraordinary evenings to devise hastily the general plot of a short operatic domestic tragedy, inform two or three others, and set us all to work immediately on an extem-poraneous performance. Walter Damrosch would per-haps preside at the piano, playing an unholy combination of old Italian opera, Wagnerian music-drama, " Ta-ra-ra-boom-de-ay," and " Danny Deever," while Marguer-ite Hall as the heroine, I as the irate parent, and Mansfield as the heavy villain would sing in faked Italian lingo, clad the while in antique armor and mediæval raiment from our host's wardrobe.

Mansfield adored his wife, and yet stories of cruelty to her became current in the daily papers. In reality there was never a kinder man in his family circle or a more genial host, though his penchant for practical joking sometimes led him to extremes of behavior. For instance, Mansfield at one of his Sunday night dinner parties, a formal occasion attended by people of distinction in social, literary, and artistic life, ordered his butler to remove every course as it came on the table before his guests had an opportunity to taste the food which, though cooked to perfection by a French chef, the fantastic Richard would declare unfit to eat. The appetite of no one present was satisfied by more than nibbles at bread, until the close of what should have been the meal, when our host permitted ices, fruits, and coffee to be served. Then the amazed disappointment of those present was assuaged by a most remarkable evening's entertainment furnished by the brilliant conversation of our eminent host. We were moved to uncontrollable laughter by his wit and to tears by his story of the care taken of him by Madame Edna Hall in Boston, when as a youth his own mother had turned him off, and the evening ended with beautiful music.

I was present in Chicago at one of his early performances of " Julius Cæsar." Mansfield had confided to me that it was his original intention to double the parts of Cæsar and Brutus. I was astonished to find that he permitted Arthur Forrest, who gave a fine performance of Mark Antony, to take every curtain call of the evening, he himself taking not one throughout the season.

This, as I afterward learned, was by way of apologizing to Forrest for what had occurred the year before when, in a moment of excitement, he had gone out of his part and taken Forrest to task in hearing of the audience for a fancied departure from the business of the scene. For-rest left the company that night thinking never to see his old friend again after supporting him for so many years. Only a little while later, Mansfield met Forrest on Broadway and, as if nothing had happened to mar the cordiality of their intercourse, offered him what the actors call the " fat " part of Mark Antony, accepting the less showy part of Brutus for himself and giving all the honors to his colleague.

On the afternoon of May 2, 1905, there took place at the Metropolitan Opera House a musical and dramatic performance, arranged by Daniel Frohman as a testimonial to Madame Helena Modjeska, who was about to leave the stage she had so adorned in the United States for many years. Many of the most noted American actors and actresses of the day were present, with visiting artists from Europe, among them the celebrated de Pachmann at the piano in place of Paderewski, who had his hand injured in a railway accident a little while before. Paderewski sent the following letter to Mr. Frohman, which I was requested to read to the audience:

Dear Mr. Frohman:

For many months I have been looking forward to the 2nd of May and anticipating one of the greatest joys of my career.

The thought of joining you all on this solemn occasion has been my pride for many months. The sudden adversity of Fate makes me feel now grieved and humiliated, and words cannot express all the bitterness of my disappointment; but there is still a pride and joy I cannot be deprived of: the pride of belonging to the country, to the same race which sent into the wide world one of the greatest and noblest artists of all times and stations; the joy of being one of the many to whom Madame Modjeska has been good, kind, and generous.

My first encouraging words as a pianist came from her lips; the first successful concert that I had in my life was due to her assistance.

Unable to be present, I beg of you to convey to Madame ·Modjeska the homage of my profound admiration and gratitude, and to extend my sincere thanks to all who contribute to make this day a day of legitimate and crowning triumph for a career great, noble, pure, and beautiful.

Sincerely yours,
IGNACE J. PADEREWSKI.

A delightful sense of humor was not the least of Madame Modjeska's many attractions. She was once asked to be the guest of honor at a reception in Boston, when her hostess, not quite aware of the *convenances,* requested her to recite. The eminent actress without hesitation launched forth in a declamation which apparently called upon every resource of her histrionic art, moving her auditors to smiles or tears as she willed. One of the company went out into an anteroom and found there Count Bozenta, Modjeska's husband, and her manager doubled up with laughter which they were trying to keep from reaching the other room. " What do you find amusing in that? " indignantly demanded the newcomer, scenting disrespect to a performance so fine. He was enlightened immediately. " Madame is repeating the numerals up to a hundred in Polish," said the Count.

Paderewski was the best balanced pianist, indeed the best balanced all round artist, that I ever knew; but de Pachmann, however distinguished, was a different sort of person. Notwithstanding his acknowledged skill, especially in the interpretation of the works of Chopin, he behaved so peculiarly on the stage, with physical and facial contortions so simian, that a witty reviewer observed that " he played in a manner almost human." At times he would place music upon the piano, though he had no need whatever for the printed page, in a minute or two convulsing his audience by a gesture of surprise, after which he would turn the music upside down and proceed with apparent relief.

I came down to a hotel breakfast once and found him finishing his own meal. As I went to shake hands with him, for I had not seen him for some time, he looked up at me as though I had been a stranger. Realizing that he was in one of his moods, I introduced myself by name; but, apparently annoyed, he shook his head violently as he consumed the last of his egg, saying: " Bismarck! Bismarck! I don't know Bismarck." Much amused, I sat at another table to see what was going to happen. When the waiter handed him his bill, he rose and made a deep bow, dismissing him at last with a large fee and an exaggerated flourish, immediately after which he came over, sat down with me, and began to talk in the most natural manner in the world.

For some time I had been corresponding with my friend Liza Lehmann (Mrs. Herbert Bedford), regarding her composing an opera for me on Goldsmith's " The Vicar of Wakefield." She asked Austin Dobson to adapt the story and write the dialogue and lyrics, but he was too busy. The preparation of the book, which was to contain instrumental and vocal music after the manner of opéra comique as known in Paris, was intrusted to Laurence Housmann, to whom and to his sister had been

traced the authorship of the beautiful anonymous work,
" An Englishwoman's Love Letters," which added a
luster to a name already made famous by their brother,
Alfred Edward Housmann, author of " The Shropshire
Lad." I had been in London during the summer of
1905 in consultation with Madame Lehmann and Mr.
Housmann. Madame Lehmann's music was beautiful
and Mr. Housmann's dialogue excellent, but it was far
too long and had to be cut severely. An offer to produce the piece was made to me by the Shubert brothers,
and another was received from a Chicago manager, who
heard of the work and came on to acquaint himself with
the manuscript and music, growing so enthusiastic that
he made me an offer I could hardly refuse. I thought it
best, however, to produce the opera in London, where I
could not only obtain a better cast than was available
in New York, but where I could have the authors' help.

Unfortunately, Mr. Housmann saw nothing of the
work until the dress rehearsal, when he was so annoyed
by what he considered the mutilation of his lines, that
he disclaimed the authorship of the book. Besides losing a season's labor and its expected emolument I lost
in him one whom I would fain call my friend, and as
beautiful a light romantic opéra comique as ever was
put upon the boards fell between the stools of grand
and comic opera and failed to satisfy the adherents of
either.

I had trouble in finding a tenor for the part of Squire
Thornhill and was about to engage Walter Hyde when
Madame Lehmann begged me first to hear a young man
whose voice had just been brought to her attention. Accordingly, one Sunday afternoon in September, 1906, I
went with my conductor, the late Hamish MacCunn, and

my manager, Bram Stoker, so long Sir Henry Irving's right-hand man, to Madame Lehmann's house at Wimbledon, where we heard several selections beautifully rendered by a young Irishman named John McCormack. After he had sung, my dear Liza took me into the next room and enthusiastically said, " David, if you don't engage him you're a fool. He has an angel's voice." " True," said I, " but he has an Irishman's brogue." " He can get over that," said she fervently. " Send him to Richard Temple for lessons." This famous artist, after years at the Savoy Theatre, upon Sir Arthur Sullivan's death became a professor of spoken English in the Royal College of Music.

I presently took McCormack aside and said, " If I engage you for this part, you must try to get over your brogue." " Sure," said he, in his delightful way, " it's no matter at all — at all! Oliver Goldsmith was born just two mile over the hill from where I came from." " True," I replied; " I know Oliver Goldsmith was an Irishman; but he wrote an English story, and it will never do for you to play the part of Squire Thornhill with a brogue."

Though Mr. McCormack accepted the part, he found it unsuitable and soon returned it. Walter Hyde, who was originally in my mind, was secured in McCormack's place and in the short time left learned the opera and gave a beautiful performance. Richard Temple was admirable as Mr. Burchell and Mr. Lander played the part of the rascally Jenkinson, which fitted him like a glove; Mrs. Primrose, the vicar's wife, was played to perfection by that most sympathetic of comediennes, Mrs. Theodore Wright; the daughter Sophia and the boys Moses, Dick, and Bill were performed as if Goldsmith's char-

acters had come to life; while in the charming Miss Isabel
Jay I had the one woman on the London stage who filled
the eye as well as the ear in her rendering of the part of
the wayward but captivating Olivia.

Keen interest was felt in the presentation. "The
Vicar" had not been seen in London since Henry Irving
had put on a version of the story under the title of
"Olivia," though Sir Arthur Sullivan, I understood, intended to set the old romance to music, and had made a
number of sketches to that end.

My production was such a surprise to a representative
of the Opéra Comique from Paris, who was in one of
the boxes on the first night, that he declared it pressed
hard anything he had ever seen at his own theatre.

After a period of fluctuating attendance and toward
the close of our two months' season, my opera was visited by agents of the Schubert brothers and these two
hardened theatregoers were so moved by the beauty and
pathos of the piece that they cabled their employers.
As a result I was again offered a New York production
by them. But I had had enough; the elusive game was
not worth the theatrical candle, which burns so readily at
both ends. "The Vicar of Wakefield" I find in my
memoranda to be numbered as the 1404th work I had
performed up to that time.

CHAPTER XXXVIII

SPEAKING WITH TONGUES

We must be free or die, who speak the tongue
That Shakespeare spake; the faith and morals hold
Which Milton held.— *Wordsworth.*

DISAPPOINTED in " The Vicar of Wakefield " in London, but aware of the need for taking the good with the ill in my journey through life, I started on my prearranged American tour in the autumn of 1907, beginning with a recital of my own at Carnegie Hall.

After wandering in my native land much farther than " from Dan to Beersheba," I found myself giving one of my recitals in Boston on December 1 at Symphony Hall, a place associated with perfect productions. I had appeared there satisfactorily on many previous occasions, but now my accompanist had no sooner seated himself at the piano and struck a full chord with his foot on the pedal than everybody knew something was wrong. The pedal stuck so that no effort induced it to let go its hold. My audience, at first patient, began to fidget, and I to perspire from sheer nervousness. Finally I asked if there were any one in the audience accustomed to pianos, begging him to come on the stage and adjust the balky mechanism. A man accordingly stepped up on the platform, got himself under the piano, and indulged in physical contortions that mightily amused the people. No other good piano being available and this instrument having failed us, in the attempt to proceed an old, dirty,

336

tuneless upright instrument was found in some out-of-
the-way place, dragged on the stage, and my concert proceeded to its uncomfortable and unworthy conclusion.

Early in 1908 I had the opportunity of meeting and
singing with Madame Teresa Carreño, under the conductorship of Wassili Safonoff, then directing the Philharmonic Orchestra of New York, and again on the occasion of a memorial concert with music by the late Edward A. MacDowell at Carnegie Hall, on the evening
of March 31, when as so often both before and since I
brought forward a number of carefully selected songs
by that representative American composer, whose career
illness ruined and death brought to a close, all too soon
for the good of our national art. Listening to the distinguished Madame Carreño play his Piano Concerto,
I could not help thinking of the story so often told of this
talented but much married lady, of whom a reviewer in
Europe once said of her concert of the preceding day
that " She performed for the first time the second concerto of her third husband."

Filled with the desire to become a tragedian or comedian, I did not care which, after my success in the
" Midsummer Night's Dream " I prepared with great
care a condensation of the dialogue of Sophocles's " Antigone," using Plumptre's translation, and performing
this for the first time it had been given in many years.
I recited it with the Orpheus Club in Philadelphia on
February 8. The chorus of the club, augmented to 120
men and conducted by Horatio Parker, gave a majestic
rendering of the noble choruses. As I delivered the
stirring lines, which I have done since many times, I could
not help contrasting my rendering of this tragedy with
Shakespeare's comedy, and remembered the story told

of David Garrick, greatest of English tragedians, who
was also a fine comedian.   It is said that when one of
his friends, congratulating him upon his skill in either
phase of the dramatic art, asked him which he preferred,
Garrick after a moment's thought replied that tragedy
with its noble lines was certainly grateful.   " But comedy?   Ah, comedy is a very serious matter."

Ever interested in the growth of music by American
composers, I gave on April 18, 1909, at Carnegie Hall
an orchestral concert on behalf of the American Music
Society, when besides orchestral music by MacDowell,
Chadwick, Arthur Powell, and Harry Rowe Shelley, I
included in the program the prelude to William J. Mc-
Coy's music drama " The Hamadryads," so successfully
performed by the Bohemian Club in the redwood forest of California.   I also recited with orchestra Poe's
" Raven " to Mr. Bergh's music, and produced for the
first time in New York the four-songs with viola obbligato
by Charles Martin Loeffler of Boston, a musician American by adoption and long residence, but most modernly
French in his compositions.

In the spring of 1909 I made one of many journeys to
the Pacific Coast and had the pleasure, on March 27,
1909, of giving a recital in the Greek Theatre at the
University of California.   Before going on the stage
I was thoughtfully taken to peep through the curtain
into the vast auditorium lest I should be overcome by
its majestic dimensions and make undue effort to fill a
space so vast.   The Greek Theatre is nearly perfect
acoustically and it was not necessary to sing more forcibly
than in an ordinary concert hall.   When I rendered in
the open air Schubert's beautiful " Hark! Hark! the
Lark," through the delicacy of the music birds could

be heard singing in the trees overlooking and overhanging the back of the auditorium. The Right Honorable James Bryce, the British ambassador, was sitting there with President Benjamin Ide Wheeler of the University, who assured me afterward that the slightest sound of my voice could be heard perfectly despite the distance that separated them from the stage.

In San Francisco that year I was entertained, for the first time since the disaster that destroyed so much of it, at the temporary quarters of the Bohemian Club, myself reciting " The Raven." After resuming my place at table I saw that my friend Charles K. Field, a kinsman of the poet Eugene Field, was writing upon the back of his menu, though carrying on an animated conversation the while. Presently he asked me quietly, " You will not mind, I hope, anything done at your expense; we chaff each other a good deal in this club." I assured him he need have no fear of my taking offense. Motioning to a clever amateur pianist, the two took the platform I had just left and gave a travesty of both the words and music of " The Raven." The accompanist had caught marvelously the principal themes, which he wove into popular music of the day, mingled with strains from the Wagnerian parts in which he had heard me, while Field not only parodied the verses, but caricatured me and satirized the management of the club, giving at the close the tragic line, " Tea and toast, and nothing more! "

Later that season I took part in the music festival given at Northwestern University in Evanston, Illinois, under such distinguished direction and general circumstances that these events have become noted throughout America for their artistic value. To Professor Peter

C. Lutkin belongs most of the credit for these dignified annual offerings.

My principal work was the rendering of the title rôle in Mendelssohn's "Elijah," so frequently performed and so grateful to me. At Evanston on June 5 I was surrounded by a truly grand chorus, accompanied by the entire Theodore Thomas Orchestra from Chicago, and had an enormous and enthusiastic audience. Only a few rows away in front of me sat the aged Mr. Kappes, who had been the intimate friend of Mendelssohn and had heard the first performance of the oratorio sixty-three years before.

After Madame Schumann-Heink had sung superbly at an afternoon performance and was receiving the congratulations of the committee and her many friends in the artists' room, she called to her side her little boy. His mother and I just prior to his advent ten years before had sung frequently together in opera. To Madame Schumann-Heink tragedy and comedy follow each other as the day the night, and after serious selections from Wagner and Schubert grandly sung, she was in one of her witty moods. As the lad came to her side, and before the assembled company, the great contralto introduced him to me as follows: "Come here, my dear, and shake hands with my old friend, David Bispham. He knew you very well before you were born."

September 21, 1909, I visited Mark Twain at his beautiful new house called "Stormfield" near Redding, Connecticut, in order to take part the next day in a concert to be given in his drawing-room for the benefit of a library he had recently founded in the village. The affair was carried through with Miss Clara Clemens, the distinguished author's daughter, and Ossip Gabrilowitsch the pianist, to whom she became engaged to be married that day.

The world-renowned novelist, whom I long had known, spent the morning half dressed in bed talking to me. Nothing could have been more charming than his casual conversation as, in slippers and dressing gown, he leaned on one elbow in his pillow smoking a great pipe, and indulged in reminiscences mingled with wit and wisdom, or with sarcasm and invective against whatever was going on in the world that did not please him.

Every room on the ground floor of the spacious house was filled to the last inch that afternoon by a crowd that spread up the stairways, on the balcony, out into the pergola, anywhere indeed from which the music could be heard, even if we performers could not be seen.

We were introduced by Mark Twain himself clad in his distinctive suit of white flannel, which served to set off his magnificent head of snowy hair, and he was in great fettle. After a little speech which convulsed his hearers, he presented us who were to make music for his guests, saying shrewd and complimentary things about each one of us men, and in conclusion: "While Mr. Gabrilowitsch and Mr. Bispham are much better known than my daughter, they are not near so good looking."

I was still concertizing all over the country and appearing with clubs, at colleges, universities, and such conservatories of music as the Peabody Institute of Baltimore, and was asked by the Harvard Club of New York to sing on January 30, 1910, at the first of what proved to be an annual series of concerts extending over nine years; and in the spring produced at the New York Theatre in connection with the Lambs Club for their Ladies Annual Gambol an excellent one act grand opera entitled "The Anniversary," by Robert Hood Bowers, which unfortunately has never been heard since.

During 1910 I was engaged by the authorities of the Ohio Valley Exposition, to be held in Cincinnati in September, for the principal barytone part of the romantic grand opera "Paoletta," written by Paul Jones, a local painter-poet, and composed by Pietro Floridia, an Italian professor in the Cincinnati College of Music. All the singers were Americans and the work was sung in English; the chorus of 150 was drawn from the ranks of the May Festival chorus, and the orchestra consisted of picked men from the Symphony Orchestra, all of Cincinnati.

I acted the part of Gomarez, an old Moorish magician of the Middle Ages, whose love for the king's daughter gets him laughed and jeered out of the court. In his despair he invokes his gods and prays for the restoration of his youth, and his prayer is granted. This powerful invocation is an admirable piece of modern declamatory writing, and I have used it frequently in my recitals.

I delighted in the impersonation of the character of the Moor and in making the quick change between age and the prime of manhood, and at the conclusion of the opera sank away in sight of the audience into senility and death. The opera as a whole contains so many beautiful passages, that I am surprised that it has never been taken up by the Metropolitan Opera Company, to whose consideration I heartily recommend it.

Ever since the production of my "Vicar of Wakefield" in London, and since the shock I received from a certain lady who spoke disparagingly of "that rotten music in English," I have been more than ever addicted to the use of our own language in my concerts, framing

DAVID BISPHAM

as Gomarez in Floridia's
"Paoletta."

GOMAREZ — REJUVENATED

*From Photographs by Bellsmith,
Cincinnati*

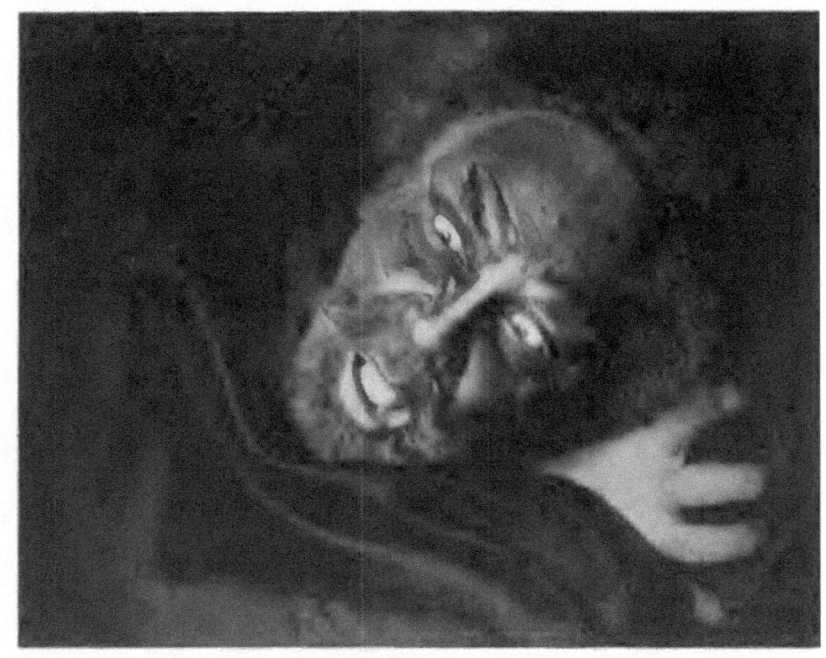

DAVID BISPHAM
The death of Gomarez in Floridia's "Paoletta."
From a Photograph by Bellsmith, Cincinnati

many programs without using any foreign tongues, even though many of the finest songs were originally written in them. Our speech, though richer than any other in its possibilities, has not been wisely used by those music publishers who seek to supply songs in foreign tongues with English versions. Instead of employing poets of musical tendency with a copious vocabulary and well-turned phrases at their command, the publishers seem to have committed German poems to men familiar enough with the original but not sufficiently conversant with English. This has resulted in operatic libretti and hundreds of songs being issued in a variety of translations, most of which are bad and some of them ludicrous. I have therefore sought out the best available versions, though my *confrères* seem unaware that many English and American poets have beautifully translated the German classics. I speak of German more particularly, because so much of the best vocal music is by Teutonic composers. While English-speaking poets of rank have translated German classics, the German composers have used the British poets. Beethoven, Schubert, Schumann, Robert Franz, and Loewe took words by Shakespeare, Burns, Scott, Byron, and Moore, turned into their own language, all of which are directly transferable to the original.

I also comment in my concerts on the subject of our language in song, giving " lecture recitals " which dwell upon the beauty of our native tongue. It would be as absurd for a lecturer before an English-speaking audience to give part of his discourse in French, part in German, and another part in Italian, as for a singer to expect unqualified welcome for songs in foreign languages which

DAVID BISPHAM
From a sketch by J. A. Cahill, San Francisco

344

he himself but imperfectly understands and which his audience does not understand at all.

The trouble has been, however, that the English language has not been properly taught in our schools. To all American singers I say, sing your songs in well-chosen English if singing to an English-speaking audience, and sing them so that every one understands your words; enunciate so clearly that the audience can tell even how every word is spelled. Get away from this foreign-language fad and you will find yourself nearer the heart of your public. I often quote from the 14th chapter of St. Paul's First Epistle to the Corinthians, where he says: " Now brethren, if I come unto you speaking with tongues, what shall I profit you? . . . Even things without life, giving sound, as with pipe or harp, except they give a distinction in the sound, how shall it be known what is piped or harped? . . . So likewise ye, except ye utter by the tongue words easy to be understood, how shall it be known what is spoken? " And the Apostle goes on to say, " I will sing with the spirit, and I will sing with the understanding also. . . . I had rather speak five words with my understanding, that by my voice I might teach others also, than ten thousand words in an unknown tongue."

Realizing how often a one-man concert becomes trying to those accustomed to a greater variety of musical fare, I find such remarks are not only appreciated by the public, but are expatiated on by the press, which, I am glad to say, is almost entirely with me. I also indulge myself in a change of concert manners by staying on the platform after most of my groups of songs, instead of leaving it every few minutes; for, as I explain, letting my audience into professional secrets, most artists after singing bow themselves off the stage to listen, unseen, for the applause they fondly hope will bring them back to take an encore. For my own part, I would rather give an encore plainly expected than to go off for rest I do not need, alone in a dark, stuffy, and generally uncomfortable waiting room.

CHAPTER XXXIX

PROGRAM MAKING

The difficulty in life is the choice.
— George Moore.

PROGRAM making is not the easy thing that it may at first glance appear to ·be.   It will not do to set down at random a number of songs and expect them, however beautiful in themselves or however well sung, to fit properly together; they must be chosen with care and with the knowledge of the literature of song, which it is better to possess than to engage another to provide.

The number of songs that I have actually sung amounts to about fourteen hundred.   My endeavor has always been to choose from these for the many song recitals I have given — some eight hundred in the past twenty-five years — so that every program shall bear a resemblance to a symphony, the four movements of which are in a manner exemplified by four song groups, each so constructed as to have a distinct character of its own and yet a direct relation to the whole scheme of sound and of sense.

Many kinds of programs may be made, some entirely classic, others illustrative of this period or that, of one school or another; but the finest program is that which has been so arranged as to contain notable examples of a variety of times and styles, so combined as not only to entertain the average person, but to hold the interest of even the most experienced concert goer.

347

The older classics of European countries, including ex-
cerpts from oratorio, should set the standard for a program of this sort. They should seldom be given at the
end of a concert, while the modern selections suitable for
the conclusion of such an entertainment should never be
used at its opening; that would be like serving dessert
at the beginning of a meal. The second group should
consist of songs representative of the great period that
began with Beethoven and continued through the Romanticists, Schubert and Schumann, to Brahms. A third
group might feature operatic selections not often heard
upon the stage, ballads by Loewe, songs by Franz, Grieg,
or Strauss — the combinations to be made are, of course,
infinite. But the last group of a recital, whether it consist of English, American, or foreign composers of the
present time, must be of such a character as to send
the people away sorry to go, but glad that they have
come. I have often found that at the end of such a
concert the homely ditties of the British Isles or folk
songs, including American negro " Spirituals," are very
useful.

Realizing that an audience may become weary of hearing even the best voice of one singer, the judicious recitalist, in all programs, will take especial care so to
combine the component parts of each group as to afford
a change of key as well as of *tempo* and general character
of the songs. Nothing is more wearisome than one long-
drawn selection following another in the same, or nearly
related, soporific key. I myself have peacefully slum-
bered under the soothing influence of an artist, rich
voiced, but regardless of the fact that variety is the spice
of life — and of concert-giving. One must remember

that while such a program is made up of a patchwork of pieces, it must, after all, have an artistic design and not resemble a crazy-quilt.

The encores to each group of songs should be very carefully considered and should be not only familiar but of the same period as the group itself and, if possible, shorter than the encored song, in order that the balance shall not be destroyed.

I cannot too strongly insist upon the recognition of the gender of songs; some are masculine and some are feminine, and the opposite sexes should not encroach upon each other's preserves. Many women in this way offend the artistic proprieties; their plea that all the best songs are written for men is not well founded, for a little investigation will serve to show our sisters that there is a wealth of womanly material open to them if they will but depart from the beaten paths. Nothing, for instance, could be more beautifully feminine, or more femininely beautiful, than Schumann's little-used cycle of eight songs known as " Woman's Love and Life " (Frauenliebe und Leben). Women will also often find melodic ground that is open to their brethren as well as to themselves, for there is plenty of vocal material of a poetic character suitable for both male and female artists; it only needs to be gathered and used. Women are not the sole offenders in the mal-selection of songs: I recently attended a recital where an experienced man sang during the course of the afternoon five songs that were suitable only for a woman to render.

I append two programs in which I have endeavored to embody my ideas of how such song offerings can advantageously be made.

PROGRAMS

MEN'S GROUP

O, Ruddier than the Cherry ....*Handel*
    ("Acis and Galatea")
The Frost Scene ....*Purcell*
    ("King Arthur")
At Last the Bounteous Sun ....*Haydn*
    ("The Seasons")
Now Your Days of Philandering.*Mozart*
    ("Marriage of Figaro")

Creation's Hymn ....*Beethoven*
    (Gellert)
The Wanderer ....*Schubert*
    (Lübeck)
The Hidalgo ....*Schumann*
    (Geibel)
May Night ....*Brahms*
    (Hölty)
Edward ....*Loewe*
    (Scotch Ballad)

When I Was Page ....*Verdi*
    ("Falstaff")
At Evening's Hour ....*Hahn*
    (Verlaine)
Autumnal Gale ....*Grieg*
    (Richardt)
Secrecy ....*Wolff*
    (Mörike)
The Stonebreaker's Song ......*Strauss*
    (Henkell)

The Sea ....*MacDowell*
    (Howells)
O, Let Night Speak of Me ..*Chadwick*
    (Bates)
The Pirate Song ....*Gilbert*
    (Stevenson)
Sleep, then, Ah Sleep .....*Branscombe*
    (Le Gallienne)
Danny Deever ....*Damrosch*
    (Kipling)

WOMEN'S GROUP

My Heart Ever Faithful ....*Bach*
    (Pentecost Cantata)
To Florindo ....*Scarlatti*
Should He Upbraid ....*Bishop*
    (Shakespeare)
I've Peen Roaming ....*Horn*
    (Soane)

Marguerite at the Spinning
  Wheel ....*Schubert*
    (Goethe)
He, the Best of All ....*Schumann*
    (Chamisso)
Dreams ....*Wagner*
    (Wagner)
In Autumn ....*Franz*
    (Müller)
Lov'st Thou for Beauty.*Clara Schumann*
    (Rückert)

He Is Kind ....*Massenet*
    ("Herodiade")
Noblest of Knights ....*Meyerbeer*
    ("Les Huguenots")
Oh, My Lyre ....*Gounod*
    ("Sappho")
It Is Better to Laugh ....*Donizetti*
    ("Lucrezia Borgia")

Orpheus with His Lute ......*Sullivan*
    (Shakespeare)
The Blackbird's Song ....*C. Scott*
    (Watson)
The Maidens of Cadiz ....*Delibes*
    (De Musset)
The Little Silver Ring ....*Chaminade*
    (Baker)
The Floods of Spring ....*Rachmaninoff*
    (Hapgood)

Of these programs the first is one I have repeatedly rendered since its original presentation at Carnegie Hall. In it, as well as in the specimen woman's program, it will be observed that in the selection of the numbers I have not been unmindful of the source of the words; fine poetry is the inspiration of fine music, and it is my invariable custom to give the poet equal credit with the composer.

The art of presenting such a song recital is much more difficult than either oratorio or opera singing, for the reason that the recitalist, unaided by scenery, costume, or the opportunity of indulging himself in action, must rely entirely upon his vocal and expressive powers. Its preparation and presentation is as serious a thing as the painting and exhibition of a picture; indeed such a collection of songs is a tone picture: it must be alive with color and must have its principal and subsidiary features; it must have incident, must have sunshine and shadow, mirth and pathos, comedy and tragedy, all mingled with that inevitable concomitant of song, love — plenty of love; for poetry and music go hand in hand with the emotions, and it is this association, this touch of nature, that makes the whole world kin.

It is my custom to keep everything that pertains to my professional life, and the collection thus gathered together makes many volumes. Besides these, a book has been kept in which all my engagements with their dates, places, and the work performed has been entered and forms what is, to me at least, an interesting and valuable addition to my musical library.

An inspection of this record shows that my public doings began principally with plays, and of these I have at one time or another acted in twenty-five, while of recitations to music I have for years used a repertory of as many more. My character impersonations in opera of all sorts — light, comic, and grand — number fifty-eight;

while of oratorios, cantatas, masses and services, madrigals and part-songs the list accounts for some two hundred. Adding to these figures the fourteen hundred songs to which I have alluded, the summary amounts to the not inconsiderable total of over seventeen hundred titles and brings home the truth of Shakespeare's assertion that " One man in his time plays many parts."

CHAPTER XL

Eftsoons they heard a most melodious sound,
  Of all that might delight a dainty ear,
Such as at once might not on living ground,
  Save in this paradise, be heard elsewhere.
                                        —*Spenser.*

ONE of my most interesting experiences was the performance in 1910 of the title rôle in " The Cave Man " for the Bohemian Club of San Francisco at its annual revel in the great redwood grove in Sonoma County, California. The text was by Charles K. Field, editor of the *Sunset Magazine,* and the music by William J. McCoy, whose music drama " The Hamadryads " had brought him so much praise a few years previously. When I had been at the club not long before, I promised to go with them to The Grove, among the hills about seventy-five miles north of the city, where the members sojourn every August. To end the outing among the giant sequoias, plays are given which have been a year in preparation, and these have grown so famous and have developed so steadily in high purpose that I was highly complimented at being asked to play the principal part in the one forthcoming. Every resource of modern art and stagecraft is brought to bear upon them, written, composed, acted, and sung as they are by members of the Bohemian Club.

" The Cave Man " took its inspiration from these sequoia groves of California, as the only existing forests resembling those of the cave man's day. Like its predecessors, the play was given on a natural stage along the majestic hillside, the proscenium arch being furnished by nature in the form of two trees fifteen feet in diameter and 200 or more in height. A fine symphony orchestra furnished the accompaniment out of sight of the audience, which is seated on felled logs in an auditorium unequaled in the world, formed by an irregular circle of giant trees.

I left Bar Harbor, Maine, for California in July for this single performance. Arriving at the Grove late in the afternoon, I went eagerly to the hillside where I was to act. Feeling very small amongst the monster trees, I shouted to the author and the composer of the play far down in the auditorium, " Can you hear me? " One of my friends asked almost in a whisper, " Charley, can you hear David? " Every syllable came to my ear. So mysteriously perfect are the acoustics among the trees that even the slightest sound is audible.

After careful rehearsal " The Cave Man " was splendidly enacted by the Honorable Henry A. Melvin, Justice of the Supreme Court of California, the gifted Richard Hotaling and many another clever singer and actor in the cast with me, and I reveled in a part of great originality and power.

The Grove Plays are given at night, the hillside being illuminated in any manner required from behind the great tree trunks. " The Cave Man " was thus enabled to pass from dawn through the blaze of noon to the approach of night, when from the spark struck by the flint a forest fire was kindled, to be quenched by torrents of rain in a terrific storm. Though at the time these plays are given no rain has been known to fall in that part of California, so realistic was the forest fire that men in the audience started to their feet to prevent the destruction of their beloved grove, until the rainstorm poured down from perforated pipes high in the surrounding trees.

My work ending with the second act, I was able to see the epilogue from the audience — as remarkable a combination of stagecraft and music as I have ever known.

The forest is dark, not a light is to be seen, spiritual voices sound:

> " What shall awaken man
> Breaking the dream of the senses? "

A star glows in the darkness and the voice of an archangel speaks from the sky in answer:

> " Behold he shall climb
> Up the hard path of the ages —
> Into the glory of mind! "

And cave men are dimly seen climbing upward until they are replaced by shepherds climbing still upward in shadow, singing as they go. As the shepherds reach a higher level they are replaced by farmers who climb in turn up the hill in a stronger light, and farmers are replaced in turn by warriors with helmets and shield. The warriors are succeeded upon a higher level still by white-robed philosophers climbing in a light which is growing ever stronger. The hillside is thronged with the processional of the ages, the chorus of voices singing in ever heightening rhapsody, which is increased by the spiritual voices of boys from a distance, singing:

> " Man awaketh from the dream of the senses;
> Time falleth from him like a shadow;
> Glory clotheth him for evermore! "

Then He who spoke the Sermon on the Mount suddenly appears upon the height of the hill above the gathered multitude. A splendor of light bursts upon the forest and a cloud of white doves hovers above the climbing host, all singing, " Hosanna ! Behold it is the sun ! " as the procession is led upward into the light.

While on the way to the Pacific Coast I stopped to wonder at the Grand Cañon of the Colorado River. Consumed with curiosity to adventure to the bottom of this mile-deep gash upon the fair face of the world, I started on horseback down the narrow trail with a companion and three guides. I am no horseman, for my legs are not long enough to go around the belly of any well-proportioned nag so as to enable me to stick on his back. As we proceeded my mount evinced a desire to gather tufts of grass which grew where flies would scarcely dare to crawl under the edge of a precipice 2000 feet in height. My heart sank into my boots and, as I shouted to my guides the order to return, my horse in putting about upon the narrow path kicked a hundredweight of stone into the abyss. I dismounted, thankful not to be following it to the premature end of my tour.

Within a few days, I contributed to the holiday jinks of the Bohemian Club an offering of my own, which came as a little inspiration and afforded me great pleasure, as it worked out with such success. Unknown to my fellow members I had a costumer build three suits of clothes one over the other upon me. These were readily detachable and gave me three changes at one appearance. When the curtain rose, the audience found a pirate at his cabin table, his bottle of rum beside him, singing Stevenson's lines, " Fifteen men on a dead man's chest," while green lights from the sea played upon him through an open porthole. The applause from the audience had scarcely died away, when the curtain rose again upon Mrs. Howard Weeden's familiar figure of Uncle Rome, the dear old darky, who visits the beloved home of the master of his youth in the sunset glow of the evening of his life. My assistants rapidly relieved me of the costume and black stockinette mask of the old servitor and, in less time than it takes to tell it, I stepped forward in the costume of Tommy Atkins to sing the perennial " Danny Deever."

Continuing my journey I found myself caught in a snowdrift near the mouth of the Columbia River on the way to concertize in Canada, and my train was detained for twenty-four hours. Fortunately I was near a station, from which I telegraphed to Vancouver, where I was due for rehearsal a full day before the performance, and was greatly complimented to learn over the wire that the concert had been postponed a day to allow me time to get there. This I did without further mishap, and chorus, orchestra, and audience returned to the hall, from which they had been sent away the night before, to hear me in a performance of " Elijah," which, spurred on by gratitude for such consideration, I felt that I had never sung so well.

Artists, however, are not always in a position to know what effect they are creating upon their hearers. My kinsman, William Bispham, told me that he once visited Edwin Booth in his dressing room during a performance of " Hamlet " to congratulate him upon his interpretation, in which he seemed that night to attain the pinnacle of his powers. To his surprise he found Booth with his head upon his hands in the deepest dejection, from which not even the praise of his old friend could arouse him, declaring himself disgusted at having given so miserable a performance. 'But later when Booth seemed to my cousin and other intimates to be in danger of losing his reputation, and they went behind to beg him to pull himself together, to their amazement they found him in the best of spirits, frame erect, glorious eyes flashing, and a smile upon his lips. As they remonstrated with him, his countenance changed and, in high displeasure at the liberty taken with him, he dismissed them from the room lest they interfere with what he thought the best performance he had ever given in his life.

Singing early in 1911 with the New York Philharmonic under Mahler and with the Boston Symphony Orchestra under Gericke, I appeared with the Philadelphia Orchestra under Carl Pohlig, with whom I had passed certain Wagnerian rôles at Bayreuth, when under consideration by Seidl, Richter, and Madame Wagner for engagement there, which unfortunately came to nothing because of the prior claims of other artists.

Besides opening the concert room of the new Brooklyn Academy of Music, I introduced at Carnegie Hall, on May 21, 1911, the retiring lad afterward known to fame as Leo Ornstein; and kept my brain fresh by producing during 1911 three noble Tennysonian poems, " Elaine," with beautiful music by Ada Weigel Powers; " Guinevere " to the touching accompaniment by the pianist Heniot Levy, and " A Dream of Fair Women " to orchestral music of great variety and ingenuity by Doctor N. J. Elsenheimer. And that summer, in further enthusiasm for the spoken work and for drama, produced the strong one-act play in blank verse by Oscar Wilde, called " A Florentine Tragedy." This had never hitherto been given in its entirety in the United States, and I heartily recommend it to the attention of actors.

After much more music-making in the course of my daily walk and conversation, I had the opportunity of introducing to the public such pieces as Stanford's fine settings for barytone voice and chorus of Henry New-bolt's " Songs of the Sea," Frederic Converse's setting of Keats's poem " La Belle Dame sans Merci " and Par-ker's " Cahal Mor," and Howard Brockway's " Agha-doe "; and ere long found myself singing in concert with my old friend and colleague of the opera, Madame Lillian Nordica. Her second marriage had taken place after great trouble with her former husband. While settling with her spouse, she was about to give one of her concerts in New York, when one day she answered a telephone call and to her amazement heard his voice bidding her good morning and asking for a box at her performance the next afternoon. Though alarmed she promised him the box; but, as he had threatened her life, her manager set detectives in the boxes on either side of his, and at the door of it as well. When she told me the story I fully sympathized with her breathlessness during the opening numbers of her recital. It is not easy to sing while looking down a pistol barrel.

Madame Nordica was determined and brave, living up to her undertakings in spite of everything, and on her last tour of the United States was so ill, during sev-eral concerts we gave jointly, that she could hardly reach the concert room. An extemporized and comfortable retreat was arranged for her behind the scenes, for dress-ing rooms are proverbially dirty in most theatres. The poor lady could scarcely struggle to her feet, but once up she went on unflinchingly behind the disguise of rouge, beautiful gowns, and jewels to sing to audiences that adored her, doing her best in selections suited to her waning vocal powers.   Coming off she sank into her easy chair, almost crying with pain, but when the audience thundered in delight she said to me, " My favorite tree has always been tre-mendous applause.   Listen to that! I must go and sing to them again; that is worth any suffering! "   Once she added, " Do you think now I am getting old I should be doing this if I didn't have to? "

When in San Francisco at Christmas time in 1911, I was asked by Joseph D. Redding, lawyer, orator, wit, writer, man of the world, and the leading spirit of the Bohemian Club, to perform again, this time in the Grove Play he had just written, entitled " The Atonement of Pan," and founded on an ancient myth.   Henry Hadley was chosen as the composer of the music.   Accordingly I found myself the next summer among the redwoods busily rehearsing what, upon its performance on the evening of August 10, 1912, proved to be the most successful play of them all.

The prologue was seriously considered by Hadley, Redding, and myself, with special attention to my predilection for the spoken word accompanied by music.   The pipes of Pan have been heard in the distance and the familiar figure of the god has been seen coming down the hill, when suddenly he appears and renders the prologue, which for effectiveness has seldom been equaled.   The blank verse delivered in speech is ere long set off by music, into which the voice presently glides in song, ending with a beautiful apostrophe to the noble trees of the forest.   My costume had been devised with great care, my head and face made up after that of the statue of Pan in the museum at Naples, which I have always greatly admired.   The story proceeds through the atonement of Pan for the sins he is supposed to have committed and for which the gods had malformed him in punishment; he is allowed to resume his former shape, and all ends happily in a burst of choral music. What a pity these splendid works cannot be heard by the general public!

The evening after we were watching a travesty on the play amusingly and cleverly performed, and I had laughed heartily at the burlesque upon myself, but as I started in the darkness toward the camp of my host, Mr. Redding, my foot slipped on a bit of rock along the hillside, turned under me, and I fell, breaking my ankle. A repetition of the play had been decided upon for the delectation of the ladies within a fortnight. The author, the composer, and the club committee were in despair, but not so I, and I promised that, come what would of it, I would appear. The part had been written for me, was of great length and difficulty, with no one at hand who could learn it in time. A medical member of the club attended to me that night and took me to a hospital in town the next day. I was commanded to keep quiet, but with me that is easier said than done. I was to open a series of concerts at Berkeley in ten days, and this I did on crutches, apologizing to my audience when my attendant took them away and left me alone by the piano, and thanking my lucky stars it was my ankle that was broken and not my neck.

At my insistence a surgical instrument maker devised a wide but softly padded strap of heavy leather strongly fixed below my knee, upon which he adjusted two steel bands outside the plaster cast around my leg and ankle and fastened them to a metal sole an inch under my foot. Dreadfully uncomfortable as I was, I was thus enabled to repeat Pan, upheld by a rustic staff which was in full keeping with the character. A few changes in stage management saved me from moving much during the performance, which I went through without any one of the audience being the wiser. I returned that night by special train with the others to San Francisco, leaving by the Overland Express in the morning for Halifax, Nova Scotia, where on the evening of my arrival I began a Canadian tour which had been arranged months before.

I had an attendant and was made as comfortable as possible on this arduous journey, during which I sang nearly every night of the week. Luckily my concerts were given in theatres, enabling me to hobble on the stage and have all signs of my injury removed before the curtain rose. I was then discovered standing comfortably in the bend of the grand piano, at which sat my accompanist ready to proceed. Not until the concert was half over and Harry Gilbert, my pianist, had to play his solo, did the audience learn that anything was wrong with me, for I could not leave the stage. After an explanation I remained on the platform seated in an armchair, rising from it to sing when my turn came again. I merely mention this by way of insistence upon the duty that every artist owes the public; from it no performer should ask or expect sympathy; but pluck it does admire.

It was this tour which led me in and out of the Middle West, into the Southern States as far as Florida, around the Pacific Coast again, until the journey drawn upon the map looks as if Puck himself had been after us and crying:

> "Up and down, up and down,
> I will lead them up and down."

I had often wondered what could be the mileage of some of my journeys, and found that in 1905 I traveled 23,000 miles. A few years later, in a little over twelve months, I covered 34,000 miles, and from the summer of 1912 to the autumn of 1913, upon my return from Australia, I attained the enormous total of 50,000 miles, equal to at least twice around the world.

CHAPTER XLI

DIVERSE INTERESTS

There is a tide in the affairs of men
Which, taken at the flood, leads on to fortune;
Omitted, all the voyage of their life
Is bound in shallows and in miseries,
On such a full sea are we now afloat,
And we must take the current when it serves,
Or lose our ventures.— *Shakespeare.*

IT had become known in theatrical circles that it was my wish to continue upon the stage, and a play with music was being sought to fit my personality. One was so strongly recommended by Madame Schumann-Heink, who knew of its success in Europe, that I eventually accepted it and signed with a theatrical producing firm to appear in it in New York in the latter part of 1913. Coincidently I was negotiating for a concert tour in Australia, whence I was to return to enter upon the rehearsals for the musical play. At the same time, also, I received the third of a series of offers for a vaudeville engagement which, as theretofore, I declined, giving as the reason my previously arranged plans. After a long tour of America I sailed for Sydney, via San Francisco, where at the Bohemian Club a farewell supper was given me — a masterpiece of ingenuity and fun concocted by my associates of several years in grove plays and High Jinks, this being as high an example of the genus jink as could well be imagined.

In great fettle I journeyed to heavenly Honolulu, where before proceeding southward down the vasty deep,

I sang to the portion of the population that holds the Islands to the United States. And then on around the curve of the world to the great continent below our feet which almost equals in extent the part of North America occupied by the United States, but whose total population is less than that of the City of New York. Once there, I was treated with the greatest courtesy and enthusiasm, but happened to arrive during the rainiest of all rainy seasons, and to encounter as well an epidemic of smallpox, which sadly interfered with my tour. After many appearances in Sydney, Melbourne, Adelaide, and other places, which demonstrated to my satisfaction the kindness of the Australians, than whom, under ordinary circumstances, no more musical people exist, I pushed through to the end, Madame Nordica following me on the list of artists that was to have toured the antipodean land. My experiences and hers which ended in her shipwreck and death as she sailed to India, deterred the rest of our associates from following us so far afield.

Just before I boarded the steamer I spent an hour with my beloved companion of so many operas. She had sung the evening before, and, though I was unable to hear her, I observed that the papers treated her with the greatest consideration, realizing what a famous woman was in their midst.

Just as I was to sail I received another letter from my insistent vaudeville promoter, to say that it was rumored that a combination of untoward happenings in America was about to result in the failure of the firm with which I had contracted for opera, and again vaudeville was suggested to me, with a figure named, by way of bait, that would tempt the veriest anchorite of them all. Though never sharing the prejudices of some of my colleagues against vaudeville, then evidently rising to the status of a fine art and enlisting many actors and musicians of distinction, yet I had held out because I feared that a lowering of my standards might be demanded of me. I thought the matter over and sent a cable to my lawyer in New York asking about the misfortunes of my managers-to-be, and at San Francisco I found an answer which decided me at once. Taking the first train east I substantiated the information, and in one week was off under the most valuable contract I had ever signed, and under conditions entirely satisfactory. I found myself treated like a prince and given every chance to sing to the public the very best in my repertory.

It is always a mistake to play down to anybody. Mediocrity attracts mediocrity. My belief is now, as it was in the beginning, that the artist with courage to sing, or play or act, the finest things he knows, will more quickly gain the ear of the public and more lastingly retain its respect. While the quality of one's performances should be like the quality of mercy, not strained, one's auditors are glad of a message that they can recognize as being higher than what they expected, and thankful to the messenger for providing them with loftier ideals. They come to be amused, they go away interested; and if they are both amused and interested, so much the better.

I changed my offerings every day, sometimes both afternoon and evening, and amply verified my faith that the classics of song do not bore people. My repertory comprised nearly a hundred selections during the course of about a year that I appeared in vaudeville, a year that I look back upon with interest and pleasure.

The spring of 1916 brought with it opportunities to appear in many of the Shakespearean celebrations in honor of the 300th anniversary of the great dramatist's death, my contributions being Shakespearean songs and my reading of "A Midsummer Night's Dream." Among the more noted events of the year was the remarkable testimonial given by the actors of New York and visiting histrions on March 14 to William Winter, so long associated with the *New York Tribune* as dramatic critic. I also helped my friend Beerbohm Tree on a Shakespeare Day at the New Amsterdam Theatre where he was ending his American engagement, while Tree and I, with Alfred Noyes, the poet, assisted shortly after at a similar occasion at the Academy of Music in Philadelphia.

Here let me pause to pay tribute, not too long deferred, I hope, to the American musical amateur. The word itself is one which in professional circles is looked down upon, as if it involved an inferior status. I hold, on the contrary, that the professional who enters upon work before the public with the sole idea of making money, and who learns and performs only what he is compelled to learn and perform, is often more ignorant of his art than he who for the love of it — and that is what the word *amateur* means — applies himself to music without the hope of personal gain, his ideals being primarily artistic. Indeed the mere possession of a voice and the ability to sing songs is but little, unless behind that there is an informing spirit, which with its magic touch irradiates everything that an artist subsequently does before the public. My father used to say, entirely apart from my musical proclivities: " Even a cobbler, if he is an educated cobbler, will make a better pair of boots because of his education; the better the education the better the boots.   A man should love his work."

That old associate of mine in opera, Albert Reiss, whose Mime has never been equaled, called on me in the summer of 1916 to lay before me his project for the revival of Mozart's opera, " Der Schauspiel Direktor " (The Impresario).   I fell in with Reiss's plan. Henry E. Krehbiel, music editor of the *New York Tribune,* provided a new English libretto, and with Sam Franko, the expert in old music, and the American soprano Mabel Garrison, we produced " The Impresario " at the Empire Theatre, New York, on the afternoon of October 26, 1916.   It was preceded by Mozart's youthful operetta " Bastien and Bastienne," with a delightfully naïve book by Alice Mattullath.

So great was the demand for a repetition of those operas, that the Society of American Singers was incorporated early in 1917, with Albert Reiss as president, myself as vice president, and with Herbert Witherspoon and George Hamlin on the board of directors.   In addition to " The Impresario " and " Bastien and Bastienne " a repertory of opéra comique in English with an entirely American cast was given for a short season at the Lyceum Theatre, New York, beginning Monday, May 7, when, again for the first time in America, was performed a double bill, consisting of Pergolesi's delightful comedy " La Serva Padrona " (The Maid as Mistress) and Donizetti's " Il Campanello " (The Night Bell). The former was sung to the English adaptation by Sydney Rosenfeld, with myself as Doctor Pandolfo, and that accomplished American singer, Miss Florence Easton, as the Maid.   These comedies again set a pace and gave the season a send-off of a classical nature, which was just what was needed to attract the attention of musical connoisseurs. In that attractive bit " The Night Bell " Miss Lucy Gates was the bride, Albert Reiss her lover, and I was the Apothecary, Don Hannibal.

Our new repertory also included, for the first time in America, Gounod's comic opera in three acts, " The Mock Doctor," founded upon Molière's satire, " Le Medicin Malgré Lui." In addition to these novelties, the American Singers revived their previous success of " The Impresario " and " Bastien and Bastienne." Our stage director was that master, Jacques Coini, who had been so long the right-hand man of Oscar Hammerstein at the Manhattan Opera House, while our musical conductors, besides Mr. Franko, were Paul Eisler and Artur Bodanzky, conductor in chief of the Metropolitan Opera House, who had generously offered his services in recognition of the artistic importance of our undertaking.

During the progress of the Great War our activities were suspended, but some reconstruction having taken place, we opened on September 23, 1918, under the presidency of William Wade Hinshaw, our second season of opéra comique at the Park Theatre, Columbus Circle, New York, with a performance of Ambroise Thomas's " Mignon," in which the accomplished Scotch soprano, Miss Maggie Teyte, gave a touching performance of the title rôle. The following evening in Donizetti's " Daughter of the Regiment," I appeared as Sergeant Sulpice, with Bianca Saroya as his adopted daughter. Our repertory was further increased by the production of " Carmen " admirably sung by Miss Marguerita Silva, assisted by Riccardo Martin as Don José. While these operas were being sung Puccini's " Madame Butterfly "

was being prepared, with Henry Hadley's prize opera
" Bianca " and Offenbach's " Tales of Hoffmann," in
which I delighted in sinking my personality in the character part of the Jew peddler Coppelius, the doll being
Ruth Miller, and Orville Harrold, as admirable as she,
as Hoffmann himself.   For over six months these works,
alternating with several of Gilbert and Sullivan's masterpieces, and other operas of the highly artistic sort known
as opéra comique, proceeded successfully, and I hope will
result in the establishment of a permanent institution.

My doings during war time continued to be varied
almost beyond belief, for it was my privilege to sing for
the men through every process of recruiting when, before huge gatherings indoors and out, I and my associates in the dramatic and musical professions did our bits.
It was all I was able to do, to hearten the younger generation for the tremendous task before it, but I feel sure
that the value of music has been greatly enhanced in
public opinion by the recognition of its power to heighten
morale as well as of its ability to incite to great deeds.
The roll of the drums, the blare of the trumpets, the
skirl of the bagpipe, and the song of the marching men
have always had their place, but the song of the individual heard by thousands, as I have been heard, is as
refreshing to them as their answering song to me when
by way of thanks the boys good-naturedly trolled out
the ditties taught them by their leaders.

During this time it fell to the lot of the young
American actor-manager, Stuart Walker, to present
that great poem, The Book of Job, upon the New York
stage, using Professor Moulton's version as the basis
of his adaptation, and accordingly in the Booth Theatre
on the afternoon of March 7, 1918, and upon other oc-

casions that Lent, this superb drama was reverently enacted. The mystery of suffering, most universal of all topics, was feelingly declaimed by George Gaul as Job, who nobly led up to the great and final message of patience, faith, and triumph, " I know that my Redeemer liveth," while Elihu was in the master hand of Walter Hampden, at that time preparing for the revival of " Hamlet," in which he was presently so successful as to gain a high name for himself in the annals of the American stage. The Eternal Voice out of the whirlwind was mine.

Of all that has come to me in recognition of my services to art, no honor, not even the praise of kings, has so touched me as a letter received as I was closing my vaudeville experience. It was from that same Isaac Sharpless who, as a professor of mathematics, leniently enabled me in final examinations to take the degree of B. A. at Haverford College, of which he had at last become the president. In it he informed me that the directors of my Alma Mater had decided to confer upon me the honorary degree of LL.D., which was duly granted me on Commencement Day, June 12, 1914. Academically gowned, capped, and hooded, I acknowledged my sense of the dignity awarded me by singing Schubert's glorious song, " Omnipotence," and the Prologue from the opera " I Pagliacci," to bring home to those not musically or dramatically inclined not only the value of song, but the fact that we upon the stage are merely men and women, and none the worse or better because of our profession.

Had anything happened to me, or was it that something had happened to Haverford? Nothing had happened to me except the daily, monthly, yearly, continual

application to musical and histrionic pursuits of a mind
that could do nothing else. Therefore something must
have happened to the college. The rising generation,
and those of the older school who remained, had lived
to see a time not contemplated by its founders, when
music and the drama had become recognized factors in
the daily life of the community. No longer are they
to be looked upon as wicked or at least idle pastimes, but
as a means of education. Hence it is, I suppose, that I as
their representative was given a place among educators,
and I was proud thus to be considered worthy of the
honor which my college had conferred upon me. The
world to come, the future life, is full of possibilities; men
and women stand upon the threshold of a new era, the
longed-for millennium. Upon the individual rests the
responsibility of making his work good, and to uplift by
his attitude everything he may lay his hand to; as says
the poet George Herbert:

> " Who sweeps a room as by God's law
> Makes that and the action fine."

Music has meant so much to me from boyhood, has
been so much a part of my youth and early manhood,
and has become so much to me in my maturity, that I cannot bring these recollections to a close without a summing-
up of my understanding of this empress of modern arts.
In our music alone does it seem certain that we have sur-
passed the ancients in the finer arts of human life, following in their footsteps the eternal quest of beauty.
He would be bold who should claim our present superiority in painting, sculpture, architecture, poetry, and drama.
In music alone can we assert ourselves as masters of a
technique finer than the world has ever known before.

We can do more. Is there a painting as delicate and descriptive as the pictures music brings to the mind's eye, a statue ennobled by poetry that will not gain by the harmonies at our command, a building whose aspirations toward the skies are not winged by solemn chants, a poem or a play that does not find its finer inspiration doubled in loveliness and in permanent value by its wedding to immortal melody? Is there a conception of life beyond the grave that does not spring from the music of eternity? Truly, as Carlyle says, " Music is well said to be the speech of angels."

THE END

INDEX

Abbot, Emma (soprano), 34
Academy of Fine Arts, 50
Academy of Music (Philadelphia), 29, 36, 52, 196, 227, 230, 367
Accident to throat, 72
Achenbach, Andreas (painter), 136
Acropolis, 24
Adams, Suzanne (singer), 292, 294
Adelaide (Australia), 365
"Adelaïde," (play, Hugo Müller), 215, 216, 217, 285
Africa, 288
African, 287
"Agamemnon," 154
"Aghadoe" (song), 359
Agnostic, the (Huxley), 73
"Aïda" (opera, Verdi), 111, 170, 187
Aïdé, Hamilton (author), 77
Albani, Madame (soprano), 113, 123, 166, 182, 183, 265, 305
Albany, 283, 317
Alberich (in "Rheingold," Wagner), 112, 123, 167, 191, 206, 208, 247, 250, 251, 253, 254, 309
Alexander, George (actor), 150, 151
Alfio (in "Cavalleria Rusticana"), 124, 139
Allen, Grant (author), 147
Alma Mater, 34, 371
Alps, 136
Alvarez (tenor), 184, 193, 292, 295
Alvary, Max (tenor), 114, 123, 136, 139, 145
Amadi, Madame (singer), 165
Amateur's Drawing-Room (Philadelphia), 42, 43
America, 12, 61, 62, 125, 129, 144, 148, 154, 156, 159, 181, 184, 186, 188, 189, 190, 197, 198, 203, 206, 209, 212, 216, 218, 224, 226, 230, 241, 260, 280, 286, 288, 291, 292, 311, 313–315, 321, 322, 324, 339, 364, 366, 368, 369

American, 10, 129, 132, 137, 182, 184, 185, 188, 197, 198, 201, 204, 208, 214, 216, 218, 225, 228, 229, 287, 294, 303, 305, 310, 367, 368, 370
American Actors and Actresses, 330
American Colony in Florence, 65
American Composers, 107, 119, 197, 290, 317, 338, 348
American Compositions, 320
American Indian, 93
American Minister, 319
American Music Society, 338
American Musician, 209, 226
American Negro Melodies, 295
American Negro Spirituals, 348
American Poets, 344
American Sage (Walt Whitman), 15
American Sculptors, 327
American Songstresses, 100
American Stage, 327, 371
American Students, 240
"American, The" (play, Henry James), 150
American Tour, 336
American Writer, 15
Americanism, 198
Americans, 135, 177, 198, 200, 227, 235, 248, 251, 253, 266, 271, 281, 283
Amfortas (in "Parsifal"), 127, 206, 310
Amonasro (in "Aïda," Verdi), 111, 112, 115, 266
Ancona (singer), 137, 183, 187
Anderson, Mary (actress), 293
Anderson, Percy (artist), 100
Anderson, Sarah (soprano), 300
André, Major, 271
Andrew the Rich, 276, 277, 278, 279
Anecdote of Edwin Booth, 357, 358
Anecdote of Mark Twain, 341, 342
Anecdote of Mme. Schumann-Heink, 341

"Angel of the House," The, 152
Anglin, Margaret (actress), 284
Anglo-Saxon Talk, 23
Ann Arbor, 218, 226
Annapolis, 132
"Anniversary, The" (opera, Bowers), 343
"Antigone" (tragedy), 310, 337
Antwerp, 259
Apollo Club, 283
"Apostles, The" (oratorio, Elgar), 311
Apostle Paul, 345
Apothecary (in "Romeo and Juliet," comic opera), 45
Apothecary (in "The Night Bell"), 369
Arbos, Señor (violinist), 131, 164
Arch Street Theatre (Philadelphia), 39
Archer, William (author), 270
"Archibald Douglas" (song), 159
Arch Street, 2
Arimondi (singer), 165
Arion Club (Columbus), 286
Arion Club (Philadelphia), 48
Arizona, 283
Armbruster, Carl (conductor), 112, 117
Arthur (in "The Scarlet Letter"), 222
Art Theatre Society, The, 275
"At Evening's Hour" (song), 350
Athenian Amphitheatres, 284
Athens, 24, 25, 276
Atlantic City, 1
Atlantic Ocean, 185, 266, 303
"At Last the Bounteous Sun" (song), 350
"Atonement of Pan, The" (music drama, Redding and Hadley), 360, 362
Auber (composer), 165
Auburn, 15
Auditorium Theatre, 241, 243
Australia, 11, 363, 364
Australians, 365
"Autumnal Gale" (song), 350

Bach Choir, 127, 163
Bach, J. S. (composer), 52, 131, 145, 180, 228, 286, 350
Bach Festival, 133, 163
Bagby, Morris, 216

Baird, Frank (teacher), 59
Balfe (composer), 88, 126
Balfour, Arthur (statesman), 266
Baliol College, 135
Ball, Thomas (sculptor), 65
Ballad Concert, 135
Balmoral Castle, 213
Baltimore, 259, 342
Bancroft, Squire (actor), 73
Bandrowski (singer), 301
Bangs, F. C. (actor), 41
    As Sardanapolus, 41
    As Mark Antony, 41
Banjo, 28
Barbirolli (pianist), 68
Bar Harbor, 354
Barili, Ettore (Patti's teacher), 48
Barker, Granville (actor), 270
Barnard, George Gray (sculptor), 4
Barnes, Jack (actor), as Romeo, 42
Barrett, Lawrence (actor), 38, 41
"Basoche, The" (opera, Messager), 81, 97, 100, 102, 108, 111
"Bastien and Bastienne" (opera, Mozart), 368, 369
Baths of Diocletian, 154
"Battle Cry of Freedom," The (song), 65
Batley, 174
Bauermeister, Miss (singer), 292
Baveux tapestry, 307
Bayard (ambassador), 304
"Bay of Biscay, The" (song), 84
Bayreuth, 58, 74, 104, 111, 112, 127, 134, 167, 190, 241, 303, 358
Beatrice (in "Much Ado"), 294
Beckmesser (in "Die Meistersinger," Wagner), 58, 111–115, 123, 137, 139, 187, 206, 208, 253, 266
Bede, the Venerable, 10, 11
Bedford, Herbert, 146
Bedford, Herbert, Mrs., 332–334
Beecham, Sir Thomas (conductor), 107
Beethoven, 29, 51, 163, 179, 204, 215, 217, 218, 219, 226, 228, 236, 250, 285, 287, 320, 348, 350
Beethoven (in "Adelaïde"), 215, 216, 217, 310, 344
Belgian, 241
"Belle Dame sans Merci, La" (song), 359

Bellincioni, Madame Gemma (singer), 166, 167
Bell Song ("Lakme"), 265
"Bells, The" (play), 66
Belmont, Mr., 274
Beneckes, the Alfred (cousins of Mendelssohn), 147
Benedick (in "Much Ado"), 294
Benoist (composer), 219
Benson, Lionel (director), 102, 106
Bergh, Arthur (composer), 280, 281, 338
Berkeley, Calif. (Greek Theatre), 25, 284
Berkeley, Calif., 361
Berlin, 108, 216
Berlin, Royal Opera, 108, 228
Berlioz (composer), 145, 159, 219, 228
Bernhardt, Sarah (actress), 232, 284, 291–293
Besant, Mrs. Anne (author), 76
"Bethlehem" (oratorio, Mackenzie), 131
Bevan, Alexander (singer), 172
Bevignani (conductor), 187
"Bianca" (opera, Hadley), 370
Bible, 194, 250
Bible reading, 89, 195
Bigod (Roger and Hugh, ancestors), 14
Bilboss (in "Joan"), 83
Bill (in "Vicar of Wakefield"), 334
Bird, Henry (pianist), 181
Birmingham, 211, 212, 288
Birmingham Festival, 61, 160, 209, 286
Biscop, Benedict (Abbot), 10, 11
Biscop (Saxon family), 10
Biscopham (original name), 11
Bisham Abbey, 12
Bishop (composer), 88, 350
Bismarck, 332
Bispham Coat of Arms, 9
Bispham, David (singer), 341, 342, 354
Bispham, David (sketch of), 5, 340
Bispham Family, 6, 10, 11, 12, 22
Bispham Hall (old home), 10, 22
Bispham Houses, 6
Bispham, John (uncle), 28, 30
Bispham, Maria Stokes (grandmother), 14

Bispham, (misspellings of — Beechmann, Besphain, Besphourm, Besthon, Bicham, Biftham, Bipham, Biscamb, Biscopem, Biscopeym, Bisfam, Bisfan, Bishham, Bishham, Bishamp, Bishphan, Biskham, Bispam, Bispame, Bisparn, Bispen, Bispin, Bisphame, Bisphan, Bisphain, Bisphen, Bispum, Bisplain, Bipsham, Bispthan, Bispthane, Bistam, Bisthiam, Bisthan, Bixham, Dispam, Dispham and Dishchan, 11, 12
Bispham, Samuel (grandfather), 14
Bispham, William (1597), 22
Bispham, William Danforth (father), 2
Bispham, William (New York), 22, 357
Bizet (composer), 301, 310
Black, Andrew (barytone), 121
Black, Mrs. Morris (singer), 290
"Blackbird and the Crow, The" (song), 295
"Blackbird's Song, The," (song), C. Scott, 350
Blackpool, 140
Blake (artist), 79
Blank, Mr. (pianist), 190, 249
Blass, Robert (basso), 294
Blauvelt, Lillian (singer), 198, 290
Blavatsky, Madame (occultist), 76
Bloch-Ernest (composer), 306
Blowitz, 151
Blue Reserves (Civil War regiment), 3
Blumenthal (composer), 88
Bodanzsky, Artur (conductor), 369
Bohemian Club, 338, 339, 353, 356, 360, 364
"Bohemian Girl, The" (opera, Balfe), 30, 84, 126, 127
Boito (composer), 228
Bologna, Italy, 68
Book of Job, The, 370
Book of Revelation, 4
"Bookworm, The" (picture), 80
Booth, Edwin (actor), 38, 40, 41, 324, 328, 357, 358
    As Brutus, 41

Booth, Edwina (Mrs. Grossman),
    324
Booth Theatre (New York), 370
Bordighera, 89
Borwick, Leonard (English pian-
    ist), 131, 163
Boston, 11, 55, 178, 199, 217, 220,
    247-249, 322, 329, 331, 336,
    338
    Museum, 39
    Public, 39
Boston Common, 248
Boston Symphony Orchestra, 55,
    128, 219, 221, 248, 260, 358
Bowers, Robert Hood (composer),
    343
Box Hill, 147
Bozenta, Count, 331
Bradford, 174
Braham (composer), 88
Brahms, Johannes (composer), 32,
    105, 134, 164, 190, 194, 195, 197,
    204, 226, 228, 250, 286, 320, 348,
    350
Brangäne (in "Tristan," Wag-
    ner), 119, 303
Branscombe (composer), 350
Brema, Marie (singer), 208, 258,
    265, 294
Brignoli (tenor), 35
"Brindisi, The" (song), 241
Britain, 10, 129
British and American Festival
    Peace Concert, 305
British Composers, 107, 177
British Embassy, 127
British Isles, 131, 313, 348
British Metropolis, 164
British Museum (London), 79,
    80
British Nation, 303
British Poets, 344
British Press, 118
British Provinces, 124
British Public, 169
British Spy (Story of), 271
British Yeomen, 15
Briton, the, 304
Broadway, 132, 330
Brockway, Howard (composer),
    290, 359
Broadway Managers (story of),
    271

Bronson, Mrs. (friend of Brown-
    ing), 66
Brooklyn Academy of Music, 221,
    250, 358
Brooklyn Institute, 249
Browning, Mrs. Elizabeth Barrett
    (poetess), 66
Browning, Robert (poet), 66, 82,
    158, 243, 248, 271, 281
Brozel, Philip (tenor), 166
Bruch, Max (composer), 52
Brünnhilde (in "The Valkyrie"),
    191, 250, 254, 256, 293, 309
Brutus ("Julius Cæsar"), 329, 330
    Davenport as, 41
    Booth as, 41
    (Speech of), 20
Bryce, Right Honorable James
    (ambassador), 339
Bryn Mawr College, 241
Buck, Dudley (composer), 53, 197
Buckingham Palace, 169, 171, 184,
    264
Buffalo, 321
Bull, John, 166
Bull, Ole (violinist), 30
Bull of Bashan, voice of, 114
Bull Run, 3
Bullet Hole Fence, 7
Buonamici (pianist), 68
Burchell, Mr. ("Vicar of Wake-
    field"), 334
Burgstaller, Aloys (tenor), 292
Burleigh, Henry (negro compos-
    er), 295
Burlington County, 6
Burne-Jones (painter), 146
Burnett, Mrs. Frances Hodgson
    (writer), 42, 89, 153
Burnett, Lionel, 153
Burns (poet), 87, 235, 344
Burton, Sir Richard, 152
Bushnell, Erickson (singer), 160
Butt, Madame Clara (contralto),
    121, 179, 305
Buzzard's Bay, 328
Byron, Lord (poet), 83, 235, 323,
    324, 344

Cæsar, 329
"Cahal Mor" (song), 359
Cahier, Madame (singer), 290
California, 338, 353, 354

Calvé, Emma (soprano), 166, 187, 193, 194, 244, 296
Cambridge, 117
Cambridge University, 117, 209
Camden, 15
Campanari (barytone), 187, 220, 296
"Campanello, Il," 368, 369
Canada, 296, 302, 320, 357
Canadian, 305
Carlyle (poet), 373
Carl Rosa Company, 106, 171
"Carmen" (opera, Bizet), 30, 124, 139, 187, 193, 369
Carnegie, Andrew (story of), 269–279
Carnegie Hall (New York), 126, 157, 197, 221, 249, 300, 318, 321, 322, 323, 336, 337, 358
Carnegie Lyceum, 197
Carpenter, John Alden (composer), 290
Carreño, Madame Teresa (pianist), 337
Carritte, Miss Nita (actress), 217
Carte, D'Oyley (manager), 92, 95–97
Cassius (Barrett as), 41
Castelmary (basso), 35, 115, 187
"Cavalier Tunes" (songs, Stanford), 82
Cathedral Glass, 10
"Cavalleria Rusticana" (opera, Mascagni), 124, 139, 166, 187
"Cave Man, The" (music drama, McCoy), 353, 354
Cecilian Society (oratorio society), 48, 52
Cedric the Saxon (in "Ivanhoe"), 92
Cellier, Alfred (conductor), 96, 97
"Centennial Cantata, The" (Buck), 53
Centennial Exposition (Philadelphia, 1876), 53
Central Park, 273
Chadwick, Geo. W. (composer), 119, 197, 338, 350
Chamberlain, Will (boy friend), 28
Chambers, Haddon (playwright), 142
Chaminade, Mlle. (composer), 350
Chappell, Arthur (director), 179
Cheatham, Kitty (singer), 217
Chester Cathedral (England), 22

Chesterfield, Lord, 234
Chew Mansion, 7
Chicago, 59, 125, 154, 155, 194, 217, 219, 220, 221, 241, 247, 283, 285, 286, 293, 324, 329, 333, 341
Chicago Orchestra, 281
Chillingworth ("The Scarlet Letter"), 222
Chinese, 325
Chinese Theatre, 234
Choate, Joseph H. (ambassador), 304
Choate, Mrs., 304
Chopin (composer), 332
"Choufleuri" (opera, Offenbach), 45
Christ Church, 50
Christie's Minstrels, 91, 295
Christmas Pantomime, 38
Church of England (music of), 49
Cincinnati, 324, 325, 343
Cincinnati College of Music, 343
Cincinnati Festival, 218, 228, 285
City of New York, 365
Civil War, 3, 7, 16, 319
Civil War Songs, 65
Clara (in play, "Adelaïde"), 217
Clarendon House, 1
Classic Theatre, 25, 269, 270, 272–274, 276
Claudio (in "Much Ado"), 294
Clemens, Clara (singer), 341
Cleveland, Grover (President), 327, 328
Coates, John (tenor), 294
Coquelin (actor), 232, 291–293
Coini, Jacques (stage director), 369
Cole, Belle (singer), 306
Cole, Rossetter G. (composer), 280
Coleridge-Taylor, S. (composer), 287–289
Colonel Berners (in "Cut Off with a Shilling"), 44
Colorado River, 356
Columbian Exposition, 154
Columbia River, 357
Columbus Circle (N. Y.), 369
Columbus, O., 286
Comédie Française, 270
"Come into the Garden, Maud" (song), 88
Commencement Day, 371
Commissioner of Parks, 154
Commonwealth of Pennsylvania, 11

Connecticut, 341
Conried (impresario), 309
Constantinople, 25
Continent, the, 286, 303
Convention Hall, 297
Converse, Frederic (composer), 359
Cooke, Jay (banker), 33
Cooper, Fenimore (author), 65
Cooper, Mrs. William (musician), 65
Cooper, William (sculptor), 65
Cope, Henry (cousin), 19
Coppelius (opera, "Tales of Hoffmann"), 370
"Coquaine" (overture, Elgar), 311
Corinthians, First, 345
"Coronation Ode" (Elgar), 311
Corsi, Pini (singer), 139
Costanzi Theatre, 24
Count Bozenta, 331
Count Montebello (in "The Ferry Girl," Hill), 82
Count Rudolfo, 84
Court Opera, (Vienna), 321
Covent Garden Opera House (London), 35, 73, 83, 85, 105, 107, 112, 113, 115, 117, 118, 124, 129, 136, 137, 139, 145, 165, 166, 170, 171, 181, 182, 185, 206, 208, 260–262, 294, 302
Cowboys, 325
Cowen, Sir Frederick (composer), 105, 134, 166, 205
"Cox & Box" (opera, Sullivan), 43
Cox (in "Cox & Box"), 43
Cramer, Pauline (soprano), 117
Crawford, F. Marion (novelist), 65
"Creation, The" (oratorio, Haydn), 52, 320
"Creation's Hymn," (song), 350
Cremonini (singer), 187, 193
Cricket, game of, 19
Croatian Singer, 291
Crœsus, 276, 279
Crookes, Sir William (scientist), 76
Cross, Michael H. (musician), 33, 47, 48, 49
Crystal gazing, 79
Crystal Palace (London), 58, 82, 124, 131, 159, 305
"Cujus Animam" (song), 69
Cupid, 323

"Cup of Tea, A" (play), 44
Cushman, Charlotte (actress), 38
"Cut Off with a Shilling" (play), 44
Cycle of Great Song Cycles, 323

Dakota, 285
Daland (in "The Flying Dutchman," Wagner), 121, 167
D'Albert, Eugene (pianist), 282
Dame Quickly (in "Falstaff"), 139
"Damnation of Faust" (Berlioz), 145, 219, 228
Damrosch, Walter (conductor), 125, 217, 219, 220, 221, 222, 223, 230, 233, 235, 236, 283, 285, 291, 296, 310, 311, 313, 323, 324, 328, 350
Dancing Dervishes, 25, 26
Dane, the ("Hamlet"), 143
Dannreuther Quartette, 217
"Danny Deever" (song by Damrosch), 230, 231, 236, 283, 317, 318, 328, 350, 357
"Danny Deever, The Hanging of" (poem, Kipling), 230
Darwin, Charles (scientist), 372
"Daughter of the Regiment" (opera, Donizetti), 369
Davenport, E. L. (actor), 41
"David" (Michael Angelo's), 65
David, the Singer of the Church, 276, 277
Davies, Ben (tenor), 100, 229, 305
Davies, Fanny (pianist), 135, 164, 180, 236
Davies, Ffrangçon (singer), 306
Davies, Walford, 158
Davis, Richard Harding (author), 230
"Death of Nelson, The" (song), 88
De Bohun, Henry (ancestor), 14
Debussy, Claude (composer), 306
Declaration of Independence, 3
De Clare, Richard and Gilbert (ancestor), 14
De Koven, Reginald (composer), 43, 197
De Lacie, John (ancestor), 14
Delaware River, 15
Delibes (composer), 350
Del Puente, Giuseppe (barytone), 56, 227

De Lucia (tenor), 165, 265
De Mowbray, William (ancestor), 14
De Nevers (in "Les Huguenots"), 124, 139, 183
De Pachmann, Vladimir (pianist), 330, 331
De Quincey, Saher (ancestor), 14
De Reszke, Edouard (basso), 129, 182, 187, 191, 244, 250, 266, 267, 290, 292, 297, 309
De Reszke, Jean (tenor), 113, 123, 129, 137, 182, 185, 187, 191, 192, 232, 244, 250, 266, 267, 292
"Der Freischütz" (opera, Weber), 136
Dervishes, Dancing, 25, 26
Dervishes, Howling, 26
De Treville, Yvonne (soprano), 217
Detroit, 285
DeVere, Clementine (singer), 190
De Vere, Robert (ancestor), 14
Dewsbury, 174
Diamond Jubilee, 264
Dibdin, Charles (composer), 84
"Dichterliebe" (song cycle, Schumann), 205
Dick (in "Vicar of Wakefield"), 334
Dickens, Charles (author), 261
Dickens's Land, 80
Dicksee, Frank (painter), 146
Dictionary of Music and Musicians, 55
"Die Frisst is um" (song), 262
Diligent Engine Company (Philadelphia), 3
Dippel, Andreas (tenor), 243, 249, 292, 296
Dobson, Austin (poet), 332
Doctor Fleming (in "Weak Woman"), 44
Doctor of Laws — LL.D. (Degree of), 371
Dogberry (in "Much Ado"), 294
Dolmetsch, Arnold (musician), 131, 145, 168, 169
Domesday Book, 10, 11
"Domestic Symphony" (Strauss), 323
"Don Carlos" (opera, Verdi), 24
"Don Giovanni" (opera, Mozart), 187, 265, 266

Don Hannibal (in "The Night Bell"), 369
Donizetti (composer), 350, 368, 369
Don José (opera "Carmen"), 369
Donoghue, John (sculptor), 153, 154
Dorking, 147
Dramatic Literature, Love for, 40
"Dream of Fair Women, A" (Tennyson), 358
"Dream of Gerontius" (oratorio, Elgar), 287, 311
"Dreams" (song), 350
Dresden, 266
Drew, John (actor), 39
Drew, Mr. and Mrs. John, the elder (actors), 39, 40
Drury Lane Theatre, 114, 136, 180, 261
Dryden (poet), 211
Dublin, 313
Dublin, University of, 117
Duc de Longueville (in "The Basoche"), 81, 97, 100
Duke of Connaught, 265
Duke of Edinburgh, 103
Dusé, Elenora (actress), 166
"Dutchman, The Flying" (opera, Wagner), 121, 167, 172, 190, 220, 228, 233, 244, 247, 260, 264, 322
Dvorák (composer), 228, 287
Dysart, Lord, 112

Eames, Emma (soprano), 137, 184, 187, 207, 220, 241, 243, 249, 250, 252, 290, 296, 309
Earthquake in Italy, 63, 64
Eastern States, 283
Easton, Madame Florence (soprano), 368
"Ecco il Leone," 295
Edgardo (Reeves as), 85
Edinburgh, 128
"Edward" (song, by Loewe), 159, 350
Edwin Forrest Home (Philadelphia), 126
"Egmont" (drama, Goethe), 310
Egyptian Mummy (poem on), 79
Eisler, Paul (conductor), 369
"Elaine" (Tennyson), 358
Elberfeld Horses, 116
Elderly Friend's Story, 53

Elgar, Edward (composer), 287, 311
Elihu (in "Job"), 371
"Elijah" (oratorio, Mendelssohn), 52, 160, 163, 211, 219, 285, 341, 357
Elizabeth (in "Tannhäuser"), 172, 207, 241
Ellis, Chas. (manager Boston Symphony Orchestra), 219, 220
Ellis-Damrosch Opera Company, 232
Elsa (in "Lohengrin"), 182, 220, 250
Elsenheimer, Dr. N. J. (composer), 358
Emperor William (Old), 32
Empire Theatre, 368
Engadine (Swiss), 72
England, 10, 11, 12, 22, 60, 61, 62, 72, 102, 105, 121, 125, 129, 131, 144, 160, 168, 172, 174, 178, 204, 205, 209, 210, 212, 224, 229, 231, 234, 236, 266, 268, 286, 289, 295, 303, 306, 311
Engle, Marie (soprano), 166
English, 207, 209, 212, 213, 214, 294, 324
English, a world language, 105, 143, 184, 334, 345
English Channel, 33, 106
English Comedies, 270
English Composers, 33, 119, 287, 303, 348
English Compositions, 320
English Ditties, 14
English Festivals, 106, 174, 210
English Lyrics, 283
English Music, 51, 168, 177, 313
English, opera in, 30, 32, 108, 123, 166, 171, 251, 294, 310
English Play, 40
English Poets, 344
English Selections, 134
English, songs in, 33, 317
English-speaking World, 95, 224
English-speaking Audiences, 105, 188, 225, 344, 345, 368
English Versions, 344
"Englishwoman's Love Letters, An" (novel), 333
"Enoch Arden" (melodrama), 280, 302, 306, 314, 320, 321
Episcopal Academy, 40

Epistle of David, the, 276
Erda (in "Rheingold"), 309
"Erl King, The" (song, Loewe), 159
"Erl King, The" (song, Schubert), 49, 104, 226
"Esmeralda" (opera, Goring Thomas), 105
"Esmeralda" (play), 42
"Eugen Onegin" (opera, Tschaikowsky), 108
Europe, 124, 133, 148, 156, 161, 181, 183, 189, 198, 200, 204, 237, 248, 266, 290, 302, 303, 315, 337, 364
European, 253, 256
European Artists, 330
European Countries, 347
European Peasants, 325
European Trip, 21-27, 57, 58, 59, 266
Europeanism, 198
"Euryanthe" (opera, Weber), 164
Eva (in "Meistersinger," Wagner), 123, 137
"Evangelimann" (opera, Kienzl), 206
Evanston, 339, 341
"Eve" (oratorio, Massenet), 219
"Evelyn Innes" (novel, George Moore), 151
Evil One, Music Wile of, 29
"Excelsior" (poem), 16

Fair Rosamund's Bower, 236
"Falstaff" (in opera, Verdi), 121, 122, 136, 139, 143, 166, 266
Cast from Milan, 124
(Opera "Falstaff"), 139, 140
"Fair Hedwig" (ballad, Hebel), 180
Fat Knight, the (in "Falstaff"), 143
Fauré, Gabriel (composer), 180
"Faust, Damnation of" (Berlioz), 145, 219, 228
"Faust" (opera, Gounod), 30, 36, 113, 139, 187, 313
Faversham, Mrs. William (actress), 216
Fechter, Charles (actor), 40, 41, 311
Feld (conductor), 172
"Ferry Girl, The" (operetta, Lady Arthur Hill), 82
Festival (New York), 52

Festival Peace Concert, 305
"Fidelio" (opera, Beethoven), 136
Field, Charles K. (author), 339, 353, 354
Field, Eugene (poet), 339
Fifth Avenue, 273
Fifth Avenue Hotel (N. Y.), 132
"First Day" (Sunday), 19
First Opera ("Martha"), 30
Fischer, Emil (singer), 220
"Floods of Spring, The" (Rachmaninoff), 350
Florence, 23, 61, 63, 64–71, 72, 74, 75, 215
Florence of Worcester, Chronicle of, 10
"Florentine Tragedy" (Oscar Wilde), 358
Florentine Singer, Story of, 69, 70
Florida, 302, 362
Floridia, Pietro (conductor), 343
Flosshilde (in "Rheingold"), 251
"Flying Dutchman, The" (opera, Wagner), 121, 167, 172, 190, 220, 228, 233, 244, 247, 260, 264, 322
Foote, Arthur (composer), 119, 197
Forbes-Robertson, Sir Johnstone (actor), 62, 73
Ford, Ernest (composer), 82, 94–96, 97
Ford, Mrs. Seabury (soprano), 225
Ford (opera "Falstaff"), 139
Foreign Composers, 348
Foreman of the Jury ("Trial by Jury"), 44
Forest, Arthur (actor), 329, 330
"Forest, The" (opera, Smythe), 303
Fort Sumter, 3
Foster, Muriel (English alto), 311
Four o'Clock Concerts, 293
"Four Serious Songs" (Brahms), 190, 194, 197, 226, 250
"Fourth Day" (Wednesday), 19
Fourth of July, 4
Fourth Symphony (Schumann), 228
Fox, George (Early Quaker), 29
"Fra Diavolo" (opera by Auber), 165, 166, 182
France, 106, 224, 270, 305
Franck, Cæsar (composer), 228
Franklin, Benjamin (statesman), 2, 27, 304, 305

Franklin Square, 14
Franko, Sam, 368, 369
Franz, Robert (composer), 348, 350
"Frauenliebe und Leben" (song), 205, 349
Free Trade Hall (Manchester), 121
"Freischütz, Der" (opera by Weber), 136
Fremstad, Olive (soprano), 303, 304
French, 139, 184, 206, 207, 224
Canadian, 182
Artists, 206
French Lessons, 17, 18
French Operas, 296
Friar, the (in "Romeo and Juliet"), 292
Friar, the (in "Much Ado"), 294
Fricka (in "Rheingold"), 256, 258
Friedrichs (as Beckmesser), 58
Friends' Meeting, 3, 20, 28, 93
Friends' School (Philadelphia), 15
Friends, Society of, 2, 6
"Frithjof" (cantata, Bruch), 52
"Frithiof's Return" (Steele), 219
Frohman, Daniel (manager), 216, 330
"From the Uplands to the Sea" (song), 158
Frost Scene (Purcell's "King Arthur"), 211, 253, 350
"Fugitives, The" (recitation, Shelley), 180
Fullerton, Morton, 151
Furness, Doctor Horace Howard (Shakespearean scholar), 45, 127
Furness, Dr. Horace Howard, Jr. (Shakespearean scholar), 45, 127

Gabrilowitsch, Ossip (pianist), 341, 342
Gadski, Madame (singer), 209, 218, 220, 247, 260, 264, 283, 290, 296, 298, 309
"Gaiety Girl" (comic opera), 263
Gaiety Theatre, 98
Galassi (barytone), 56
"Gallia" (cantata, Gounod), 52
Galveston, 325
Garden, Mary (soprano), 304, 307

Gardener, The (in "Sweet-
hearts"), 43
"Gardy" (Reeves's pet name), 85
Garrick, David (actor), 40, 261,
338
Garrison, Mabel (soprano), 368
Gates, Lucy (singer), 369
Gatty, Alfred (composer), 295
Gaul, George (actor), 371
Gave up smoking, 99
"Gems of Song in English," 225
General von Rosenberg (in "Her
Bitterest Foe"), 44
Genius of Cold (in "King Ar-
thur"), 253
Gericke (conductor), 358
German Actor, 280
German Classics, 344
German Composers, 344
German Element, 313
German Horseman, 23
German Language, 123, 139, 182,
206, 207, 224, 226, 251, 303,
324
German Lesson, 19
German Music, 208,
German Opera, 260
German Poems, 344
German Singers, met, 74, 129, 267
Germantown, 7, 48
Germantown, Battle of, 7
Germantown Opera House, 45
Germany, 106, 216, 224, 256, 295,
303
Gertrude (in "Romeo and Juliet"),
292
Gettysburg (Battle of), 3
Ghibelline Battlements, 307
Gilbert, Harry (accompanist), 362
Gilbert, W. S. (composer), 142, 143,
350
Gilbert and Sullivan's operas, 42,
83, 370
"Sorcerer," 44
"Trial by Jury," 44
Gilder, Richard Watson (editor-
poet), 230
Giles, Edward (teacher), 47
Gilmore, "Pat" (conductor), 29
Glacial Epoch, 253
Gloucester Cathedral (England),
51, 173
Gloucester Festival, 174
Gloucestershire, 236

Gluck (composer), 124, 285
Godowsky, Leopold (pianist), 92
Goethe, 161, 291
"Golden Haired Gertrude" (oper-
etta, Parrish), 43
"Golden Legend, The" (cantata,
Sullivan), 159
Goldschmidt, Otto, 205
Goldsmith, Oliver (author), 258,
332, 334
Gomarez, 343
Gordon, MacKenzie (tenor), 217,
225
Gospel according to Andrew, 276
Gosse, Edmund (author), 15
"Götterdämmerung, The" (opera),
167
Gounod, Charles (composer), 52,
131, 135, 160, 219, 265, 292, 302,
313, 350, 369
Gozlan (writer), 293
Grand Cañon, 356
Grand Opera, 105
Grant, General Fred, 319
Grant, U. S. (President and Gen-
eral), 3, 49, 50, 319
Grau, Maurice (director), 186, 187,
189, 218, 219, 220, 245, 246, 250,
259, 266, 301, 309, 310
Great Britain, 95, 266, 319
Great Eastern Steamship, 22
Great War, 369
Great White Way, 238
Greek Theatres, Athens, 24
Greek Theatre, University of Cali-
fornia), 25, 284, 338
Greek Tragedies, 25, 89
Green Drawing-Room, 267
Greene, Plunkett (singer), 121, 159
Gregorian Music, 10
Gregorian Chants, 10, 68
Gregorowitsch (Russian violinist),
197
Griddley (in "Sixty-Six"), 44
Grieg, Edvard (composer), 219,
228, 286, 350
Grisi, Madame (soprano), 83
Griswold, Putnam (basso), 294
Grossman, Mrs. (Booth's daugh-
ter), 324
Grove, The Bohemian Club, 353-
354
Grove Plays, 354, 360
Grove, Sir George (editor), 55

Grosvenor Gallery (London), 82
Guetary (tenor), 123
Guitar, 28
"Guinevere" (Tennyson), 358
Gura (singer), 58
Gurney, Edmund (scientist), 76

Haddow, W. H. (writer), 117
Hadley, Henry (composer), 197, 226, 360, 370
Hagen (in "Götterdämmerung"), 167, 250, 309
Hahn, Reynaldo (composer), 350
"Hail Smiling Morn" (madrigal), 87
Halifax, Nova Scotia, 362
England, 174
Hall, Madame Edna (teacher), 329
Hall of Fame, 281
Hall, Marguerite (contralto), 135, 197, 225, 328
Hallé, Lady (Madame Norman Neruda, violinist), 125, 179
Hallé, Sir Charles (conductor), 120, 121, 159
"Hamadryads, The" (music drama, McCoy), 338, 353
Hall of Song, the, 298
Hamburg, 113, 136
Ham House, Richmond, 112
"Hamlet" (Booth as), 38, 142, 357, 358
 (Fechter as), 311
 (Hampden as), 371
 Opera (Thomas), 187
 (Sarah Bernhardt as), 291
Hamlet's Soliloquy (Shakespeare), 20
Hamlin, George (tenor), 368
Hammerstein, Oscar (impresario), 369
Hampden, Walter (actor), 371
Handel Festival (London), 58, 305
Handel, G. H. (composer), 47, 52, 124, 219, 228, 306, 350
Handelian Singer, 53, 54
Handel and Haydn Society, of Boston, 248
Hans Sachs (in "Die Meistersinger"), 58, 74, 111, 123, 137, 139, 167
"Hansel und Gretel" (opera, Humperdinck), 181

"Hark! Hark! The Lark" (song), 338
Harley, Orlando (tenor), 132
"Harold" (opera, Frederick Cowen), 166
Harris, Sir Augustus (impresario), 106, 107, 112–115, 186
Harris, Victor (teacher), 225
Harrold, Orville (tenor), 370
Hartford, 249
Harvard Club, 342
Harvard Stadium, 154
Haverford College (Penna.), 16, 18, 19, 20, 31, 33, 34, 241, 371
Haverford Station, 31
Havergal, Frances Ridley (poetess), 161, 163
Hay, John (ambassador), 304
Haydn, Michael (composer), 47, 52, 350
Haymarket Theatre, 140, 143
Hawkesley (in "Still Waters Run Deep"), 44
Hearst, Mrs. Phœbe, 284
Hearst, William Randolph, 284
"Heart Bowed Down, The" (song), 126
Hebbel (poet), 180
Hedmondt, E. C. (tenor), 123, 171, 172
Heine (poet), 205
Heinrich, Max (barytone), 31, 32, 33, 34, 47, 49, 52, 56, 129, 299
"He is Kind" (song), 350
"He Jests at Scars," 313
Henley, 259
Henschel, Georg (conductor), 55, 56, 103, 104, 128
Henschel, Mrs. Georg (singer), 129, 135, 164
Herald ("Agamemnon"), 155
Herbert, George (poet), 372
"Her Bitterest Foe" (play), 44
Hereford, 173
"Hereward" (cantata, Prout), 159
Herford, Oliver (humorist), 99
Herkomer, Herman (artist), 101
Hero (in "Much Ado"), 294
Hertz, Alfred (conductor), 309
"Herodiade" (opera, Massenet), 145
Hester (in "The Scarlet Letter"), 222
"He, the Best of All" (song), 350

"Hiawatha" (cantata, Coleridge-Taylor), 288
"Hidalgo, The" (song), 350
Higbee, Miss Beulah, 16
Higbee, Miss Lill, 16
Higbee, Mrs. (friend), 16
Higginson, Colonel, 178
High Jinks, 364
Highland Poachers, Story of, 271
High Priest (in "Passion Music"), 52
Hill, Lady Arthur (composer), 82
Hill, Lucille (soprano), 100
Hinshaw, William Wade (impresario), 369
Hofmann (composer), 159
Hoffmann (opera, "Tales of Hoffmann"), 370
Holbein Room, 268
Holman, Joseph (cellist), 82, 236
Holy Trinity Church (Philadelphia), 49
Homer, Madame Louise (contralto), 266, 296, 301
"Home, Sweet Home" (song), 34
Honolulu, 364
Honorary Degree LL.D., 371
"Hora Novissima" (oratorio, Horatio Parker), 209
Horn (composer), 350
Hotaling, Richard, 354
"Hound of Heaven, The" (poem), 63
Housmann, Alfred Edward (poet), 333, 334
Housmann, Laurence (author), 332
Howard, Esmé (diplomatist), 127
Howells, W. D. (author), 44
Howling Dervishes, 26
Hub, the, 248
Huddersfield, 174
Hudson River, 20
Hume (medium), 77
Humperdinck (composer), 181
Hunding (in "The Valkyrie," Wagner), 123, 252
Hungarian Gypsy tunes, 164
"Husband in Clover, A" (play), 44
Huss, Henry Holden (composer), 126, 226
Huxley, Prof. Thomas (scientist), Preface, 3, 72
Hyde, Walter (tenor), 333

Hyde Park Corner, 120
"Hymn of Longing" (song), 322
"Hymn of Love" (song), 322
"Hymn of Praise, The" (cantata, Mendelssohn), 52
"Hymnus" (song), 291, 306
Hypnotism, 74, 75, 77

Iago (in "Othello"), Verdi, 266, 295, 309
"I don't want to stay here no longer" (song), 295
"I know that my Redeemer liveth" (song), 371
Illinois, 339
"I Maestri Cantori" (opera, Wagner), 137
"Impresario, The" (opera, Mozart), 367, 369
"In a Balcony" (Browning), 271
"In Autumn" (song), 350
Indianapolis, 218, 226
Indians, 6, 325
"In Memoriam" (song cycle, Lehmann), 290
"I Pagliacci" (opera, Leoncavallo), 139, 180
Ipswich, 85
Irate Hibernian, 314
Ireland, 117, 121, 144, 295
Irish Ditties, 121, 317
Irish Opera ("Shamus O'Brien," Stanford), 120
Irish Stories, 313
"Irish Symphony" (Stanford), 313
Irish, the, 313
Irving, Laurence, 155
Irving Place Theatre, 310
Irving, Sir Henry (actor), 62, 65, 142, 155, 178, 194, 207, 334, 335
  As Mathias, 66
Isle of Wight, 151, 265
Isolde (Albani as), 182, 183
  (Lehmann as), 58, 256
  (Nordica as), 254
  (Sucher as), 58
"Israel in Egypt" (oratorio, Handel), 52, 306
Italian, 136, 139, 182, 184, 207, 224, 296
Italian Cities, 23
Italians Critical, 69
Italian Government, 127
Italian Lakes, 64

Italian Language, 112, 123
Italian Manner, 130
Italian Opera, 73, 295, 296, 313, 328
Italian Repertory, 285
Italian Riviera, 63
Italian School of Music, 68
Italian Selections, 134
Italian Singer, 267, 292
Italy, 22, 61, 62, 64–71, 88, 90, 127
" It is Better to Laugh " (song), 350
" Ivanhoe " (opera, Sullivan), 92, 106
" I've Been Roaming " (song), 350

James, Francis (artist), 77
James, Henry (author), 150, 151
Janotha, Mlle. (pianist), 86, 90, 92
Janson, Agnes (singer), 164
Japanese Language, 123
Jarrow (monastery of), 10
Jastrow, Prof. (Shakespearean scholar), 127
Jay, Isabel (singer), 335
Jefferson, Joseph (actor), 326–328
Jefferson, Thomas (House of), 2
Jefferson, William (actor), 327
Jenkins (composer), 168
Jenkinson (in " Vicar of Wakefield "), 334
Jensen (composer), 320
Jeremy Crow (in " Meg's Diversion "), 44
Joachim, Joseph (violinist), 30, 90, 125, 131, 144, 163, 179, 237, 288
" Joan; or, The Brigands of Bluegoria " (opera, Ford), 82
Job, Book of (drama), 371
" Job " (oratorio, Parry), 159
Johannes (in " Evangelimann "), 206
John Precentor, 10
Johns, Clayton (composer), 235
Johnson House, 7
Jones, Paul (artist), 343
Jones, Sir Lawrence, 153
" Joshua Fit de Battle of Jericho " (song), 295
Journet (basso), 207, 297
Juch, Emma (singer), 124
Judas (in " Passion Music "), 52
    (in " The Apostles "), 311
" Judas Maccabaeus " (oratorio, Handel), 52

'Julius Cæsar" (play, Shakespeare), 41, 329
    Quarrel scene of, 20, 98

Kaighn, Bartram (schoolmaster), 16, 17, 18
Kalisch, Paul (tenor), 303
Kansas, 253
Kansas City, 297, 299
Kappes, Mr. (Mendelssohn's friend), 341
Kaun, Hugo (composer), 228
Kean, Edmund (actor), 40, 261
Keats (poet), 359
Kellogg, Clara Louise (soprano), 30
Kembles, The (actors), 40, 261
Kensington Gore, 137, 146
Kensington Palace Gardens, 146
Kentucky, 293, 296
Kienzl (composer), 206
King, The (in " Lohengrin "), 250, 267
" King Arthur " (cantata, Purcell), 211, 253
King Edward VII, 305, 311
King George V, 268
" King Robert of Sicily " (poem, Longfellow), 280
" King Robert of Sicily " (recitation, Rossetter Cole), 280
Kingston, Beatty (writer), 143
Kipling, Rudyard (poet), 230, 231, 236
Kitchener, Lord, 265
Klafsky, Katharina (soprano), 136
Klingsor (in " Parsifal "), 242
Kneisel String Quartette, 198, 285, 286
Knight of the Swan (" Lohengrin "), 182, 259
Kobbé, Gustave (writer), 53
Korbay, Franz (composer), 164
Korbay, Madame, 164
Korsakoff, Rimsky (composer), 228
Kraus, Ernst (tenor), 220, 222, 292
Krehbiel, Henry E. (music critic), 368
Kubelik (violinist), 286
Kundry (in " Parsifal "), 242
Kurwenal (in " Tristan and Isolde," Wagner), 111–115, 117, 145, 182, 183, 206

Ladies' Annual Gambol, 342
Lady Allcash (opera "Fra Dia-
    volo"), 165
Lady Chapel (Chester Cathedral),
    22
"La Donna é mobile" (song), 24
"L'Africaine" (opera), 187
Laird of Skibo, 272
Lake District, 10, 11
Lake Michigan, 243
Lake Mohonk, 125
"Lakme" (opera), 265
Lamb, Charles, 261
Lambs' Club, 342
Lament of Amfortas (opera,
    "Parsifal"), 167
Lamperti, Francesco (teacher), 59,
    69, 88, 122, 218
Lancashire, 10, 11, 22, 140, 179
Land of Song, 24
Lander, Mr. (actor), 334
Landgrave (in "Tannhäuser"),
    172, 207, 241
Landi, Signorina (contralto), 180
Laniere (composer), 168
Lang, B. J. (conductor), 61
"L'Arlesienne" (drama), 310
La Scala Theatre, 121
"La Sonnambula" (opera, Bel-
    lini), 83
Lassalle, Jean (barytone), 113,
    123, 187
"La Traviata," opera, 187
Lawes, Henry (composer), 168
Lawes, William (composer), 168
Lawrenceville School, 3
Lawson, Corinne Moore (singer),
    198
"Lay on, Macduff!" 275
Leach (artist), 91
League of Nations, 121
"Le Cid" (opera), 187
Lee (General), 3
Leeds, 174
Leeds Choral Society, 174
Lehigh Valley Railway Co., 58
Lehmann, Lilli (soprano), 104, 191,
    244, 256, 257, 258, 266, 303
Lehmann, Liza (singer-composer),
    131, 146, 225, 250, 290, 332–
    334
Lehmann, Marie (singer), 257, 258
Leighton (painter), 146
Lemoyne, Sarah (actress), 271

Lennox, Cosmo Gordon, 83
Leonato (in "Much Ado"), 294
Leoncavallo (composer), 119
"Les deux Grenadiers" (song),
    103, 180
"Les Huguenots" (opera, Meyer-
    beer), 124, 139, 183, 187
"Lesson in Love, A" (play), 44
"Let the Dreadful Engines" (Pur-
    cell), 168
Letter from Paderewski, 330, 331
Levitation, 77
Levy, Heniot (pianist), 358
Liberty Bell, 3
Liceo Musicale (Bologna), 68
Life Guards (officers of), 78
Lincoln, Abraham (President), 4, 6,
    319, 320
Lincoln, Colonel Robert (Minister
    to England), 319, 320
Lincoln, "Tad," 319, 320
Lind, Jenny (soprano), 48, 205
Lippincott Family, 14
Liszt (composer), 104, 228, 302
"Little Lord Fauntleroy" (novel),
    89
"Little Silver Ring, The" (song),
    350
Litvinne, Madame (singer), 187
Liverpool, 10, 22, 83, 178, 212
Liverpool Orchestral Society, 177
Liverpool Philharmonic, 178
LL.D., Doctor of Laws, 371
Lloyd, Edward (tenor), 121, 287
Lloyd, Madame, 287
Lodge, Sir Oliver (scientist), 76,
    116
Loeffler, Charles Martin (com-
    poser), 338
Loewe, Carl (composer), 124, 158,
    159, 190, 320, 344, 348, 350
Loge (in "Rheingold"), 250, 252,
    309
"Lohengrin" (opera, Wagner),
    129, 180, 182, 187, 221, 243,
    249, 250, 259, 267, 296, 302, 303
London, 7, 22, 27, 55, 57, 59, 62,
    63, 72, 75, 77, 78, 79, 82, 83, 90,
    93, 100, 105, 108, 110, 122, 124,
    125, 127, 131, 134, 135, 140,
    149, 150, 157, 164, 165, 166,
    177, 179, 180, 181, 183, 185,
    190, 195, 198, 199, 200, 204,
    205, 209, 212, 216, 217, 220,

225, 226, 235, 260, 265, 266, 286, 288, 289, 294, 295, 303, 304, 307, 309, 313, 333, 335, 336, 343
London Audiences, 107
London Directory, 11
London *Times*, 106, 118, 151
Longfellow (poet), 280, 287
Lord Allcash (in "Fra Diavolo"), 165, 182
Lord Dundreary, 166
"Lord is a Man of War, The" (duet, Handel), 53, 306
Lord Touchstone Pepper (in "A Reformer in Ruffles"), 44
Los Angeles, 283
"Lost Chord, The" (song), 184
Lotos Club, 323
Louisville, 293, 296
Lourdes, miracles of, 116
"Love Songs" (Brahms), 164
"Lov'st Thou for Beauty" (song), 350
"Lucia" (opera, Donizetti), 85, 187, 293
"Lucifer" (oratorio), 219
Lung' Arno, Florence, 72
Lutkin, Professor Peter C., 341
Lyceum Theatre (New York), 216, 368
4th Ave. and 24th St., 216
Lymington, 152
Lyric Club (London), 102
Lysiart, aria of ("Euryanthe"), 164

"Macbeth" (play, Shakespeare), 182
McClellan (General), 3
McCormack, John (tenor), 334
McCoy, Wm. J. (composer), 338, 353
McCullough, John (actor), 38
MacCunn, Hamish (conductor), 333
MacDonald, George (poet), 89
MacDowell, Edward A. (conductor), 337, 338, 350
MacIntyre, Margaret (singer), 172, 229
Mackenzie, Sir Alexander (composer), 75, 102, 119, 122, 131, 164

Macready (actor), 40
"Madame Butterfly" (opera, Puccini), 123, 369
Madison Square, 133
Madison Square Theatre, 42
Madrigal Society, 48
Mad Scene (from "Lucia"), 293
Maeterlinck (author), 116
Magdalena (in "Evangelimann"), 206
"Magelone" (Brahms), 190, 204
Magna Charta, 14
"Magpies, The" (club), 102, 103, 106
Mahler, Gustav (conductor), 114, 321, 358
"Maid as Mistress, The" (opera, Pergolesi), 368
"Maidens of Cadiz, The" (song), 350
Maine, 125, 354
Main Street (Moorestown), 7
Maitland, J. A. Fuller (critic), 106, 118
Mancinelli, Luigi (conductor), 180, 187, 207, 267, 295
"Mandalay" (song), 230
"Manfred" (play, Byron), 323, 324
Manhattan Island, 274
Manhattan Opera House, 369
Manns, August (conductor), 58, 82, 124
"Manon" (opera, Massenet), 304
"Manru" (opera, Paderewski), 301, 302
Mansfield, Richard (actor), 328, 329, 330
Mantelli, Madame (singer), 184, 187, 193
"Manzoni," Requiem Mass (Verdi), 227
Marcello (in "Les Huguenots"), 183
Marchesi, Madame Blanche (singer), 236
"Marguerite at the Spinning Wheel" (song), 350
Marguerite de Valois (in "Les Huguenots"), 183
Mario, Signor (tenor), 83
Marius, Monsieur (comedian), 97, 98

Mark Antony (Speech of), 20
F. C. Bangs as, 41, 329, 330
"Marriage of Figaro, The" (opera, Mozart), 187
Mars, 323
Marschener (composer), 228
Marseilles, 27
"Martha" (opera, Flotow), 30
Martin, Riccardo (tenor), 369
Martin, Robert (playwright), 82
"Martyr of Antioch, The" (oratorio, Sullivan), 159
Mascagni (composer), 123
Massenet (composer), 145, 219, 304, 350
Master of the Gods, 208
Master of Skibo, 269
Master of the Queen's Musick, 171
Materna, Madame (singer), 191, 242, 243
Mathias (in "Evangelimann"), 206
Mattullath, Alice (translator), 368
"Maud" Song Cycle (Somervell), 290
Maurel, Victor (barytone), 115, 118, 119, 122, 257, 266, 295
Maurice Grau Opera Company, 241
Mayer, Daniel (manager), 113
May Festival, Cincinnati, 343
"May Night" (song), 350
"Medicin Malgré Lui, Le" (play, Molière), 369
"Mefistofele" (opera, Boito), 187
"Meg's Diversion" (play), 44
Meisslinger, Miss (singer), 182, 244
"Meistersinger, Die" (opera, Wagner), 58, 111, 113, 139, 144, 167, 173, 182, 187, 188, 260, 266
Melba, Nellie (soprano), 121, 183, 187, 191, 192, 220, 232, 254, 290, 293, 296
Melbourne (Australia), 365
Melodrama, 282
"Melusine" (opera, Hofmann), 159
Melvin, Honorable Henry A., 354

Mendelssohn, Felix (composer), 32, 52, 93, 147, 159, 160, 219, 310, 311, 317, 341
Mendelssohn Hall, 225, 232
Mendelssohn Scholarship, 59
Mephistopheles ("Faust"), 96, 113, 139, 145, 313
Mercantile Library, 40
Meredith, George (novelist), 147, 148, 149, 150
Mersey River, 22
"Message, The" (song), 88
"Messiah, The" (oratorio, Handel), 52, 58, 88, 127, 211, 219, 221, 232, 249, 250, 300, 318
Metropolitan Opera Company, 343
Metropolitan Opera House of New York, 132, 186, 187, 190, 193, 197, 218, 219, 232, 247, 251, 257, 260, 269, 289, 292, 301, 309, 310, 330, 369
Meyerbeer (composer), 350
Michael Angelo's "David," 65, 80, 271
Middle West, 132, 320, 362
"Midsummer Night's Dream, A" (music by Schumann), 153, 310, 337, 367
  Pyramus, 153
  Thisbe, 153
"Mignon" (opera, Thomas), 30, 369
Mikado's subjects, 123
Milan, 58, 59, 121, 122, 124
Millais (painter), 146
Miller, Ruth (singer), 370
Milton, John (reading from), 87
Milwaukee, 221
Mime (in "Siegfried"), 253, 309, 368
Minerva, 323
Minneapolis, 285
Minstrels, Christie, 295
"Missa Solemnis" (Beethoven), 219, 228
"Mock Doctor, The" (opera, Gounod), 369
Modjeska, Madame Helena (actress), 330, 331
Mohammedan Religion, 25
Molière (dramatist), 369
Monckton, Paul (playwright), 83

Monday "Pop." (concerts), 91, 125, 163, 179
Montholon, General, 153
Moor, The (in "Otello"), 295
Moore, George (author), 151
Moore, Tom (poet), 235, 344
Moorestown, 6, 15, 16, 17, 29, 38, 42
Moorestown (Episcopal Church), 28, 31
Moorestown School, 16, 17, 18, 20
Moorish magician, 343
Morgan, J. Pierpont, Sr., 247
Morgan, Tali Esen (choral director), 160
Morris, Major (U. S. A.), 16
Morris, William (poet), 158
"Mors et Vita" (oratorio, Gounod), 52
"Moses in Egypt" (oratorio, Rossini), 52, 159
Moses (in "Vicar of Wakefield"), 334
Moss, Hugh (stage director), 97
Mother in England, My, 93, 94
Mottl, Felix (conductor), 134, 167, 206, 260
Moulton, Professor, 370
Mozart (composer), 51, 180, 228, 307, 350, 368
Mr. Babblebrook (in "A Lesson in Love"), 44
"Much Ado about Nothing" (opera, Stanford), 294
Muck, Doctor (conductor), 260, 262
Mühlmann, Adolf (singer), 267
Müller, Hugo (playwright), 215
Müller, Lieder (songs, Schubert), 204, 205, 247, 250
Müller, Professor Max, 117, 205
Müller, Wilhelm, 204, 205
Musical Art Society, 102
Musical Fund Hall, 48
Musical Mornings, 216
Myers, Professor F. W. (scientist), 76
"My Heart Ever Faithful" (song), 350
"My Pretty Jane" (song), 88

"Nadeshda" (opera, Goring Thomas), 105
"Nan, the Good-for-Nothing" (play), 44
Naples, 360
Napoleon, 153, 267
Narrator (in "The Redemption"), 52

Nashville, 221
Natchez, Tivadar (violinist), 120
Negro, 317
Negro Minstrels, Distaste for, 39
Negroes, 325
Neilson, Adelaide (actress), 38, 42
  as Juliet, 41
  as Viola, 41
Neilson, Robert and William (friends), 42, 43
Neruda, Madame Norman (pianist), 125
Nevada, Madame Emma (singer), 265
"Nevermore," 281
New Amsterdam Theatre, 367
Newboldt, Henry (poet), 359
New England town, 312
New Jersey, 6
New Theatre, 327
New Thought, 76
New World, 145, 276, 278
New York, 42, 52, 61, 102, 108, 125, 127, 132, 154, 157, 160, 164, 186, 187, 188, 189, 197, 198, 199, 201, 204, 209, 212, 217, 218, 219, 220, 221, 225, 230, 231, 232, 233, 238, 245, 247, 248, 249, 250, 256, 259, 260, 273, 284, 285, 289, 290, 291, 295, 296, 297, 300, 301, 309, 311, 318, 322, 333, 335, 338, 342, 358, 364, 365, 366, 367, 368, 369, 370
New York College, 280
New York Symphony Orchestra, 323
New York Theatre, 342
New York Times, 367
New York Tribune, 368
Niagara Falls, 20
"Niebelungen Ring" (Wagner), 171, 222, 309
Niebelungen (story), 253
"Night Bell, The" (opera, Donizetti), 368, 369
Nilsson, Christine (soprano), 36
"Noblest of Knights" (song), 350
Nordica, Lillian, 127, 129, 188, 189, 220, 232, 244, 247, 250, 254, 255, 256, 266, 267, 290, 292, 293, 309, 359, 365
Norman Ancestors, 12
North America, 185, 315, 365
North American Indian, 317
Northwestern University, 339

Nova Scotia, 362
"Now your days of Philandering" (song), 350
Noyes, Alfred (poet), 367
Nuremburg, 173

Oberländer (tenor), 117
Oberlin College, 241
"Odysseus" (cantata, Bruch), 52
"O Ewigkeit" (cantata, Bach), 163
Offenbach, Jacques (composer), 42, 370
Offertorium, 68
Ohio, 286
Ohio Valley Exposition, 343
"Oh, Let Night Speak of Me" (song), 350
"Oh, My Lyre" (song), 350
"Oh, Rest in the Lord" (aria), 93
"Olaf Trygvasson" (song), 219
Old World, 176, 307
Olitzka, Rosa (contralto), 187, 290
Olivia ("Vicar of Wakefield"), 335
Olympus, 323
"Omnipotence" (song), 371
"On Wings of Music" (song), 317
Opera Comique, 81, 83, 304, 335
Opera in English, 30, 107
Opera, French, 107
   German, 107
   Italian, 107
Opera House (Blackpool), 140
Opp, Julie (actress), 216, 236
Orange, N. J., 249
"Oratorio, Opera Spoiled," 61
Oratorio Society (The Cecilian), 48
Oratorio Society of New York, 127, 221, 310, 324
Orchestra Concerts, Crystal Palace, 82
Order of Runnymede, 14
Oregon, 285
"Orfeo" (opera, Gluck), 124, 285
Ornstein, Leo (pianist), 358
Orpheus Club of Philadelphia, 47, 48, 49, 50, 196, 230, 337
"Orpheus with His Lute" (song), 350
Ortrud (in "Lohengrin"), 182, 243, 250, 256, 303

"O, Ruddier than the Cherry" (song), 350
Osborne House, 265
O'Sullivan, Dennis (singer), 165
Othello, Salvini as, 65, 295
Ottokar (in "Der Freischütz"), 136
Ouida, Madame (novelist), 66, 67, 105
Overland Express, 362
Oxford, 134, 154, 158
Oxford Street, 80
Oxford University, 117, 135, 178

Pacific Coast, 233, 283, 284, 290, 338, 356, 362
Paderewski, Ignace (pianist), 301, 302, 330, 331
Paganini (violinist), 30
"Pagliacci, I" (opera, Leoncavallo), 118
Pagliano Theatre, 68
Palace Theatre of Varieties, 97
Palestrina's High Mass, 127, 128
Pallisser, Esther (soprano), 100, 117, 300
Palmer, Lady, 149, 286
Palmer, Sir Walter, 286
Pandolfo, Doctor (in "Maid as Mistress"), 368
"Paoletta" (opera, Floridia), 343
"Paradise and Peri" (cantata, Schumann), 219, 228
Paris, 23, 27, 58, 108, 198, 266, 277, 304, 335
Paris, Wagner in, 103
Parisian production, 206
Park Theatre (New York), 369
Parker, Horatio W. (composer), 119, 209, 337, 359
"Parlor Car, The" (play, W. D. Howells), 44
Parratt, Sir Walter (conductor), 171, 265
Parrish, Miss Elinor (author), 43
Parry, Sir Hubert (composer), 119, 159, 287
"Parsifal" (music drama, Wagner), 127, 167, 206, 219, 228, 241, 310
Passion Music ("Messiah," Handel), 88

Passion Music, St. John (oratorio, Bach), 180
Passion Music, St. Matthew (oratorio, Bach), 52, 131, 163, 180, 286
Patmore, Coventry (poet), 152
Patti, Adelina (soprano), 48, 169, 170, 171
"Paul et Virginie" (opera), 34
Paur, Emil (conductor), 221, 291
Peabody Institute, 342
Peace Concert, 305
Peace Conference, 302
"Peasants, The (Bauern) Cantata" (Bach), 145
Pearse, Mrs. Godfrey, 83
Peile, Kinsey (playwright), 83
"Pélleas and Mélisande" (opera, Debussy), 306
Pendleton, Elliott, 43
Penn Club (Philadelphia), 65
Pennshawken Creek (New Jersey), 6
Pennsylvania, 3
Pennsylvania Railroad, 19, 31
Penn, William, 6, 11
Penn's Surveyor (Skull), 12
Pergola Theatre (Florence), 69
Pergolesi (composer), 368
"Per questa bella mano" (song), 180
"Persian Garden, In a" (song cycle, Liza Lehmann), 225
Peter (opera, "Hänsel and Gretel"), 181
Peter (in "Passion Music"), 52
Pevny, Olga (singer), 241
Philadelphia, 1, 6, 11, 15, 16, 22, 27, 29, 39, 45, 48, 50, 53, 57, 58, 59, 62, 65, 126, 161, 196, 217, 219, 221, 227, 243, 248, 249, 276, 293, 337, 367
Philadelphia, Map of, by Nicholas Skull, 12
Philadelphia Orchestra, 311, 358
Philadelphia Public, 39
"Philemon and Baucis" (opera, Gounod), 135, 139, 187
Philharmonic Orchestra of New York, 157, 190, 291, 322, 337, 358
Philharmonic Society (London), 134, 164, 180
Phrenologist story, 80, 81

Piano, 28
Piano Concerto, 337
Piatti, Signor (cellist), 90, 180
"Pied Piper of Hamelin, The" (Browning), music by Bergh, 281
Pigeon (in "Golden Haired Gertrude"), 44
"Pilgers Morgenlied" (song), 291, 306
Pilgrims, The (Dramatic Society, Germantown), 43
Pinero, Arthur (playwright), 150
Pini, Corsi (singer), 166
"Pirate Song, The" (song), 350
Pittsburgh, 274
Pizarro (in "Fidelio"), 136
Plains of Lombardy, 64
Planchette Story, 110–116, 121, 295
Plançon, Pol (singer), 137, 183, 184, 187, 193, 232, 245, 292, 294
Players, The (club), 326, 328
"Pluie et le Beau Temps, La" (Gozlan), 293
Plumptree, 337
"Plus grand dans son Obscurité" (song), 265
Poe, Edgar Allan (poet), 280, 281, 338
Poet Laureate, 90, 151
"Poet's Love" (song cycle, Schumann), 205
Pogner (in "Die Meistersinger"), 137
Pohlig, Carl (conductor), 358
Polish singers, 129, 182
Ponchielli (composer), 228
Pope Leo XIII, 127, 128
Pope's Choir (St. Peter's), 24
Portland, 285
"Portrait of Dorian Gray, The" (novel), 150
Possart, Ernst (actor), 280, 324
"Postal Card, The" (play, W. D. Howells), 44
Powell, Arthur (composer), 338
Power, Sir George (singer), 83
Powers, Ada Weigel (composer), 358
Powers, Hiram (sculptor), 327
Poynter (painter), 146
Premier of Poland, 302
Press Club, 155

Primrose, Mrs. (in "The Vicar of Wakefield"), 334
Prince Arthur (story of), 103
Prince Consort, 171
Prince of Darkness, 96
Princess Christian, 102
Princess Louise, 102
Prince of Wales, 103, 165, 169, 184, 265, 268
Prince and Princess of Wales, 173
Princeton University, 3, 16, 230
Prologue (opera "I Pagliacci"), 371
"Prospice" (song), 158, 243
Prout (composer), 159
Providence, 322
Puccini (composer), 369
Puck, 362
Punch (magazine), 91
Purcell (composer), 124, 168, 211, 350
Pyne, Minton (organist), 51

Quakers, 2, 3, 11, 15, 19, 22, 25, 34
Quakerism, 73, 152
Quaker ancestors, 54, 76
Quaker City, 65, 219
Quaker meeting, 39, 93, 268, 286
Quartettes (Brahms), 164
Queen Alexandra, 90, 295, 305
Queen Victoria, 85, 90, 102, 120, 171, 173, 213, 214, 265, 267, 268, 295
Queen Victoria's Diamond Jubilee, 170, 264
Queen's Hall, 88, 131, 134
Queenstown, 212
Quince, 183

Rachmaninoff (composer), 350
Radleigh College, 154
Randegger, Alberto (teacher), 102, 106, 120
"Rantzau, I" (opera, Mascagni), 123
Raven, The (Poe), Bergh's setting, 280, 281, 338, 339
Ravogli, Julia (contralto), 124, 139
Recoschewitz, Madame (singer), 172
Redding, Jos. D. (author), 341, 360, 361
"Redemption, The" (oratorio, Gounod), 52, 131, 160, 219, 302

Reeves, Sims (tenor), 83-88, 90, 121
Reeves, Mrs. Sims, 85
"Reformer in Ruffles, A" (play), 44
Reger, Max (composer), 307
"Reine de Saba, La" (opera, Gounod), 265
Reiss, Albert (tenor), 296, 309, 368, 369
Remenyi (Hungarian violinist), 30
Renaud, Maurice (barytone), 266
"Requiem" (Brahms), 287
"Requiem" (Verdi), 159, 302
Resolution, To Act and to Sing, 25
Restoration Period, 29
"Reverend Mr. Bispham, The," 99
Revolutionary times, 271
"Rheingold, The" (opera, Wagner), 112, 167, 250, 253, 302
Rhine, 251
Rice, Wallace (author), Preface
Richings-Bernard Opera Co., 30
Richmond, 112
Richter, Hans (conductor), 134, 144, 167, 171, 178, 190, 191, 209, 211, 212, 286, 288, 358
Richter, Mrs., 212
Ricordi (publishers), 121
Riddle, George (elocutionist), 155, 280
"Rigoletto" (opera, Verdi), 187, 266
"Ring, The" (cycle of music dramas, Wagner), 244, 250, 258
Ristori, Madame (actress), 38, 40
Rochester, 285, 286
Rocky Mountains, 297
Rodewald, Alfred (patron), 178
Rodick's Hotel (Bar Harbor, Maine), 43
Roman Catholic Cathedral, 33
Roman Catholic Practices, 28, 128, 152
Roman Church, Music of, 24, 49
Romanticists, 348
Rome, 24, 58, 127, 128, 154, 248, 276, 327
"Romeo and Juliet" (comic opera, Charles C. Soule), 45
"Romeo and Juliet" (opera, Gounod), 187, 292
Ronalds, Mrs., 96

Roosevelt, Theodore (President), 283, 305, 317, 318, 319
Roosevelt, Mrs. Theodore, 283, 317
Root, Geo. F. (song writer), 65
Rosenfeld, Sydney (playwright), 368
Ross, Betsy (House of), 2
Rossini, G. (composer), 52, 69, 120, 159, 302
Royal Academy of Music, 75
Royal Albert Hall, 131, 146
Royal Amateur Orchestral Association, 103
Royal Carl Rosa English Grand Opera Co., 106, 171
Royal College of Music, 55, 287, 334
Royal English Opera House, 81, 92, 97, 98, 106
Royal Institution, 122
Royal Italian Opera, The, 171
Royal Opera, Berlin, 32, 108, 286
Royal Opera, Covent Garden, 117, 135
Rubaiyát of Omar Khayyám, 225
Rudbeck, Baron, 110, 111
Rudolf (in " Der Wald "), 303
Runciman, John (critic), 163
Runnymede, Order of, 14
Russell, Ella (soprano), 305

St. Botolph Club, 199
St. Clement's Church, 51
" St. Elizabeth " (oratorio, Liszt), 302
" St. Francis " (oratorio, Tinel), 159
St. Giles (Cathedral), 144
St. Helena, 153
St. James's Hall, 84, 90, 125, 135, 164, 179, 185, 205, 235, 306
St. James's Theatre, 150
St. John Passion (oratorio, Bach), 180
St. John's Church, 35
St. John's Day, 173
St. Louis, 221
St. Mark's Church, 28, 51, 59
St. Martin's Lane (Friends meeting), 93
St. Matthew Passion (oratorio, Bach), Judas, Peter, High Priest, Christ, 52, 131, 163, 180, 286

St. Paul, 285
St. Paul (First Corinthians), 345
" St. Paul " (oratorio, Mendelssohn), 52
St. Peter the Apostle, Church of, 10
St. Peter's, 127, 128
St. Peter's (Pope's Choir), 24
Sachs, Hans (in " Meistersinger "), 266
Safonoff, Wassili (conductor), 337
Sailors' Home, 232
Saint Gaudens, Augustus (sculptor), 326
Saint-Saëns (composer), 145, 228
Sala Filarmonica, 68
Salem County, 6
Salignac (tenor), 187, 220, 244, 292, 296
" Sally in Our Alley " (song), 84
Salvini, Tomaso (actor), 65
" Samson " (oratorio, Handel), 52
" Samson et Delila " (opera, Saint-Saëns), 145
San Bris (in " Les Huguenots "), 183
San Francisco, 339, 353, 360, 362, 364, 366
San Remo (Italy), 88
Santissima Annunziata (Florence), 68
Santley, Sir Charles (barytone), 30, 53, 121, 145, 305
Santo Spirito (Florence), 68
Santuzza (in " Cavalleria Rusticana "), 166
" Sardanapalus " (play, Byron), 41
F. C. Bangs as, 41
Sargent, John S. (painter), 66, 146, 154
Saroya, Bianca (singer), 369
Sat. " Pop." (concerts), 179
Saturday Review, 163
Sauer, Emil (pianist), 157, 163
Sauret, Emil (violinist), 120
Savage, Henry W. (manager), 310
Savoy Theatre, 82, 94–96, 334
Scalchi, Sophia (contralto), 285
Scarlatti (composer), 350
" Scarlet Letter, The " (opera, Damrosch), 222
Schalk (conductor), 241
" Schauspiel Direktor, Der " (opera, Mozart), 368

Scheff, Fritzi (singer), 297, 301, 321
Scheidemantel (barytone), 266
Scheldt River, 259
Schelling, Prof. (Shakespearean scholar), 127
Schiller (author), 291
Schillings, Max (composer), 281
Scholastic work, 18
"School for Scandal" (scene from), 44
Schubert, Franz (composer), 29, 32, 51, 124, 134, 158, 159, 179, 190, 204, 205, 214, 219, 226, 228, 235, 247, 250, 320, 338, 341, 344, 348, 350, 371
Schumann, Clara (pianist), 350
Schumann-Heink, Madame (contralto), 129, 206, 208, 243, 250, 254, 266, 267, 290, 293, 296, 309, 341, 364
Schumann, Robert (composer), 32, 103, 124, 134, 135, 180, 226, 228, 235, 320, 323, 344, 348, 349, 350
Schumann, Paul (stage manager), 260
Scotch ballads, 159
Scotch soprano, 369
Scotch stories, 87, 88
Scot, 269
Scotia, 269, 276
Scotland, 87, 144, 265, 269, 270
Scots Guards Band, 84
Scott, Cyril (composer), 350
Scott (poet), 344
Scotti, Antonio (barytone), 295
Scottish orchestra, 128
Scull, David (grandfather), 7, 17
Scull, David (uncle), 8, 21
Scull, Edward (uncle), 8
Scull Family, 6, 12, 14
Scull, Gideon (uncle), 8
Scull, Jane Lippincott (mother), 2
"Sea, The" (song), 350
Seargent Sulpice (in "Daughter of the Regiment"), 369
"Seasons, The" (oratorio, Haydn), 52
"Secrecy" (song), 350
Seguin, Zelda (alto), 30
Seidl, Anton (conductor), 187, 190, 191, 208, 216, 217, 221, 358
Sembrich, Marcella (soprano), 88, 218, 244, 254, 255, 296, 301

Senta (in "Flying Dutchman"), 264
Seppilli, Armando (conductor), 118, 119
Sermon on the Mount, 355
"Serva Padrona, La" (opera, Pergolesi), 368
"Seven Ages of Man" (Shakespeare), 20
"Seven Ages of Man" (song, Huss), 126, 226
Seventh Regiment Armory (New York), 52
Shaftesbury Avenue, 92
Shakespeare (poet), 20, 60, 89, 126, 127, 142, 143, 153, 235, 270, 275, 294, 310, 313, 337, 344, 367
Shakespeare Day, 367
Shakespeare, William (teacher-tenor), 59, 60, 61, 69, 74, 92, 120, 135, 164, 236
Shakespeareana (Furness Collection), 45
Shakespeare Travesty ("Romeo and Juliet"), 45
"Shamus O'Brien" (opera, Stanford), 120
Sharman, Percy (violinist), 86
Sharpless, Isaac (President Haverford College), 371
Shaw, George Bernard (author), 117, 163
Sheffield Festival, 305
Shelley, Harry Rowe (composer), 180, 235, 338
Sheridan (General), 3
Sherman (General), 3
Sherwin, Amy (soprano), 86
"She Stoops to Conquer" (play, Goldsmith), 258
Shoreham Hotel, 255
"Should He Upbraid" (song), 350
"Shropshire Lad, The" (poem), 333
Shubert Brothers (managers), 333, 335
Sickert, Walter (painter), 151
Sidgwick (Professor), 76
"Siegfried" (opera, Wagner), 123, 187, 249, 250, 253, 302
    Jean de Reszke as, 191, 192, 250, 292
Siegmund (in "Valkyrie"), 252

Sieglinde (in "Valkyrie"), 252, 256, 309
Sierra Leone, 289
"Signa" (opera, Cowen), 105
Silva, Margerita (singer), 369
Simpson Auditorium, 283
Sindaco, of Florence, 69
Sir Bloomfield Brambleton (in "Who's Who"), 44
Sir Charles Seymour ("A Cup of Tea"), 44
Sir Peter Teazle ("School for Scandal"), 44
Sistine Chapel, 128
"Sixty-Six" (opera, Offenbach), 45
Skeneateles Color, 15
Skibo Castle, 269
Skibo Estate, 274
Skinner, Otis (actor), 271
Skull (or Scull), 12
Skull, Nicholas (Penn's Surveyor), 12
"Sleep, then, Ah Sleep" (song), 350
Smetana (composer), 228
Smith, Harold (pianist), 325
Smythe, Ethel M. (composer), 303
Sociables, 31
Society of American Singers (Opera Co.), 368, 369
Society of Friends, 2
Society for Psychical Research, 76
Sola Virtus Invicta (Bispham Coat of Arms), 9
"Solo Pianist" (Janotha), 86
Somervell, Arthur (composer), 119, 290
"Song of Hiawatha" (cantata, Coleridge-Taylor), 287
"Songs of the Mill" (cycle by Schubert), 204, 205
"Songs of the Sea" (songs), 359
Sonoma County, 353
Sophia (in "Vicar of Wakefield"), 334
"Sophocles," 154, 310, 337
"Sorcerer, The" (opera, Gilbert and Sullivan), 44
South African War, 305
Southampton, 152
Southern Negro Melodies, 317
Southern States, 362

Southport (Eng.), 178
Spain, 286
Spaniard, 292
Spaniards, 123
"Spectre's Bride, The" (cantata, Dvorák), 287
Spencer, Herbert (author), 147
Spiering, Theodore (conductor), 293
Spirit of Flame, 253
"Spirit, The," 154
Spiritualistic Séances, 76–81
"Spirituals" (American negro), 348
Spirit Voices, 324
Spofforth (composer), 87
Spong, Hilda (actress), 217, 285
Springfield, 125
Squier, William Barclay (librarian), 106
Squire Thornhill (in "Vicar of Wakefield"), 333, 334
"Stabat Mater" (oratorio, Rossini), 52, 69, 302
Staple Inn, 145
Stanford, Sir Charles Villiers (composer), 82, 117, 119, 127, 133–137, 163, 288, 294, 313, 359
Stanley, Professor Albert A., 226
Stars and Stripes, 2
State Concert (Buckingham Palace), 169, 171, 184
State House, 3
Steersman, The (in "Odysseus"), 52
Stehle (composer), 219
Steinert, Morris (collector), 217
Stein, Gertrude May (singer), 209
Stengel, Doctor Sembrich, 255, 256
Sterling, Antoinette (contralto), 93
Stevenson, Robt. Louis (author), 356
Stewart, Sir Robert (conductor), 117
"Still Waters Run Deep" (play), 44
Stock Exchange, 245
Stock, Frederick (conductor), 281
Stoker, Bram (manager), 334
Stokes, Emma (great-aunt), 28
Stokes Family, 14
Stoll, William, Jr. (conductor), 161, 163

"Stonebreaker's Song, The,"
    Strauss, 350
"Stormfield," 341
Story of British Spy, 271
Story of Broadway Managers, 271
Story of Carreño, 337
Story of De Pachmann, 332
Story of "Flying Dutchman," 260-
    264
Story of Highland Poachers, 273
Story of Joseph Jefferson, 326, 327
Story of Modjeska, 331
Story of President Lincoln, 319
Stories of Richard Mansfield, 328-
    330
Story of Saint Gaudens, 326, 327
Story of Richard Strauss, 321-322
Story, Roosevelt at White House,
    317
Stradivarius, 286
Strauss, Richard (composer), 280,
    291, 302, 306, 320, 321, 322,
    323, 348
Strong, Susan (singer), 208
Studebaker Theatre, 293
"Student's Companion, The," 16
Sturgis, Julian (author), 294
Sucher, Rosa (soprano), 58
Sullivan, Sir Arthur (composer),
    43, 92, 94, 96, 97, 100, 159, 174,
    334, 335, 350
Sullivan, Barry (actor), 40
Sunday School Concerts, 31
Sunset Magazine, 353
Supreme Court, of Calif., 354
"Swan and the Skylark, The"
    (cantata, Thomas), 159
"Sweethearts" (play, Gilbert), 43
Swinburne (poet), 302
Switzerland, 23, 72
Sydney (Australia), 364, 365
Symphony Concerts for Young
    People, 311
Symphony Hall, 336
Symphony No. 5 (Beethoven), 228
Symphony Orchestra (Cincinnati),
    343

Tadema, Alma (painter), 146
Taft, William H. (President),
    318, 319
"Tales of Hoffmann" (opera, Of-
    fenbach), 370

Tamagno (tenor), 69, 292, 295
Tannhäuser (opera, Wagner), 111,
    136, 172, 187, 206, 241, 244,
    260
Tannhäuser (in "Tannhäuser"),
    207
Tarkington, Booth, 230
"Ta-ra-ra-boom-de-ay" (song),
    328
Teck Theatre, 321
"Te Deum" (Berlioz), 159
"Télémaque," 17
Telramund (in "Lohengrin"), 180,
    182, 206, 208, 221, 249, 267
Temple, Richard (actor), 334
Temple unto Thespis, 276
Tennyson, Alfred Lord, 90, 151,
    280, 290, 306, 316, 358
Tennyson, Hallam, 90
Tennyson, Lady, 90
Tercentenary of Dublin University,
    117
Ternina, Madame Milka (so-
    prano), 291
Terry, Ellen (actress), 148, 149,
    194, 195, 286
Teutonic, 129, 251
Teutonic composers, 344
Texas, 325
Teyte, Maggie (soprano), 369
Thames River, 12, 259
"That Lass o' Lowrie's" (novel),
    89
Theatre Royal, Drury Lane, 106
Theodorus the Strenuous, 276
Theodore Thomas Orchestra, 341
Thirty N. 7th St. (birthplace), 2
Thomas, Ambroise (composer),
    369
Thomas, Goring (composer), 105,
    119, 159
Thomas, Theodore (conductor),
    29, 52, 125, 228, 285
Tinel (composer), 159
Tiresias (in "Agamemnon"), 155
Tite Street, 150
Titjens, Madame (singer), 35
"To Florindo" (song), 350
"Tom Bowling" (song), 84
Tommy Atkins, 357
"Tom the Rhymer" (song), 159
Tonio (in "I Pagliacci"), 118, 139
"To Parents and Guardians"
    (play), 42

Toreador (in "Carmen"), 124, 139
Tosti, F. Paolo (composer), 120
Tosti, Madame, 120
"To the Distant Beloved" (song), 179, 204
"The Toys" (poem), 152
"La Traviata" (opera, Verdi), 187
Tree, Sir Herbert Beerbohm (actor), 8, 140, 142, 143, 367
"Trial by Jury" (opera, Gilbert and Sullivan), 44
Trilogy (Wagner), 250
"Tristan and Isolde" (opera, Wagner), 111, 114, 117, 187, 244, 249, 260, 291, 292, 303
Tristan, 145
　　Jean de Reszke as, 182
　　Edouard de Reszke (as King), 182
　　Madame Albini (as Isolde), 182, 183
"Trovatore, Il" (opera, Verdi), 187
Troy, 250
Tschaikowsky (composer), 108
Tuckey, Doctor (friend), 74, 76
Turkish Music, 25
Twain, Mark (author), 15, 341, 342
"Twelfth Night" (play, Shakespeare), 208
Twelfth Street Meeting House, Philadelphia, School at, 15
"Two Grenadiers, The" (song, Schumann), 49, 103, 312

Ulana (in "Manru"), 301
Uncle Rome (poem), 356
United Kingdom, 133
United States, 11, 60, 197, 204, 210, 224, 225, 230, 241, 243, 249, 288, 313, 315, 323, 327, 330, 358, 359, 365
United States Naval Academy, 132
University Club (St. Louis), 45
University of California, 338
University of Dublin, 117
University of Michigan, 226
University Musical Club (Oxford), 134
University of Pennsylvania, 42

Urok (in "Manru"), 301
Utopia, 279

Valentine (in "Faust"), 139
Valentina (in "Les Huguenots"), 183
"Valkyrie, The" (opera, Wagner), 112, 123, 144, 167, 172, 192, 208, 252, 260, 293
Vancouver, 357
Vanderdecken (in "The Flying Dutchman," Wagner), 121, 262, 264
Van der Stucken (conductor), 226, 324, 325
Van Dyck Beard, My, 99
Van Dyck, Ernst (tenor), 167, 206, 207, 208, 241, 243, 247, 250, 252, 290, 292, 296, 309
Vannuccini, Maestro (teacher), 61, 68, 69
Van Rooy, Anton (barytone), 244, 247, 250, 266, 309
Variorum Shakespeare (Furness), 45
Vassar College, 241
Venerable Bede, The (monk), 10, 11
"Venetian Lion, The," 295
Venice, 23, 24, 66, 118
Venus, 323
Venus de Milo, 161
Venus (in "Tannhäuser"), 172, 241
Venusberg ("Tannhäuser"), 172
Verdi, Giuseppe (composer), 24, 111, 115, 121, 122, 143, 159, 227, 295, 301, 302, 350
Verona, 23, 307
Vezin, Herman (actor), 97, 98, 180, 181
"Vicar of Wakefield, The" (opera, Liza Lehmann), 306, 332, 335, 336, 343
"Vicar, The" ("Vicar of Wakefield"), 335
Vienna, Court Opera, 321
Viennese actor, 215
Villa Wahnfried (Wagner's), 104
Vine Street Hall, 31
Violetta (in "Traviata"), 254
Virginia, 11
Vitam Impendere Vero (Scull Coat of Arms), 13

Voice trials, Savoy Theatre, 94–96
Von Bülow (pianist, conductor), 104, 105
Vulcan, 323
Vulcan (in "Philemon and Baucis"), 135, 139

"Wachet Auf" (cantata, Bach), 163
Wagner family, 104
Wagner, Madame Cosima (Wagner's wife), 104, 129, 130, 190, 191, 303, 358
Wagner, Richard (composer), 74, 103, 104, 105, 111, 112, 115, 121, 127, 134, 171, 172, 180, 182, 187, 190, 206, 222, 228, 261, 263, 264, 291, 301, 302, 309, 341, 350
Wagner, Siegfried (son), 134, 167
Wagner Society, 112, 228
Wagnerian Concerts, 134
Interpreters, 144
Operas, 136, 272
Selections, 283, 339, 358
Singer, 303
Wagnerian music dramas, 218, 220, 328
Waistcoat Story, 312
"Wald, Der" (opera, Smythe), 303
Waldorf-Astoria Hotel, 216
Waleen, Baron, 110
Walker, Ernest (musician), 117, 158
Walker, Stuart (actor-manager), 370
Wall Street, 246
Wallingford, 45
Walnut Street Theatre, 38, 39
"Walpurgis Night" (cantata, Mendelssohn), 159
Walter, the Musician, 277
Walther (in "Meistersinger"), 113, 123, 137
Waltraute (in "Rheingold"), 309
Wanamaker's Store, 322
"Wanderer, The" (song), 350
Wanderer, The, 247, 250
Wanderer, The (in "Siegfried"), 191
Wartburg ("Tannhäuser"), 172
Warwickshire family, 61
Washington, D. C., 221, 254, 318

Washington, George (General and President), 50, 305
Waterloo Bridge, 98
Waterloo Chamber, 267
Waters (Philadelphian), 161, 163
Watts, Frederick C. (painter), 146, 148, 149
"Weak Woman" (play), 441
Weber (composer), 164, 228
"Wedding Song" (song), 159
Weeden, Mrs. Howard (poetess), 356
Weingartner, Felix (conductor), 321
Weld, Doctor (clergyman), 28
Wells College, 241
Welsh enthusiast, 160
Welsh tenor, 290
"Were We Hypnotized?" Article, 77
"Werther" (opera, Massenet), 187
Wesley, S. S. (organist), 51
West Indies, 11
Westminster Town Hall, 76
Wetzler, Herman H. (composer), 197, 290
Wheeler, Benjamin Ide (Univ. of Cal.), 339
"When I Was a Page" (song), 350
When other hearts (song), 84
Whiffen, Mrs. (actress), 216
Whistler (painter), 146
White House, 283, 317, 318
White, Stanford (architect), 273
Whiting, Arthur (musician), 247
Whitman, Walt (poet), 15, 50, 198
Whitney, Myron (basso), 53, 54, 56
"Who is Sylvia?" (song), 214
"Who's Who" (play), 44
"Why do the nations" (song), 312
Wiegand (basso), 123
Wigan, 10
Wilde, Oscar (author), 149, 150, 154, 358
Wildenbruch (author), 281
Wilhelmj, Auguste (violinist), 120
William the Conqueror, 10
William the Conqueror (in opera "Harold"), 166
Williams, Evan (tenor), 209, 290
William Tell Overture, 29
Wilson, George, 125
Wilson, Miss Margaret, 319

Wilson, Woodrow (President), 121, 318, 319

Wimbledon, 334

Windsor Castle, 171, 267

Winnipeg, 285

"Winter Journey, The" (song cycle, Schubert), 205

Winter, William (dramatic critic), 367

Wister, Mrs. Caspar (authoress), 45

"Witch's Song, The" (Wildenbruch), 281

Witherspoon, Herbert (singer), 368

Wolcot, Charles (actor), 42, 43

Wolcot, Mrs. Charles (actress), 216

Wolff, Hugo (composer), 306, 320, 350

Wolf, Johannes (violinist), 82, 120, 236

Wolfram (in "Tannhäuser"), 111, 112, 115, 136, 139, 172, 180, 206, 241, 297, 298

"Woman's Love and Life" (song cycle, Schumann), 205, 349

Wood, Henry (conductor), 305

"Woodman, Spare that Tree" (poem), 16

Wool Business, Engaged in, 21

Woolson, Constance Fennimore (novelist), 65

Worcester Cathedral, 209

Concerts, 209

England, 173

Festival of the Three Choirs, 209

Massachusetts, 209, 212

World's Columbian Exposition, 125

Workingmen's Club, 43

Wotan (in "Valkyrie"), Wagner, 112, 172, 180, 192, 206, 208, 250, 260, 293, 309

Wotan's Farewell, 167

Wright, Mrs. Theodore (actress), 334

Wüllner, Dr. Ludwig (singer), 129

Yankee Doodle (song), 78, 317

Yarnall, Mr. and Mrs. Ellis, 33, 34

Young America Cricket Club, 45

Ysaye (violinist), 221, 282

"Zampa" (opera, Herold), 30

Zerlina (in "Fra Diavolo"), 166

Zermatt, 23

Zither, Lessons on, 28, 31

PRINTED IN THE UNITED STATES OF AMERICA

Reprint Publishing

FOR PEOPLE WHO GO FOR ORIGINALS.

This book is a facsimile reprint of the original edition. The term refers to the facsimile with an original in size and design exactly matching simulation as photographic or scanned reproduction.

Facsimile editions offer us the chance to join in the library of historical, cultural and scientific history of mankind, and to rediscover.

The books of the facsimile edition may have marks, notations and other marginalia and pages with errors contained in the original volume. These traces of the past refers to the historical journey that has covered the book.

ISBN 978-3-95940-134-0

www.reprintpublishing.com